THE TIGER IN THE ATTIC

THE TIGER IN THE ATTIC

Memories of the Kindertransport and Growing Up English

~ Edith Milton

The University of Chicago Press • Chicago and London

The University of Chicago Press, Chicago 60637
The University of Chicago Press, Ltd., London
© 2005 by The University of Chicago
All rights reserved. Published 2005
Paperback edition 2006
Printed in the United States of America

14 13 12 11 10 09 08 07 06   2 3 4 5
ISBN: 0-226-52946-0 (cloth)
ISBN-13: 978-0-226-52947-9 (paper)
ISBN-10: 0-226-52947-9 (paper)

Library of Congress Cataloging-in-Publication Data

Milton, Edith.
    The tiger in the attic / Edith Milton. — 1st ed.
        p. cm.
    ISBN 0-226-52946-0 (cloth : alk. paper)
    1. Milton, Edith.   2. Jews, German—England—Biography.   3. Jew-
ish children—England—Biography.   4. Refugee children—England—
Biography.   5. Refugees, Jewish—England—Biography.   6. Kindertrans-
ports (Rescue operations)—England.   7. World War, 1939–1945—
Children—England.   8. Jews—United States—Biography.   I. Title.
    DS135.E6M555 2005
    940.53′18′092—dc22

2005002110

For Peter and Jeremy and Naomi.
And for Ruth, who was there.

CONTENTS

ILLUSTRATIONS

Following page 114

ACKNOWLEDGMENTS

I'm most grateful to Mimi Schwartz and Janet Neipris, who read the manuscript with such care and gave me much excellent advice for its improvement; and also to Jocelyn Bolle, who took up the challenge of my pathetically flawed German. Without the enthusiasm and guidance of my editor, Susan Bielstein, *The Tiger in the Attic* would never have survived to see the light of day. And without the generosity of the Ticehurst family there would be no photographs: I'm especially grateful to George Ticehurst and also to Kathleen Smith.

But I will never find thanks enough to cover the debt I owe to Rosellen Brown: it was through her energetic urging that the book was started, her faith that got it completed, and her hard work that steered it into print.

GETTING THERE

～ The first thing I remember about being in England is Aunt Helen trying to put me on her lap. We are on a train taking us from London to Swansea, and since I speak no English it is difficult to resolve my urgent need to get off the lap of this woman I have never seen before. Not, at least, without becoming impolite about it. I have been warned of dire consequences if I fail to be polite when I get to England.

Luckily, my sister Ruth is along. Ruth speaks English. "I have to go the bathroom," I tell her in German. She translates this for the woman with the lap, who threatens to get up and take me there. "Not her. *You* have to take me," I say to Ruth.

My poor sister—she is thirteen, an awkward age at best, and the Basic English she has learned at school has never been tested on a native speaker. I have admired and adored her from afar for years—my handsome, scornful, heroic sister, six years older than I am and good at sports—but at that point she must be loathing me. "If you don't make that woman put me down," I tell her when we are finally alone in the corridor heading towards the toilet, which in fact I do not need, "I will start screaming."

But by the time we get back to the compartment, nothing needs to be explained after all: the woman's lap has been magically withdrawn from combat and is no longer a menace. It is filled with egg salad sandwiches, and I can settle down in my own and distant corner to eat one without fear of further interference.

✳

I do not remember the journey before that, though I know it was a journey of children: children of every age and size and condition. I vaguely recall weeping adults, my mother presumably among them, although I do not remember her. They stood, blocked by wooden barriers, as we were taken along the platform and put into railway compartments, which I seem to remember had hard, slatted seats. There was a boy, a country boy I suppose, with a huge basket of strawberries that he handed around to us all. The guard came by now and then and made jokes, and the officer in uniform and with a swastika armband who collected our papers at the border looked upon me with what I took to be parental concern as he handed back my passport, which under my name—augmented by the Jewish "Sara" mandated by the Third Reich—had been stamped STATELESS. I remember feeling a shy affection for him, a sense of safety in traveling in this carriage under his care.

I know that to cross to England we boarded the boat at Rotterdam. I know this because I had thought we would go through Amsterdam, which I had read about in the *Bibi* books of Karen Michaelis; Rotterdam, unsung in literature, was a great disappointment, which I resented enough to file firmly in memory. But the crossing itself is a blank. Probably we were all asleep. The next day comes to mind as the revelation of a huge London station with massive steel arches overhead. Liverpool Street Station. There were, I think, people at tables who shuffled through papers and who spoke an incomprehensible language that I knew must be English. I was wearing a brown hat with a rolled-up brim, and there were labels pinned to my collar and dangling from the various buttons of my new brown coat.

And then a tall, thin, aquiline woman, encased in a tweed suit that looked as if it would cause severe abrasions to any skin with which it came in contact, emerged from the crowd to lay claim to this refugee package from Germany, and she led us away.

✫

That point of my life is where my real memory begins. My earlier recollections are not much more than mental snapshots of discrete moments, deprived of emotional content and affect. Or if there is any emotion, it tends towards shame, which I have somehow breathed in during my last year there, from the air of Karlsruhe. I understand, for instance, when my best friend Ursula no longer comes to my house, that shame must be the element that most properly belongs to me. When I go to visit her, her mother will not open the gate, and when on my way home three children call out names at me which I completely fail to comprehend, I nevertheless know them to be shameful.

One day, coming home from school, I see a quartet of Hitler *Jugend* knocking on the door; they are rattling coins in round tins marked with swastikas in which they are collecting money for some worthy Nazi cause. I have been told that we never give money to the Hitler *Jugend*'s worthy causes and that we regard swastikas as hostile emblems. I shrink against the privet hedge, trying to be invisible, and am preparing myself to run away when, to my embarrassment, I find that terror has just made me pee in my pants. Luckily, however, the *Jugendbund* has given up knocking and is running down the path, going right past me on their way out. They are chatting and still rattling their tins and seem totally unaware of my shame: my twin shames, actually—of being Jewish and being incontinent. But even when they are gone, I am so overwhelmed by humiliation that for several minutes I can't move.

Shame is there in abundance. Other emotions, other moods, seem to have evaporated from the scenes I call up for myself.

My father's death, for instance, is encapsulated in a single image of a featureless figure wrapped head to toe in bandages, looking, I have lately come to think, more like the Michelin man or the Pillsbury Doughboy than a human being—though unlike the Michelin man and the Doughboy this creature does not have a face. I suppose I am extrapolating from the bandages around my father's head at the time he died—of uremic poisoning from a carbuncle at the base of his neck. In my waking life there were never any particular feelings associated with this apparition—no fear or affection or yearning—though throughout my childhood it consistently invaded my dreams and led them into nightmare.

Up to that moment when Aunt Helen collected us it is as though I had flattened everything out for easy storage, and to make things simpler I seem to have removed the sound track as well. But in that second-class compartment, halfway between London and Swansea, my memory springs into three dimensions—becomes, I suppose, normal. It decorates itself with words and sounds and feelings; it attaches itself to things like regret and pleasure. None of this is entirely reliable, of course—over the years the landscape of memory shifts and its details rearrange themselves; or it fails to shift and one knows that what is being remembered is not a memory anymore at all—that it has petrified into myth.

But, as I say, all that is normal, more or less. And in some way impossible to define my life begins when I am seven going on eight—when I have just set foot in England. It is 1939—the end of April or perhaps the beginning of May. By the time the train has arrived in Swansea and the taxi has driven us to Aunt Helen's house, it is early evening.

The house is huge, much grander than anything we have ever lived in in Karlsruhe. A young woman wearing a black dress and a little white apron opens the door for us and takes our bags; she is wearing a starched white cotton tiara thing on her head like the women who served *Mandeltorte* and *Schillerlocken* in the *Konditorei* on Kaiserstrasse. Aunt Helen has taken my reluctant hand and is leading me upstairs, followed by two of our suitcases under the care of the young woman in black. Ruth trails behind; the rucksack containing our papers and disposable treasure (two Swiss watches and some gold and platinum jewelry in case there should be an emergency need for ready cash) is clutched to her heart. Aunt Helen did try at the door to separate Ruth from the rucksack, a move that established an even firmer bond between them. Ruth and rucksack are now inseparable.

But when we get to the room where we are to sleep, she loosens her clutch a little; the two beds are turned down and there are two bowls of steaming, creamy mushroom soup on the bedside table. There is a fire in the fireplace too, and the curtains breathing at the slightly opened window frame a twilight view of a walled spring garden beyond which there is a distant glimmer of sea.

✲

There were four Harveys. Aunt Helen you have already met, but at her introduction she was wearing a Harris Tweed suit—topped by a sprightly fedora that I did not mention, with a rakish little feather in it announcing its readiness for battle. But that was a different Aunt Helen from the one who floated in through the firelight an hour later to kiss us goodnight—our soup finished, our cup of Horlick's drunk, our pajamas already on. This white-gowned woman, the new Aunt Helen, had about her the aroma of something wonderful: roses, perhaps, and lavender.

I had never eaten mushroom soup in bed before or drunk Horlick's; I had never walked down two miles of corridor before to go to the bathroom. I had certainly never been kissed before by someone wearing an evening gown. Kissed, more or less, by two people in evening clothes, because right behind Aunt Helen came Uncle Bourke, and he was wearing what I know now beyond a reasonable doubt to have been a dinner jacket. Not that it was exactly me he kissed. It was the air three inches above my right ear and three inches to the right of the spot of my scalp that still held the memory of Aunt Helen's good-night on it.

It was a ritual, an unaltering expression of affection balanced exquisitely with reticence, which was conducted every night for the seven years we were in England.

By then we had already been introduced to the other two Harveys, Valerie and Diana, whose room—not surprisingly, considering the distance covered—was on the way to the bathroom. Aunt Helen, who was then still in her tweed persona, had stopped by during our induction into the arcane British mysteries of having the bath and the toilet in separate enclaves.

Both the girls had been in bed reading when she had knocked on their door. "Here they are, girls," she announced, and they had both looked up from their books and told us "Hullo" with a show of some enthusiasm. Their hair, I noted with envy, was light brown and long— Valerie wore hers in two fat braids, and Diana had a single elegant braid so long that it disappeared under the blanket. It was what I had longed for since birth or maybe before. Briefly, just after my grandfather, Opa, died and when my father was sick, while the grown-ups, in fact, were thinking of other things, I did achieve two short little plaited stubs that stuck out proudly like low-slung horns just above my ears, but normally my fashion-conscious mother would take me off to be bobbed or shingled or curled, and the Heidi look I yearned for would escape me once more.

Valerie was nine, Diana eleven at the time, and I saw them both immediately as My Ideal. True, at first, it was only a matter of hair, but coiffure goes a long way, even when you are seven. It tells you almost everything you need to know; and I recognized at once that most of my life I would strive to be exactly like them, and that I would fail.

✡

The two smiling, interchangeable, pajama-clad little girls with those long brown braids I so much coveted, turned out, of course, not to be quite as much alike as my first, admiring assessment of them told me they must be. I suppose, through the sense of my own difference, I saw them as a matched set of sorts; it took familiarity to recognize their distance from each other.

Diana, even at eleven, had something of her mother's chiseled profile, softened by childhood and by an extraordinary gentleness of disposition into cameo perfection. She had the face that, traced in marble, hovers above the tombstones of those who died young—and she had the quiet, softly melancholy soul to go with it. Valerie was made of harder and brighter stuff. At the age of nine she was already looking out at the world through the little, round spectacles with tortoise-shell rims that stayed with her for the rest of her life and that seemed to sharpen any landscape she saw and transform it into something rich with potential amusement. She was quick and clever at everything that mattered to me, from word games to playing cricket. Both girls liked to draw and paint, but while Diana worked on surprisingly accomplished portraits of horses, Valerie created zoos of invented monsters and a Noah's ark filled with gryphons and unicorns, afloat on a foaming turquoise sea.

Diana was shy and somehow still; Valerie sparkled. It was not always with the sparkle of happiness, either—particularly not when I was around. With dismal regularity over the years she would cast a shining load of scorn upon me with the casual delivery of those who are without doubt. "You're hopeless," she would tell me, referring to

my style of running or dressing or failing to wash behind the ears—
to anything that caught her fancy in fact. I was not offended: I respected her greater knowledge and her directness, and I rather enjoyed
the attention paid to me, even if it was negative. Besides, I had one advantage: I'd always been the youngest in my family and I was still the
youngest in this new and larger one. I knew where I belonged and was
content to stay there. It was Valerie, after all, who'd been ousted.

✫

At that time, when Ruth and I first made our appearance, the four
Harveys were sharing the house with various servants and two Welsh
terriers. But as spring turned to summer and summer turned to fall, a
wave of guests began to wash in at the door: relatives, friends, people
from India and Africa and Australia, and most of them with children
and nannies in tow. As fall turned to winter and the war began, one by
one the servants disappeared, while the guests remained.

We had spent that summer, the summer before the war, under
the shadow of Mount Snowden at a farm that took in paying guests:
Clennenna. Although North Wales is not known for its good weather,
I remember those weeks as a time of unremitting sunshine. In my
memory, the hillside fields where sheep grazed among dapples of leaf
shadow and stone are unalloyed by sorrow, and the two Welsh terriers—mother and daughter, Lassie and Vixen—frolic at my side.

My memory, however, does not entirely agree with other people's
account of the time, particularly Valerie's. Later, over the years, I saw
Diana, who was gentle and always rather shy, only very occasionally;
but I kept in better touch with Valerie, who had grown into a lovely
woman, full of good cheer and brimming with fun. And she assured
me that I was a champion whiner, that for months after my arrival in
Swansea I sniffled mournfully after Ruth—who seems, thankfully, to
have forgotten about it—whenever she left my sight. I know that

when Uncle Bourke, a specialist in nicknames and neologisms, coined the verb "to corncrake," he was inspired by me. You will find "corncrake" in the dictionary as a noun signifying a game bird closely related to the grouse, particularly as to its vocal characteristics. This may strike the unbiased etymologist as evidence that I at least sounded miserable and that therefore in all probability I *was* miserable.

But that is not how I remember it—in the *chiaroscuro* of my recollection it is the *chiaro* that prevails. Wearing Valerie's outgrown shorts held up by an elastic belt with an S-shaped fastener—a fashion statement unheard of in Germany or anywhere else I can think of—I sat astride my first horse. A photograph exists suggesting simultaneous pride and petrifaction. The horse is a carthorse, a huge Clydesdale mare, and she is smiling. So are the two little blonde girls sitting behind me, Harvey cousins who are on a visit from Kenya and who are spending a week with us. I seem to recall that later, when we have all got down from the horse, the little girls lower three kittens down a well to see what will happen and that what happens is that the kittens drown. Valerie and Diana weep for the kittens, and after lunch I hear Aunt Helen furiously berating the parents of the little girls. The parents seem bemused and quite nonchalant about this fuss being made over three dead kittens, but Aunt Helen is close to tears.

There are other children at Clennenna. They stay with us for a few days and then move on. Most of them have their parents with them, though one or two, like Ruth and me, are alone, and many, like Ruth and me, have grown up in some other place than England. Native to distant continents, they suppose themselves British but are in fact homeless. In some ways the United Kingdom, which they have visited only briefly and sporadically, is as strange to them as it is to me.

The owner of the farm is a weathered old man who speaks mostly Welsh—Mr. Jones, let us say—who for some reason has taken a fancy to me. Perhaps because I am small and dark, as he is and as his children and grandchildren are, he supposes me among these tall blond paying guests to be the least likely to turn into an imperialist. He puts his calloused hands around mine: "Ura notta notta gurral," he says, affectionately and incomprehensibly. "Ura notta notta gurral."

But a problem is weighing on Mr. Jones's mind. There is no inside toilet on the farm, and even the paying guests have to make do with the chamber pot under the bed or use the outhouse. The outhouse for the wing where the guests sleep is quite beautiful, with vines trailing over the roof and through cracks to make this humblest of sheds into something of a bower. Many of the adult guests are quite happy to wander out there even late at night, even in the hours just before dawn, sauntering through the moonlight and humming to themselves. Usually, smitten by beauty or by the intensity of their own needs, they leave the outhouse door ajar when they depart.

This dismays Mr. Jones. The chickens are mysteriously attracted to the place, and they have taken to lurking nearby and stealing in when they see an opportunity. Then they roost in the outhouse corners and lay their eggs in secret and unreachable places, never to be redeemed.

"Were you out there?" Mr. Jones inquires of us each morning as Mrs. Jones sets out our lavish breakfast. "Were you out there?" It is the cry of the centurion in Thomas B. Costain's *The Robe* seeking some other witness to the Crucifixion, and like the centurion's his question has metaphysical overtones. In fact, whenever Mr. Jones speaks English his words are so essentially mysterious that they often suggest a cosmic dimension—as when he takes my hand in the leather of his and tells me, "Ura notta notta gurral." He may be saying, to tease me, "You're a naughty, naughty girl," or he may be saying, to comfort me, "You're not a naughty girl." Magically, it does not matter, because he has in some nonverbal way assured me that I am exonerated from all guilt, that he holds me blameless for the world and for the open door of the outhouse and for many other things that I cannot yet even imagine.

By now I take it for granted that the two tall strangers who three months ago, when I could hardly understand them, suggested we call them Uncle Bourke and Aunt Helen are indeed Uncle Bourke and Aunt Helen.

✡

That fall I begin to forget my German.

This is in part because my German is being replaced by English, which I now speak without having to think about it. But there may have been an almost willed though unconscious element in my assiduous forgetting of the first language I spoke and wrote and read. On September 9, 1939, England declares war on Germany. When I hear about this I am very alarmed. I stand by the window for hours, searching the skies for airplanes and waiting for bombs to fall. Nothing happens. No one else seems at all worried about bombs—or about the war, for that matter. All of the grown-ups here have been through the First World War, and they see war as something you go out to not as something that comes to you. If they knew why I was standing at the window they would think me silly and quite amusing.

But I know better. I have heard my mother and our housekeeper Stasie talk in the kitchen in Karlsruhe about falling bombs and about soldiers falling from the sky. I keep a lookout. And I know that it is the fact that I worry so much—the fact that unlike all the others I am afraid—that makes me an enemy alien. This is what worries me most of all—I am an enemy alien, and I am proving that I am an enemy alien by being such a coward about bombs and other things falling from the sky. I would like desperately to disguise myself as a little English girl, but I know that I would convince no one, since the very act of trying to disguise myself proves I am not English.

Nevertheless, I suspect it is as a first quite unconscious step in my attempt to be less foreign that I am setting about forgetting all my German.

✜

Little by little, prodded by war, things changed. Our mother's sister, Aunt Liesel, had come to England with our cousin Clare several months before Ruth and I did. Aunt Helen had taken us once to visit them when we first arrived in spring. We had a picnic by the sea and my grandmother, Oma, was also there, a small square package of disapproval punctuated by pearls. In my memory, the day is equivocal, as colorless, odorless, and neutral as my days in Karlsruhe. Aunt Liesel and cousin Clare looked like Aunt Liesel and cousin Clare, but they were in a strangely diminished mode, deprived of their ambience of shining clothes and polished corridors, of translucent china cups and the soft aura of lilies of the valley that had belonged to them in their house in Limburg.

Later that year, after the war had begun, I saw Aunt Liesel and Clare once again; this time they came to Swansea. They came to say good-bye to us, having been accepted by America. Even Uncle Julius, even cousin Kurt who had been, until now, at school in Switzerland, were going to go to America. Aunt Liesel and cousin Clare still looked like Aunt Liesel and cousin Clare, but aside from the superficial visual similarity, they were utterly estranged from themselves. In every memory I had of them, in every memory I had of Limburg, order prevailed; there was a softly repressed luxury that pervaded everything there, from the even rows of the waves in my aunt's coiffure to the satin ribbons that adorned my cousin's hand-crocheted frocks, from the yearning morning song of the caged canary to the muted up and down of scales on the piano—Clare's afternoon practice, stifled in velvet drapery.

In Limburg, the grandfather clock in the hall offered its mellow baritone announcement every hour, and the household obeyed that rhythm. No meal came late. No child went unbathed to bed. Everything was under control.

When I was six and very ill with scarlet fever, my Aunt Liesel, who was a fine watercolorist, had written and illustrated a book for me: *Der Blaue Ballon*. It was about *das kleine Edithlein*, Little Edikins, who is given a blue balloon filled with helium. The balloon is so beautiful that the cherubs in heaven crave it and set it free when *das kleine Edithlein* is looking the other way. The balloon floats upwards, out of reach and out of sight; it is the exact blue of the heavens and has become invisible, indistinguishable from them. The cherubs have possession of it. Briefly *Edithlein* bewails her loss, but the cherubs send her a very jolly multicolored soccer ball to console her—and everyone ends up happy.

Cherubs, alas, are not the only danger to one's earthly belongings. My mother shipped *Der Blaue Ballon* to America, to the house of a friend to hold until she could claim it herself. The friend's cellar was damp, and in the course of several years of storage the *Ballon* was totally eaten away by mildew, as were a valuable leather-bound set of Goethe and the entire archive of our family's photographs.

But I am sure, from what I can remember of it, that the little book and its pretty, delicate illustrations contained my aunt's quintessential philosophy: beware of loving anything too much or the angels will envy you and claim it as their own.

This philosophy had, on occasion, led my aunt to clip the wings of her canary and other creatures she loved, to keep them from flying away—though that, of course, is a very uneasy solution to the problem. And I have always wondered if a sort of abnegation—a resignation of herself to the tediously possible—underlay Aunt Liesel's apparent serenity. It may have been the prospect of going to America—of going to New York, unruly and rife with choices, possibilities, dreams, nightmares—that shattered her calm. Under the circumstances there was nothing she could resign herself to except chaos. In any case, saying good-bye to us in Swansea, the people who looked like Aunt Liesel and Clare seemed distraught. Bereft of everything that was theirs in

Limburg, they had turned into Aunt Liesel and Clare's disorderly opposites, exiles about to start on a new migration and at the edge of panic.

And I suppose that it did not help that I was no longer *das kleine Edithlein* myself, but some monster hybrid halfway between an enemy alien and an English schoolgirl and that I would no longer speak German to anyone.

✳

This is perhaps the place to confess that it took me more than forty years to understand that our transposition to England, mine and Ruth's, was a fragment of a larger and extraordinary history. The *Kindertransport*—which allowed some ten thousand Jewish children to get out of Germany, Austria, and Czechoslovakia and find shelter in England before the war put an end to the program—has been the subject of a fair amount of recent literature and of several films. It could, in fact, be counted as a sort of miracle, and I am still amazed at my own bland passivity and ignorance about my escape, my total numbness. Children, I suppose, tend to accept as normal whatever world they happen to find themselves in, whether they are terrified of it or confused by it or delighted by it, and for decades the nature of my survival simply failed to strike me as noteworthy in any way.

But that Ruth and I were even on the *Kindertransport* was itself surprising; that we ended up with the Harveys was a complete fluke. At the time, given the emergency, it was quite difficult to find people in England willing to take in this sudden flood of refugees wanting to come there. The first plan, for me, had been to ship me to Liverpool to be adopted by a childless Orthodox Jewish couple. As for Ruth, she wasn't planning on England at all: she'd enrolled in a program run by a Zionist organization, the Hachshara, and she'd been packed for months to go to Sweden with a friend. In Sweden they were supposed to learn about farming and then they were to go on to Palestine—to become kibbutzniks, I suppose. The departure for Sweden kept being postponed, and so my mother, expecting the worst, put Ruth's name in for the *Kindertransport* along with mine.

The *Kindertransport* had placed a couple of older girls at Saint Margaret's, which was Di and Val's school, and since the school no longer had room for more refugees, it sent an announcement to all the parents listing the teenage girls who were looking for homes. Ruth took—and still takes—an excellent picture, and on the evidence of the photograph the Harveys volunteered to have her live with them. At that point, Mother sent them some more snapshots, several including me, and when they realized that Ruth had a sister, the Harveys insisted that they would take me in as well.

And that is the story about why I am not an Orthodox Jewish Liverpudlian.

As for all the children who had signed up with the Hachshara, they never left for Sweden after all. Almost all of them, including Ruth's friend, died in Auschwitz.

EGGS

      Aunt Helen used to tell us that she had never boiled an egg before the war started.

This was because before the war started there had been a cook to boil the eggs—as well as everything else. Boiling, in England in those days, was the preferred method for intimidating raw nature until it would sit down at the table. There were two maids to clean—one for upstairs and one for downstairs—who also helped Cook in this taming of ingredients by peeling, chopping, and beating them up. And there was a gardener who persuaded the earth to yield many of those fruits that were later to be humiliated in the kitchen.

In addition there was a charwoman. The dictionary will tell you that the name of this institution describes a woman who does chores. But this strikes me as far too colorless, and I have always supposed that the word, charwoman, had something to do with charcoal and soot, that it was associated with things of such dark and secret character that they had to be confined to the back of the house and never allowed to look in at the front door—let alone walk through it with the doctor, the vicar, and other respectable people. In the days when there were still the cook, the gardener, and the two maids—in the few months, that is, after Ruth and I had arrived at the house but the war had not yet started—the charwoman, universally referred to as "the char," was an anonymous, shapeless, and unmemorable bundle of clothes attached to a mop or a scrub brush, which she applied to the floors midmorning after the two maids had got brass polish on them or the cook had spilled soup in the scullery.

After the war was well underway—when the cook, the gardener, and the maids had long since left for the armed services or munitions work—the char remained. I mean a char remained. And when we moved to Leeds there was a new char—or probably even a series of new chars, one of whom I remember quite well and rather fondly: Mrs. Pearson. I went to stay in her house once or twice, when Aunt Helen had to go away overnight somewhere. And when Mrs. Pearson came to our house to clean, she came through the front door like everyone else.

But that was later. Much later, when almost everything had already changed.

☆

The day on which Aunt Helen was first forced to consider seriously the boiling of eggs—the day Cook left and the maids departed—fell during the week before Christmas in 1939.

There was a crowd of visitors at the Harveys' house.

I think that Aunt Helen's goddaughter, sleek, dark Kat was there, and if she was she must have brought a friend along, as she always did, to keep her company. And possibly there may have been Aunt Violet and Uncle Clyde and Aunt Margaret and Aunt Hilda or any of the Harveys' ten or so variously virginal and solitary siblings who often came for the Holidays if there was a bed available for them. Since the cook and the gardener and the maids had left empty the iron cots up in the attic rooms that had once been their mysterious habitat, there would in all likelihood have been beds available—and beds to spare.

I know that Aunt Peggy was there, and so were her four children: Robin and Dickon, who were twelve and thirteen, went to Public School; but Joy and Beechie, who were six and three, didn't. Their father was the Bishop of Simla, and he had naturally had to stay in India to take care of local morals and various other responsibilities. Meanwhile, the rest of the family was planning to spend the war with us, a month or two it was assumed, after which, God being on their side, His Majesty's Armed Services would have restored tranquility sufficiently for everyone to go back to Simla again.

There were also, of course, Ruth and me. I know now that the bedroom we had appropriated, the room that overlooked the garden and glimpsed at a corner of the sea, was the largest bedroom in the house, the formal front guest room, kept for worthy visitors. The two of us had been taken on for an unknown duration, the understanding being that our mother might, with luck, sooner or later manage to reach America and that she would send for us if she ever got there. No one at that point was making plans for the future around the dire possibility of extermination—that came later. But when England declared war on Germany in September the Harveys must have suspected that Ruth and I would be parked with them for the duration, if not forever.

I have still reached no firm conclusion as to why we were given the best room, or why, when the house began to overflow with December guests, when it was bereft of cook and gardener and maids, two unattached children, there on sufferance, were allowed to stay there. I can only tell you that no one suggested we should be sent to one of the attic rooms, and I am fairly sure that no one even thought of suggesting such a thing; if they had thought of it, if the mere idea had even crossed anyone's mind, my sister would have known right away. She had embraced her new refugee status by wiring herself exquisitely with alarms that sounded a warning at the least hint of resentment or bias. For instance, soon after our arrival Uncle Bourke, who had just finished serving up a dessert of deep-dish apple pie at dinner, asked if anyone would like some more juice, and Ruth, leaping from her chair, shouted, "Jews! Jews! What did you say about Jews?"

So she would have sensed at once any feeling on the part of the houseguests that we didn't know our rightful place in the household. She would have made me pack my bag and, unasked, carried it for me to the new location she would have chosen for us in one of the stark, cold cells in the attic.

But she remained tranquil. And we slept on soundly in the big mahogany beds.

At the time, I think even Ruth must have accepted the room as a matter of course, as one of those inevitabilities, good or bad, that you accommodate in youth, having no choice in the matter. I was younger than she was and more passive, and I let sixty years go by before I began to see how odd it was, in fact, that we were allowed to flourish undisturbed in luxury while the world was tumbling down around us and the cook was gone. We probably owe it to a central idiosyncrasy of Aunt Helen's character—the core of her being that was left unperturbed by war and guests and the lack of egg-boiling expertise: she believed, with the deep, visionary comprehension that is true faith, that the least significant of children was worth one hundred of the most impressively important of adults. It wasn't so much that she loved children—she was quite fond of them, I am sure, as she was fond of dogs and delphiniums and the works of Angela Thirkell—but if she had found herself transported to a world from which everyone under the age of fourteen was banished she would have borne up quite well. She might even have enjoyed herself. Her passionate response to any child's helplessness, her sense of the ultimate predominance of the comfort of children over the conventions and convenience of adults was not really a matter of taste or preference. It was a fact of biology, like blue eyes or a strong dental structure. It went deeper than love. She couldn't help herself.

She had another innate and rather extraordinary quality that perhaps explains why her houseguests failed to rebel at our favored accommodation in their crowded midst: a handsome, tall, somewhat stern-looking woman, Aunt Helen, quite unconsciously, emanated an aura of almost imperial authority. During the days of rationing, butchers and grocers and dairymen constantly sought to propitiate her with offerings of illegal extras—which, having been born to a cricket-playing nation and class, she naturally declined. Also, to my frequent embarrassment, our neighbors and the parents and teachers at my school tended to become all unctuous and began to grovel at her approach. She was totally unconscious of the effect she had on people, but she struck awe into those among whom she walked. And it must have seemed obvious to her guests, as it did to the general public, that to enter into battle with her would lead not only to defeat, but to making oneself look something of a worm.

✶

On Christmas Eve I came down with the whooping cough, which Diana and Beechie both caught. Two weeks into the New Year I got the measles as well. And I suppose it was not so long after that that the Germans started bombing the harbor, one corner of which Ruth and I could glimpse from the bay window of our splendid room. Before this happened, however, at the moment the measles appeared, poor Aunt Peg, concerned for the health of her children, dared to question Aunt Helen's Prime Directive and suggested that I should be sent to the hospital to prevent further contamination.

To no one's surprise, not even her own, it was Aunt Peg who was dispatched instead. She went back to India with the girls while the boys finished the year at Marlborough and stayed with us during holidays. By the summer, the mined seas had become too dangerous for them to travel back and forth, even for the sake of Public School, and when they returned to Simla at the end of term they stayed there until the end of the war.

✳

There was only one cookbook in the kitchen when Aunt Helen took over, the book by Isabella Beeton, who died astonishingly young after leaving the world her advice in *Mrs. Beeton's Book of Household Management*, which was published in 1835. Things had been changing steadily, of course, since then: servants were becoming fewer over the decades and so were flatirons and coal cooking stoves. The iceman had entered the kitchen along with the gas man. Then came electric refrigerators and more and more commonly—even in England—machines to do the laundry. But Mrs. Beeton's advice was still to be found in almost every respectable English kitchen, having been given to every proper English bride on her wedding day. Her publisher, however, had been rather conservative in editing it to keep abreast of the times.

The copy in our kitchen was well worn—consulted, one assumes, by Cook, Aunt Helen being innocent in such matters. But left in sole charge of a dozen or fifteen houseguests she recognized that it was now time to make its acquaintance. Cautiously, she took down the sacred volume, and, tradition has it, it fell open to the page on "baking a plain cake." This sounded encouraging.

I should add here that the fact that Aunt Helen had never boiled an egg was not, at this particular point in history, significant. An army marches on its stomach, Napoleon is supposed to have said, and even though the war had not been going on for very long, a few months of trying to feed an army has its impact on the civilian population. There were no longer any eggs to boil.

Mrs. Beeton did not worry about such things: she had written for herself and her friends, women of a class and time that didn't consult twentieth-century concepts of economy or health in their culinary decisions. She began her directions for "baking a plain cake" with the instruction "take a dozen eggs."

Underneath this, in the margin, Aunt Helen noted, "put eleven back."

In retrospect I understand now that the instruction to "take a dozen eggs; put eleven back"—which is in every way, except purely mathematically, the exact opposite of the instruction to "take one egg"—was the guiding principle behind our life in England.

I suppose that most of the people I know these days, modestly affluent types who travel a fair amount in the third world, feel themselves pretty lucky to be one-eggers in a largely eggless world. I also know a couple of twelve-eggers who live lives of excess, wallowing in soufflés. But the Harveys fell into neither of these two categories. They belonged to the "take twelve eggs put eleven back" school of thought, which was nurtured in another class and another culture than any now in existence.

Brought up in the tradition of the English Public School, they had been taught to believe that a gentleman—or more incidentally, a gentlewoman—was someone who took responsibility: for the weaker, the younger, the poorer, and the less fortunate, but also, and most emphatically, for his own actions. Rudyard Kipling's "If" gives you the general idea, which if you care to you can trace back without effort to Thomas Arnold's innovations at Rugby in the 1830s: making the older boys answerable for the younger; exacting a price of obligation in exchange for a position of privilege.

But then Kipling and Arnold themselves must have had a precedent to follow, something that makes their particular model of honor so specifically English, so unlike the hairsplitting that Corneille's heroes go in for or the revenge and bloodletting that does the trick in Hispanic societies. Sir Philip Sydney, with his last breath sending the water bearer over to a common soldier—"his need is greater than mine"—might have been made a saint in any country, but I suspect that only the British would ever see him as a hero, a man not only to admire and emulate but someone to make the heart beat faster.

Who knows why? A democratic gene in the gene pool of the upper crust? A history of peasants rising to the trades and the trades rising to nobility? A wet climate and short seasons forcing every Briton, Celt, and Gael from time immemorial to work in the fields together regardless of social position? Whatever the reason, I am hardly the first to notice that the well-documented and appalling snobbery of the English upper and middle classes has its roots in a sort of dialectic opposite, in an ideal of absolute democracy hard to find anywhere else on earth.

Of course, of course—it remains largely that: an ideal, not universally, not even for the most part, not even very frequently lived up to. But the fact remains: Aunt Helen cooked and lived by the "take a dozen eggs" principle of those who are born to plenty, and she put eleven back because, where she came from, that same principle obliged her to do so.

THE SECOND YEAR OF
THE WAR

⌒‿‿ My Uncle Bourke was a prison gover-
nor. When Ruth and I came to England in 1939 he was the head of
Swansea Prison. In the autumn of 1940 he was posted to Leeds and
then, at the end of the war, to Dartmoor.

Being a prison governor was a job that, though not particularly
glamorous, was considered a respectable career for a graduate of Sand-
hurst whose main experience in life had been in the Indian Cavalry.
Having risen to the rank of major, and more formally addressed as
Major George B. Harvey, Uncle Bourke brought an aura of class to a
position that very probably shared with many other high offices in His
Majesty's Civil Service of that time the fact that it existed largely to
have an aura of class brought to it.

As far as I could tell, there were no pictures of Major George B.
Harvey in his prison governor persona, but many had been taken of
him when he was still in India. In three or four of these he was shown
in uniform, one of a group of other men also in uniform, some of
them standing, some proudly on horseback, all of them always leather

belted and leather besashed with little wands under their arms in case they needed to hit anyone.

Judging by the photographic evidence, however, Uncle Bourke did not spend much of his time in uniform: mostly he seemed to dress in short-sleeved shirts and jodhpurs, which allowed him to sit on a rather small pony while sticking his long legs out at either side to keep them out of the way. While he sat on the pony he always wore a round white hat like a brimmed pudding, wielded a mallet, and looked abashed; the pony appeared to be in a state of perpetual dejection.

The number of these photographs and the fact that they were all framed and hung might have led you to the conclusion that this part of his life—the years at play for the British Raj—had somehow been its zenith and that the rest of it—the years spent governing various penal institutions—was simply what he did afterwards. But such a conclusion would have been false. The number of photographs of his polo-playing years was due to the fact that the British Raj was what photographers took photographs of; the British penal system was not. And it has to be remembered that the pictures, after all, were hung not in the full splendor of the downstairs hall (which was reserved for a suite of eighteenth-century hunting prints) but in the passage to the upstairs bathroom. There may even have been a slight, though quite unconscious, self-mockery about their display; and when I think back now on those images of the bemused man three sizes too tall for his despairing pony, they always evoke the faint image of Don Quixote superimposed on the shadow of Sancho Panza—of honor, humor, sweetness, and nuttiness combined in exactly equal parts.

I doubt, in fact, that Uncle Bourke took polo seriously or that he was particularly good at it, but I am certain that he was a devoted and excellent prison governor. He had a rare quality for a man—rarer still for an administrator—that suited him perfectly to such a job: he took himself lightly. Lightly enough to be able to lay himself aside cheerfully whenever his faults threatened to get in the way. He didn't seem to feel any need, for instance, to hide the fact that he relied heavily on his deputy governors, who had all the training and experience he himself lacked: he was quite open about his dependency on them. He acknowledged it casually, as a matter of course, to us, and I am sure that his gratitude for his staff's indulgence must have gone on public record and certainly must have become known to them as well.

Now and then one or another of the prison officers would stop by our house on business, and when they did you could sense the result of this lack of defensiveness about his shortcomings in their palpable affection for him, a sort of slightly amused and slightly concerned respect. I think it was a form of the same protective fellowship that his subjects enjoyed in those loyal and happy days with George VI, their unexpected king. Being a bit of a duffer has probably never stood in the way of good leadership, although trying to pretend you are not one is certainly lethal.

☆

The year Uncle Bourke became the governor of Leeds Prison, the year we all moved to Yorkshire, was 1940. It was also the year of the Battle of Britain. By that spring, the Germans had taken Poland, Norway, Denmark, and the Low Countries. In mid-May, the British forces, entrenched in eastern France behind the Maginot Line of defenses, were cut off by the advancing Germans. Stranded on the wrong side of the North Sea, they made their way as best they could to Dunkirk, the single port still left open to them. In their now legendary rescue, the ships of the Royal Navy were joined by fishing trawlers, yachts, rowboats, and pleasure craft to ferry the men back to British soil.

France was about to fall, but Hitler, expecting a polite surrender by England, was disappointed.

Meanwhile, my mother, entrance visa in hand, had just arrived in New York. The American laws of immigration at the time were not notable for their generosity, but luckily she had been born in Alsace, and for the purpose of getting an entrance visa she was therefore considered French. My sister and I, both born in Karlsruhe, would have had to wait years for one. The quotas of natives of Germany, Austria, Czechoslovakia, and, of course, Poland, were filled for eons into the future, but French and Italian Jews were not yet in full flight and space in the French and Italian quotas was often still available.

My mother had originally booked her passage through Holland, and most of the possessions she planned to bring to the United States were already on the Dutch ship she had been expecting to board within the week. But she was something of a clairvoyant—a talent sharpened by the fact that she also had a strong bias towards expecting the worst—and shortly before she was to leave she was overwhelmed by a sense that she should abandon her goods and chattels to their own devices and go off in the opposite direction herself. She was on a train to Marseilles with one small, late-packed trunk and a couple of suitcases when she heard that Holland had fallen and that the ship carrying her belongings had been bombed and sunk. If she had gone in the direction she had originally planned she would have been caught in Amsterdam.

The Germans meanwhile were moving with astonishing speed: by the time my mother arrived in Philadelphia a few weeks later, they were already well established in Paris.

✫

Swansea was an important harbor, and during that summer and early fall the air-raid siren sounded every night, sometimes twice. Now and then, after a night of bombing, there would be gaps in the street where houses had been before and a sickening smell of rot and burning would announce yet more death and destruction. The beach, where we used to have our picnics, had been put out of bounds after a storm washed ashore two huge metal balls with spikes sticking out of them; they looked like maces wielded by giants, and so I suppose they were. We still went swimming—but further up the coast away from mines and air raids. Once, while we were sitting peacefully drinking barley water under the cloud-specked sky, two planes appeared, from nowhere it seemed, from behind us, speeding past us into the west. We could hear a sound like some mad chorus of woodpeckers as the planes raced by above us toward the horizon, but before they reached it there was a puff of smoke that fell from the air into the water. The one plane remaining swooped out of sight, and the world was silent again and serene.

We heard that some people—Londoners, mostly—had taken to going to sleep in their cellars so as to save themselves having to get up again. But we kept on going to bed as if we were expecting a perfectly normal night. Then, when the alert went off, we put on our dressing gowns over our pajamas and made our way down to the part of the cellar we used as our shelter. There were mattresses on the floor and cots set up, so we could go to sleep again until the All Clear allowed us to go back to our beds. After a week or two we had become used to it, to the occasional boom of bombs and the constant crackle of antiaircraft fire.

In any case, however disturbed our night may have been, we got up at the same time as always, dressed as usual, and went to kneel around the big bed in Aunt Helen 's and Uncle Bourke's room to say the morning prayer for the day, before we began our breakfast, laid out for us in the dining room, at exactly eight.

True, by the summer of 1940 some things had begun to change. To begin with, we were often sleepy in the morning and we were sent to bed a bit earlier than before. There were no eggs for breakfast and no bacon, and the meat in the sausages was, as Aunt Helen put it, a case of "here am I but where are you?" She rang the breakfast bell now herself, as one of the maids used to do when there were still maids to do it. And in the garden where delphiniums and golden rod had flourished Uncle Bourke now planted tomatoes and beans and lettuces.

We had all been given our own tiny squares of garden in which to grow whatever we liked—mine supplied the family with any mustard and cress they might need in the course of their lifetime—and we helped with the big garden too. When an infestation of caterpillars struck, Uncle Bourke offered us a bounty—a penny a dozen—for any we drowned in a bucket of salt water provided for the purpose. Robin, who was waiting for his passage back home to India, had been given a BB gun for his thirteenth birthday, and he thought it would be sporting to shoot the caterpillars instead of drowning them. He began from a distance—to practice marksmanship, he said—and then moved in to closer range for efficiency. He may have got a caterpillar or two, though I doubt it, but he certainly did nothing to improve the tomatoes.

In retrospect, it occurs to me that he may have been aiming so as to miss the caterpillars in the first place but trying not to look too resistant to adult protocols while he was doing it. As a product of the English Public School system, Robin was a bit off center. He looked out at the world past a thick forelock of dark hair that did nothing much to hide the fact that he thought a lot of very grave things quite funny and that he felt unduly sorry for unpopular scraps of creation—like caterpillars—often overlooked by the general population. He once—much later—told me that what Marlborough had taught him was to make good toast over an open fire and to read poetry in secret; and he is probably the only person since John Stuart Mill to have had a subversive passion for Wordsworth.

He was, in fact, a Romantic: not the sort of Romantic who makes the exotic familiar, but one of those who finds sublimity in the mundane. He had a passion for names, for instance—for names like Eastcheap and Cheapside, Maidenhead and Biggleswade and Wormwood Scrubs.

He therefore considered Merthyr Tydfil—a short distance from Swansea by train—extraordinarily promising as a tourist attraction, and when he noticed in the paper that *The Spy in Black* was playing at the Merthyr Tydfil Cinema, he decided that an urge to go to the Saturday matinee would make a convincing excuse to get the grown-ups to let him go there. The Spy in Black was a German spy, so he thought it would be nice if I went with him; he was even willing to pay for me out of his own pocket money.

From what I remember of it, Merthyr Tydfil fully lived up to its nominal expectations. It lay on the railroad line through the Rhondda Valley, a tormented landscape of barren hills whose grayness was broken only by telephone poles and black mounds of sludge. It was a monotony of ugliness so generous that it achieved a sort of grandeur, the mythic stature of the perfectly hideous on which nothing could improve. Robin loved it.

And the town of Merthyr Tydfil matched its ambience. The railway seemed pretty much its center and its purpose and the streets of the little black houses with their little black yards seemed not quite to know where to go to find the middle of town. When they did find their unruly way there at last, the Merthyr Tydfil Cinema revealed itself lurking in an unpromising corner, with *The Spy in Black* in three dimensions slightly aslant, up on the marquee.

There was a poster tacked up next to the box office. It said, NO MATINEE TODAY SOCCER WITH PORTHCAWL COME BACK AT 6.

I suppose at that point we would both have liked to go home; but it said COME BACK AT 6 in black and white on the poster, and Robin and I were both, in our different ways, children who had been left on our own—not for the afternoon, I mean, but for life. We already recognized the written word as being a relatively reliable guide through the fragile and alien universe, and we tended to follow such signs as we were given, whether they said, "The world is too much with us; late and soon, / Getting and spending we lay waste our powers" or NO MATINEE TODAY SOCCER WITH PORTHCAWL COME BACK AT 6. We therefore came back at six.

Meanwhile, we spent our time at Woolworths. Robin had discovered Woolworths when he was in London. That is, Robin had discovered while he was in London that the Woolworths next to his family's hotel there was exactly the same as the Woolworths in Bombay where he had spent an hour or two before boarding the ship. If he found himself, while he was in London, missing his old life, all he had to do was go to Woolworths and think he was back in India again. Or, all Woolworths being equal, if he went to Nairobi he could go to the Woolworths in Nairobi and feel as if he were in London, or the one in New York, which would be just like the one in Nairobi.

It is a concept now made trite by the universal shopping mall filled with Gaps and Brookstones and Benetons—but in 1940 it was still a novel idea.

It had begun to rain, and the streets of Merthyr Tydfil were turning to black mud, but inside Woolworths it was bright and comforting. We were in the Land of Plenty, even in Merthyr Tydfil, even in the depths of war. We fingered the rows of pencils arranged according to hardness and the pens with little boxes of pen nibs next to them, the pen wipers and ink bottles and inkwells, the various sizes of notebooks, lined and unlined, and all the other paraphernalia for writing in those times, as if we were comparison shoppers, making critical choices.

"Can I help you, is it?" asked the sales clerk, and she pointed toward the toy section where we comparison shopped for another hour among pink celluloid dolls and jigsaw puzzles and many different versions of Snakes and Ladders and Old Maid.

When Woolworths closed, Robin bought us a dozen cream buns to share between us for our tea, and then it was time for the film.

All I remember of *The Spy in Black* now is that he was played by Conrad Veidt and that he could not say "butter" properly. I believe that is why he was caught, and I remember thinking that it was silly to try to be a spy if you could not pronounce "butter" in a manner that accorded with local standards. I had learned to say "butter" properly myself. But this was early in the war, when the patriotic myths and righteous emblems that would soon light the way to thought, deed, and the plotting of films were still quite dim. The Spy in Black may even have been a quite ambiguous character. I think I quite identified with him (though not as much as I did with Dumbo, who appeared next year). This may, of course, simply have confirmed my status as an enemy alien.

When we came out of the Merthyr Tydfil Cinema it was still raining and pitch dark; since we had expected to be home by teatime, we had of course brought no torches with us to find our way through the blackout, and the dating couples frolicking through the mist and muck showed no interest in shining any beacons for us to follow. For some reason I remember no details at all of our trip back, though I think a policeman may have had something to do with it. There must be some cogent need to brush such details from my mind—embarrassment, perhaps? relief? the desire for a guilt-free ending? I know we did get back safely after all, though when we knocked on the door and Aunt Helen and Uncle Bourke answered it, it was clear they had been waiting up for us. I knew they had been waiting for us because they were both downstairs, but dressed in their bathrobes and ready for bed.

✡

I suppose for the Harveys themselves and for those who had always lived lives very much like theirs, the changes in the daily rituals during that year must have seemed cataclysmic. But for Ruth and me, who had happened by less than twelve months ago, things looked miraculously stable: the schedules unchanged, the meals on time, the rooms dusted daily, the Hoover brought out to roar once a week as if there were still a cook and two maids around to see to such things.

Indeed, despite their absence, servants were still in some way at the center of our universe, whose skeletal structure for centuries before they at last disappeared must have been formed around them. The routine of the household remained, dictating the life we lived as if it had been written on a stone tablet—not only because it had become habitual but because, like the Ten Commandments themselves, it made a great deal of sense. I suppose all of us who grew up there—in that household, in that culture, at that time—still find ourselves vacuuming weekly, having our three daily meals more or less on schedule, and changing the bed linens at regular but rather distant intervals as behooves those without washing machines. We were handed this calendar when we were children filling in for the domestic staff, who—having given us the blueprint to live by—were, however, now gone from the world forever.

✶

We drove from Swansea to Leeds in the Austin 6, its last trip before gas rationing put it up on blocks for the duration. We drove through a countryside ready for invasion. There were no signposts, and if you asked the way, the native population—young boys and old farmers beyond the age of joining in the fight—regarded you with deep suspicion. By then I had pretty much entirely forgotten my German and spoke accentless English, but clearly no one in the heat of their patriotic fervor cared about such fine points. They were only eager to do away with foreign interlopers in general—whether they came from Germany or merely from another part of England.

"Aff aroond a-oilan," we were told in Shropshire, when Aunt Helen inquired as to which road led northward. "Aff aroond a-oilan." We were told this reluctantly by a very old sheepherder who obviously regretted having to give out such dangerous information. Only an ancient habit of politeness forced him to give any answer at all to this woman with four children and two dogs in the car—an excellent disguise for a spy.

After going several times around it we decided that "Aff aroond a-oilan" must mean "half around the island," which is what the English call a traffic circle. We thought the old man was hilarious. "Aff aroond a-oilan," we told each other for the rest of our northward trip and for months, for years to come. We shrieked with delight as we aped his dialect, quite unaware that our own, snerdy Public School twang must have sounded just as silly to him. We were not ready, not quite yet, to give up the rivalries of region and class.

If an American child made such loud fun of a regional idiosyncrasy, any enlightened American parent would smack it upside the head. But then, of course, the enlightened parents of an American child would also strive mightily not to get lost in locales given to strange dialects in the first place, where, if they asked directions, they would probably be shot. Given the complex hostilities of human behavior, these things tend to balance themselves out.

✳

When she was not pausing to ask directions, Aunt Helen made headway at an alarming pace. She was famous for it; no one who has ever driven with her forgets the experience, and even my husband Peter, who was warned ahead of time and drives like a maniac himself, was impressed during the few miles she drove us from her house in Felsted to a nearby inn for lunch. At that point she was eighty and driving slowly—at a nearly normal speed. But her spirit remained unbowed, and when a bicyclist gave us a timid hand signal—he had been made fearful by our forceful descent into an intersection where he was trying to make a turn—she rolled down her window to put him right. Not that she disputed his clear right-of-way; it was his style she questioned. "Why ever are you flapping your hand at me, you silly man," she called out as, alarmed by this frontal challenge, he flapped more desperately and wobbled by. And I recall that just after the war, when the relaxation of petrol rationing allowed us to use the car again after its years on blocks, she would drive at sixty miles an hour through those narrow English lanes where hedgerows make it impossible to see ahead or into curves. Nothing daunted, she would honk the horn, confident of victory, and the poor drivers going in the opposite direction from us would shrink into the bushes, waiting for us to go by. "Coward," Aunt Helen shouted at them joyously as we passed. "Poltroon!"

It should be noted that she never had an accident. Although, of course, there is no way of assessing the psychological damage inflicted on those who happened to be in her way.

LEEDS

Leeds has undergone an architectural and cultural renaissance since I lived there, but at the best of times it is a dark city, in the north, in a valley, socially shadowed by the history of the woolen mills that have made its fortune since the Black Prince took them under his protection in the 1300s. Nor has it been blessed by nature, placed as it is under the bleak majesty of moorland totally unchanged since Heathcliff strode about on it gnashing his teeth, though now that I think of it, Heathcliff lived well south of Leeds, in a relatively sunny and hospitable spot.

In the 1940s, before its reclamation, Leeds was unequivocally a dump. Some of its residents lived in little semidetached villas with little semidetached gardens, out of range of the worst of the soot—generated by mills and railway—that fell from the sky and spread a pale gray wash over everything. But the vast majority of its inhabitants lived in streets of row houses. These had nothing in common with the august, Georgian curves of Oxford Street or Bath, nor even with the modest white-cuffed regiments of Baltimore or Philadelphia. They were an unruly hodgepodge of brick mined from Yorkshire's clay hills, gardenless, sunless, with high walls hiding the intimate lives of each from all the others.

I suppose they were built as factory houses during Dickens's time, and they were the sort of places Dickens imagines, though the sort of places Dickens imagines no longer existed, even then, in the towns he wrote about: richer and more progressive towns than Leeds whose greatest contribution to urban culture would seem to have been the walled-in backyard. These wretched little flagstone squares offered each resident family just enough space for an outhouse and a rubbish pile, hidden from prying eyes by their high brick barricades that lined the warren of narrow little streets.

Before we moved there, Aunt Helen had come up to see for herself where the governor of Leeds Prison was supposed to live. She had been duly appalled by the Governor's House, which, being next to the prison, was also in one of the worst neighborhoods in a town where there were no good ones. We therefore eschewed the Governor's House and went to live at Twenty-Three the Towers instead.

✫

You come to Twenty-Three the Towers by way of an avenue of venerable and huge horse chestnut trees. They lead to a driveway lined with still more trees: a sort of park, in fact, for a few houses whose conception is rather grander than the final result. My old friend Smigs, who was born in Leeds and still lives there, went by the place a few years ago to see if it still existed; when she found out that indeed it did, she sent me a photograph of it to prove the point.

The photograph was reassuring; I was not making things up. Twenty-Three the Towers really did have yearnings to look like a lesser version of Brideshead in *Brideshead Revisited* without the fountain. Or perhaps, more exactly, like a lesser version of Brideshead in *Brideshead Revisited* if it had been built in 1848, as an imitation of the original and

not as a single, massive castle but as three adjacent blocks of preten-
tiously ordinary townhouses.

But you get the idea. The scale of the edifice is impressive, what
with its towers and the fake crenellations on the roof. The buildings
are up on something of a hill, so the rather scrawny lawns stretching
towards the driveway are terraced and each house has a row of steps,
punctuated by the occasional stone bench, rampant lion, or other object of distinction to take one down in style. But since The Towers was
home to at least ten or twelve families, even in 1940 before the advent
of condominiums, the grandeur of the outside was largely an illusion.

The horse chestnuts, however, were real.

In spring, they blossomed with pyramids of white candles.
When the petals fell and covered the ground in white, you could already see the tight green buttons of the chestnuts beginning to form.
In time, they swelled up, until by late summer they were the size of
golf balls. They had also developed spikes and looked very much like
miniature green cousins of the mines that had washed ashore in
Swansea Harbor. In fact, the green, spiked shell of these chestnuts *did*
hide a weapon of war, the beautiful, gleaming brown nut that spilled
out when the shell cracked—or was cracked by us—in early fall.

We called the nuts "conkers" because they were used to conk
each other and also because, as far as we were concerned, their exis-
tential purpose was to conquer. We strung each one singly onto a
strong length of twine, knotted at one end, and chose ourselves an an-
tagonist. Then swinging them on their strings like cowboys twirling
lassos, we would bash at each other's conkers until one of them
cracked while the other was pronounced the victor. You could do
things to make your conker a winner: choosing a big, particularly shining one was a good idea; but you could also soak it in vinegar for a day
or two. Conkers gained reputations—like fighting cocks—and it occurs to me that, like fighting cocks, the concept of cracking nuts has
its overtones.

Looking back, I am astonished, in fact, at how many of our

games reflected the hostile, punishing world we were growing up to, though perhaps that is putting it backwards and it is the hostile world that develops out of games like ours, out of some inborn impulse, endemic to human nature, waiting from our infancy to grow up into war. The Harveys' household was perhaps as peaceful and pleasant as any household on this earth, but the games we played were not. Even our usual card games suggested an agitated sensibility unsuitable, one would have thought, for such a sedentary form of entertainment, and they had names like Double Demon and Oh Hell.

Our favorite game by far was a species of hide-and-seek. We called it Kickapeg. One player was "it." The others went into hiding while the "it" person tried to find them and corral them, one at a time, onto the upstairs landing, which was our designated "prison." The "prisoners," however, could be set free again by a touch of the fingers of those still unfound, and then they could go and hide all over again. And since the game was only officially over when everyone had been put into "prison," it could go on indefinitely with hardly a pause for lunch. Most of us as the years went by found things to do while we were in our hiding places—reading, knitting, crossword puzzles—illuminating such avocations with our blackout torches.

Sometimes on winter weekends Kickapeg was simply a framework for our everyday existence: life rearranged by make-believe into something just slightly more coherent than the real world of growth and decay and war and separation. It was a kind of pleasant and rather aimless transformation of the reality both of Uncle Bourke's daily occupation as prison governor and of our nights of hiding out from the German bombs.

There were more formal games too, of course, and seasonal rituals like the charades we put on at Christmas. These were not the mimed charades one plays at nowadays, but a species of instant theater involving two teams staging impromptu dramatic skits involving multiple characters who were costumed in the old clothes stored especially for the purpose in the two big trunks up in the attic.

Our charades went like this: suppose, for instance, that team A has decided on a word, "pensive," say, for team B to guess. In scene 1, Uncle Bourke turns himself into a schoolboy by way of putting on a jacket five sizes too small for him, hitching up his trousers, and decorating his nose with ink, while Ruth, ruler in hand, is transformed into a schoolmarm. "Where is your pen, Leonard?" she asks. In scene 2, Leonard, having become a pastry chef with the help of a tablecloth tied round his neck and a half cup of flour paste stuck to his face, moans that he "can't find a sieve." And, in the final scene, incorporating the whole word, Aunt Lil, seated, with chin in hand and a sheet draped modestly around her vest and knickers, attempts to look enough like Rodin's *The Thinker* so that I can wander by and comment, "Ain't she pensive?" Casting, dramaturgy, and set decoration naturally take much longer than the actual scenes, and team B has probably wandered off to get itself slices of plum cake during the entr'acte. Still, with the help of prompting, groaning, eye rolling, and other aids, team B usually guesses the right word or phrase.

Afterwards, to end these winter evenings on Christmas or New Year's or Boxing Day, Val or Di would put the record of the Sir Roger de Coverly on the gramophone and we would get into two lines and dance. On the left side of the globe the Sir Roger de Coverly is known as the Virginia Reel, but in those days our part of the world was still nostalgic for a time when ladies were escorted in to supper and titles mattered.

✳

In summer we played outside—not on the terraced lawn with its pretensions, but in the lower garden behind the garage, where the little Austin 6 had been put away. Though the lawn there was just big enough for tennis or badminton, the game we played most was cricket, family style—one set of wickets, adjustable rules, and a highly variable number of players per team.

In place of the Austin we had procured bicycles. Aunt Helen cut a dashing figure as two or three times a week she rode to the greengrocer and the butcher and the fishmonger to exchange our ration coupons for cooking supplies, which she carried home in the large wire basket attached to the handle bars.

She was the only one who used her bicycle regularly and for practical purposes. The rest of us took ours out only on weekends and holidays; but still, in their way, though they were mere machines and kept for occasional use, they represented us and suggested some of our quintessential differences. Uncle Bourke, of course, had a man's bike, larger than any of the others. It had a bar between front and saddle, and Uncle Bourke would mount it smartly, left foot on the pedal, right leg swung over the bar, as if he were mounting a horse. The ladies' bikes, however, were built to allow one to get on without an undue show of crotch, and we would sneak our right leg daintily behind our left, through the space provided. In those days, feminine delicacy was still more important than the structural safety that makes most bicycles these days rather more unisex.

And our bicycles displayed idiosyncrasies aside from gender characteristics. Those of all four Harveys, for instance, were slim, with large, narrow-rimmed wheels, thin tires, and slender saddles on which one perched, upright and stiff as if in a straight-backed chair. They were graceful and simple, single-geared English devices with rear-wheel brakes and good English names, like Raleigh. My sister's bicycle, to the contrary, was German. I am not sure how or why she had brought it over with her, but there it was, short, thick, and heavy, with fat, deeply cleated tires so foreign that it was impossible to get replacements for them. It had double brakes, front and back, three gears, and a grim, Teutonic seriousness of purpose that always got her wherever we were going long before anyone else.

Finally, then, we must come to me. My bicycle was a pathetic thing with no nationality and no style except that it was as close to being a tricycle as you can get without having three wheels. My legs were too short for a grown-up bike, and so I had been given an old, discarded one of Val's. I pedaled on it furiously, trying to keep up while the others sailed blithely ahead. Breathless with effort and the fear of abandonment, I would arrive at the hilltop to find everyone waiting for me. Or they might already have gone and I would find Uncle Bourke, one foot on the pedal, the other on the ground, waiting for me alone.

In those days, handicapped by being the youngest and the shortest, I was usually also the last. Scenes of the period rise up in my memory covered with the pale wash of other people's strained patience. Valerie, who had been the youngest and the shortest before I arrived—and who was, I can now see, somewhat ambivalent about passing that honor on to me—observed my panting progress with a smug disdain I very much admired. But being the youngest is at least a restful place to be, a relaxing position that rarely needs defending, and I settled in very comfortably as Valerie's henchman, a quite willing toady, happy to have her to follow. Ruth and Diana had moved to some antechamber of the adult world where neither Val nor I had any wish to spend much time. For want of a better alternative, therefore, we spent most of our days together and I think, by and large, despite her disdain— or more likely because of it—she was pleased to find me reliably trailing behind her.

So I took my place as the smallest, slowest, and last, content at least to have a position so definitive in the great family scheme. Occasionally, Aunt Helen or Uncle Bourke had to intervene on my behalf—they would insist I be given a head start in rounders, for instance, or that a visiting cousin should, literally, go to bat for me. And often Uncle Bourke would wheel my little bicycle for the last few yards up the more difficult hills along with his own.

There was a family code for such indulgences: "f'ing G." If one of the visiting cousins questioned these favors or looked annoyed, or if Valerie or Diana objected, Uncle Bourke needed only to say "f'ing G," and the matter was dropped. In those days of blessed innocence, "f" was as blameless as any other letter of the alphabet and there was

certainly not the slightest hint that "f'ing" might imply something un-
toward, but I never found out what exactly it did mean. When, years
later, I asked Valerie, she said she remembered something about "f'ing
G," but she had no idea what it could have stood for. We both agreed
that "G" was for Granny, the nickname Uncle Bourke had bestowed
on me my first Christmas in England, when I would sit up in bed,
feverish and coughing whoopingly, with a bed shawl over my shoulders. I suppose "f'ing G" meant something like "favoring Granny," or
"fathering Granny," or possibly "fooling Granny." In any case, whatever it meant, it served to get me through.

✫

Robin and Dickon were by now settled back in Simla, but there were
more houseguests than ever: relatives and godchildren of relatives and
relatives of godchildren—home on leave, or regrouping after some
private, minor disaster of war, or escaping the bombs that seemed to
fall relentlessly on every city but Leeds. Leeds apparently was so hidden by so much smoke and grime that those aiming for its destruction
inadvertently cast their weapons onto the moorland sheep instead, and
after a year or so they gave up, as we—after a year or so of heading
dutifully for the cellar whenever the siren sounded—gave that up and
instead turned over and went back to sleep.

Meanwhile, the Harveys' friends and relations who lived in the
south of England sent their children up to be safe with us for the holidays, and as often as not they came up with them themselves. Michael
was a frequent visitor but usually arrived without his mother who wore
wonderful hats because she was an actress; and because she was an actress, she had to remain in London. Peter and Marjorie and their
little brother Charlie stayed with us often, sometimes with their im-
perious and elegant mother and always with Charlie's nanny, Nanny
Webb, who smoked so much that her white hair had turned yellow.
She had an edge of satire that touched her trim, tart, tailored persona

with a slight aura of wickedness. Elizabeth came now and then. She was even worse at games than I was and less resigned to her lack of talent. When challenged, she tended to retire into dudgeon. Her mother, Aunt Doll, was Uncle Bourke's sister and was married to an earl or a viscount or something of that sort; and she was very deaf, so she had to carry around with her a little black box that she could turn on whenever she wanted to hear better—which she never did.

Usually, therefore, we had enough people around to get up a game of cricket—even though Charlie was too young and Elizabeth dudgeon-bound. If there were not enough for two teams, we played in rotation—one batter, one pitcher, and assorted fielders, taking turns.

And there was also Smigs.

✫

Smigs's real name was Kathleen Merryweather. She was in the same year as I was at West Leeds High School, but she was in the section focused on something called Domestic Science and other practical disciplines, while Ruth and Valerie and Diana and I were all learning Latin and French and various convolutions of science and math aimed towards an academic future.

Smigs was brilliant at sports, particularly swimming. Later, as a young woman, she swam for Leeds and Yorkshire and was the Yorkshire Junior Champion for a time. I was hopeless at anything involving balls or sticks, and my preferred method of water locomotion has always been the dead man's float. I don't know why she came back with me for tea one day, but she did. Uncle Bourke, who was often home at teatime, opened the door for us, and after he had looked Smigs over for a moment he said, "How nice to meet you. Do come in. You must be Smigly Rydz."

We all, even Aunt Helen, followed the custom of the day in accepting him, the resident wage-earning male, as the head of our tribe; but he was a man with the eternal light of boyhood twinkling in his

eye, and when we followed enthusiastically where he led us it was often to find ourselves in the world of Oswald Bastable and Stalkey &
Co., in the world of Peter Pan, in short, where boys never grow up.

For example, Uncle Bourke was the instigator of the butter dripping competition, which evolved from Aunt Helen's comment that we
could do whatever we liked with the two pats of the rationed butter
each of us was allotted for our tea. I think she had in mind a choice
between eating them now or saving them for a later meal, but Uncle
Bourke recalled that at Marlborough they used to shoot butter up
from the ends of their knives to hit the ceiling just above the chandelier so that as the meal progressed the butter would melt and drip
down on people's heads. The winner of the competition was the butter flipper who got his pat of butter closest to Chandelier Center.

I have no idea why Aunt Helen did not immediately put a stop
to it—I suppose her promised word, that we could do whatever we
liked with our butter, meant more to her than a buttered dining room.
And after a week or two of flipping and being dripped on we got tired
of it, and of our butterless bread, on our own. She did put an end to
the darts hurling affair. That was while we were still in Swansea, and it
involved extending the enormous, twenty-place dining-room table to
its full length, standing at one end, and shooting darts at a target
erected on the other end—a picture of Hitler was the bull's-eye while
other, lesser wartime villains radiated outwards from him. These were
hit rather less often than the table itself, and by the time we moved it
to Leeds its gleaming mahogany surface had developed an interesting
inlay of something that looked like birds-eye maple.

But Uncle Bourke's greatest tribal leadership was exhibited in his
genius for neologisms: complaining of your lot in life was corncrak-
ing; public toilets became bonga-bonga houses; getting bits of food
out from between your teeth was bonnifacing, while leaving a crumb
on your cheek was a paralyzed face; I was Granny, Ruth was Chyfe—
and Kathleen Merryweather, age nine, was Smigly Rydz.

Later research revealed Smigly-Rydz (in a variety of spellings) to have been a power in Polish politics in the 1930s. And I don't have a clue why a small girl standing shyly in the doorway should have brought him to mind. But Smigly Rydz she became and Smigly Rydz she more or less remained. True, in her most recent Christmas cards and letters, she signs herself "Kathleen," but she is careful to add "Smigs" in parentheses, in case of doubt.

She was a fair-haired, brown-skinned, compact little girl—the only daughter and youngest child in a family of sons. One escaped harm and survived the war, although his ship was sunk during the evacuation of Dunkirk; another was killed off the coast of Ceylon in 1942; the third worked at the prison under Uncle Bourke, until he too joined the navy; and the youngest, Jimmy, curly haired and cornflower eyed, often came with her to the Towers. When I was twelve, we were alone one evening in the Merryweathers' house—one of the larger houses with indoor plumbing in among those dark rows of brick just above the railroad tracks—and he read aloud "The Fall of the House of Usher," dramatizing it with appropriate sound effects and terrifying both of us. I got a brief crush on him, but that was unsurprising in a year when I had a crush on any male humanoid in whose presence I remained for more than ten minutes.

Smigs's father was a commercial traveler, a job that kept him away from home for a large part of each week, and her mother's schedule as a nurse also involved strange hours and late, long shifts. It was therefore Smigs's Auntie who kept house—and who made the best Yorkshire pudding you are likely to taste this side of Heaven.

I suppose it was made, like all Yorkshire puddings, from a batter of a cup of milk and two eggs to each cup of flour, poured over the beef drippings, and baked at as a high a heat as the oven and conscience would allow. But, unlike Aunt Helen's Yorkshire pudding, it was not an incidental accompaniment for the Sunday roast. Aunt Helen had become a very good cook—she became, in fact, a superb cook in time, after throwing out the pernicious influence of Mrs. Beeton— but she had been born in that part of England that produces trifle and lemon curd and beef with horseradish sauce, a part of England where Yorkshire pudding never amounts to more than an insincere reduction of a French cream puff. Auntie's pudding, a single dense, crisp, gravy-bathed circle centered on a large dinner plate, arrived solemnly in solitude, as the first course brought in before the meat was carved. It was a serious creation that surpassed all one's expectations; it filled one's hunger.

And not just the hunger for food. A sense of sparseness, a sense of things getting smaller, narrower, scarcer, and more dangerous, had begun to pervade the atmosphere. Perhaps it was just that we were growing up, and looking into the mirror we could already see the outline of our limitations, the setting mold of what we would grow into. We had come to an age when children begin to reach for solace, and in our wartime world there was not much solace to be had. So the perfection of Auntie's Yorkshire pudding—as good now as it had been in the days when slabs of meat hung, unsold, in the butcher's window and there were two eggs apiece for breakfast every morning—comforted and consoled us.

✶

When Val and I took the dogs for their walk after tea, Smigs would often join us, and she made up the quorum for cricket and rounders on summer weekends. A slightly acrid edge surrounds my nostalgia for those summer games. I was bad at them: terrible at rounders, disastrous at cricket. I'd be out as soon as I was in, and usually I brought the entire team down with me—though I did, once, make a single, stupendous, astonishing catch that stung my hands for hours afterwards and earned me a lifetime's sliver of glory.

At winter games I did better, especially at Double Demon, at which I was brilliant. But the balance of our days—after school, after dog walking, after helping around the house—was not, after all, devoted to these community pastimes. Though the games that included all of us—family, guests, visitors, friends—appear in my memory as the warp on which we wove the pleasant fabric of our leisure, I can now see, when I consider those days more analytically, that by far the largest part of our spare time was spent in solitude. Occasionally we listened to the wireless—but there were no serials, no *Lone Rangers* or *Green Hornets* or *Shadows* in England. Sometimes we would knit: dexterous Di was turning out pairs of socks for soldiers; Val had finished several balaclavas—an early, military version of the ski mask. I was still confined to lumpy squares to be sewn into blankets for bombing victims. We drew; we made scrapbooks of the royal family and horses.

Mostly we read.

Our tastes diverged according to age and character. Ruth, years ahead of the rest of us, was reading *Trent's Last Case* and was a fan of Dorothy L. Sayers. Diana favored animal stories like *Owd Bob, Old Yeller,* and *Black Beauty,* while Valerie was particularly fond of *Swallows and Amazons,* the adventure series by Arthur Ransome, which is notable not just for its portrait of six very interesting children but for the fact that the most commanding of them are girls.

As for me, I would read anything. Print was what mattered, not content, and I devoured whatever lay within reach with equal appetite, from the stuffed-animal exploits of *Winnie-the-Pooh* and *Mumfy Goes to War* to the romantic swashbuckle of Jeffrey Farnol. It was not so much that my taste was still unformed, as the fact that my appetite for text—book or newspaper, fact or fiction—was too huge ever to be satisfied.

Like everyone else in the family, I had read Sellar and Yeatman's *1066 and All That.* We declaimed bits of it aloud over our tea, and I still know sections of it by heart—as did Valerie, ten years ago, when she gave me a new, elegant edition to replace my old one that had long since fallen apart. "History is not what you thought," we reminded each other. "*It is what you can remember.* All other history defeats itself."

That errant philosophy, imbibed in childhood, has probably become part of me over the years. I suppose in its antic way it guides any account of the past I try to write for myself, including this one.

✶

In Swansea we had gone to a private day school run by the Parents National Educational Union, whose philosophy was progressive and whose methods were productive. But there were no PNEU schools near us in Leeds, while Twenty-Three the Towers was a mere ten-minute walk from West Leeds High School, one block to the left of the end of the avenue of horse chestnuts.

West Leeds High School, whose philosophy was getting through the day, the year, and the curriculum as calmly as possible, was not a bad school despite having a gym teacher whose name was Miss Battle and a hideous uniform consisting of a box-pleated dark blue tunic worn over a striped, square-necked blouse. The crest on the ribbon around our navy felt hats was embroidered with the West Leeds High School motto, *non sibi sed ludo* ('not for oneself, but for the game') a sentiment that did not engage my sympathies, since my only relationship to *ludi* was to stay out of them as much as possible.

In imitation of Rugby, Eton, and Harrow, we were each bound over to a "house," a rather inchoate institution halfway between a team and a club—the idea being that you were supposed to be faithful to the death to whatever house you were put in. But the principles of sport and loyalty developed by Doctor Arnold rather depend on the closeness of daily living in real houses. Without real houses the whole thing loses its urgency; and besides, to be aroused to serious to-the-death loyalty towards something invented for the sole purpose of arousing serious to-the-death loyalty to it, you probably need to be a boy.

We were all pretty flabby about the house thing. I think I was Rose—which would have been for England. But I may have been Thistle, for Scotland. I know Smigs was a Welsh Daffodil and that they always won.

My own talents lay in other directions. I was a genius at day-dreaming and at those disciplines ancillary to daydreaming—reading, playacting, and pretending not to be there. It would take hours for Aunt Helen calling me to take the dogs for a walk to penetrate the vacuum insulating my ears from the rest of the world. My favorite pastime was to go into the garden, wandering up and down the steps and into the laurel bushes while I told myself the story of Doctor Edith Cohn and her Island of Abandoned Children. Doctor Cohn was in charge of curing them of varying lethal ailments, of getting them through hurricanes, plagues, and invasions by hostile tribes. She always prevailed.

I varied the plots according to my mood, sometimes stretching one narrative over a period of several days. I had a few basic plots—Storm Hits Island, More Children Shipwrecked, Epidemic Strikes, and so on. But there were two concerns to which I reverted most often that were not plots at all: first was the accommodation and healing of some deviant, defiant, or depressed child who had happened to come to Doctor Cohn's island and moved her to try innovative and ingenious therapies; and second was the continual arrangement and rearrangement of various domestic details. I became the architect and interior designer of mud huts and straw bungalows, developed an island cuisine around fish and fruit, and spent days working out, mentally, how to weave fabric from leaves and grass, make crockery from seashells, and construct furniture from twigs and slabs of stone.

During these bouts of fantasy, which lasted for hours, I would talk to myself, speaking for the various personae in my mind. I think I recognized myself that this was somewhat eccentric behavior, and I tried to hide it by jumping rope when I was, mentally, otherwise engaged or by whipping a top on the hard surface of the upper driveway. I became a superior rope jumper and I was probably the unrecognized champion top spinner of northern England.

As I got older, Doctor Cohn was increasingly aided by someone else, a male someone else, who was sometimes another doctor and sometimes a strong, jolly, handsome and slightly piratical rogue who knew how to sail in a high wind. In time, this invented male, whatever his calling, insisted on taking charge and Doctor Cohn began to simper at his approach.

And that was the end of that.

DOWN IN THE FOREST

⟿ I suppose identity is always something of a compromise, a complex accommodation between what other people call you and what, usually taking the cue from them, you end up agreeing to call yourself.

Having been called several contradictory things in two languages by the time I was eight, I found the question of my identity particularly complicated. My sister, who had just reached her teens when she came to England, had already pretty much decided by then who she would be when she grew up. Though most of the people she has known most intimately, her husband and her husband's friends, have their equivocations, of course, their equivocations are unequivocally German-Jewish. She does not entirely go along with these, but she at least has a template to work from.

I, to the contrary, have never had a clue.

Still, my attempts at anglicizing myself, though ultimately doomed to failure, were not entirely futile: and, like many other aspects of my growing up, they often stretched the possibilities beyond the obvious into the unexplored—into the terra incognita of the immigrant, the refugee, and the expatriate, which is perhaps the New World of our age, the place in which a greater and greater number of us seem to live and to which more and more of us think about moving. With luck, by the next millennium, we will all be there.

✶

To help define my shaky identity, I of course consulted books and, even more persuasively, films. Books and films might not resolve my agonized self-translations and redefinitions, but at least they could suggest alternative personae and alter egos that I could try on for size. They also demonstrated, dramatically and therefore cogently, various ways one might want to look at life. Though most of these were too noble, too simple, or too athletic to suit, occasionally one would turn out to be a fine signpost to point my way towards a Weltanschauung.

For instance, *Pimpernel Smith.* It was made in 1942, and until Laurence Olivier came out with *Henry V* two years later it was my favorite film. Leslie Howard, who both produced and directed it, was also its star, playing a 1930s reincarnation of the Scarlet Pimpernel, which—as we all knew, having seen *The Scarlet Pimpernel* at least seven times—was who Leslie Howard actually turned into when he stopped being an actor and went home to brush his teeth. Mature reflection causes me to wonder whether equating the French Revolution with Hitler's Germany was entirely appropriate. But never mind—Leslie Howard was almost as good a Pimpernel in Harris tweeds as he had been in a brocade waistcoat, and rescuing the elite from the *Lumpenproletariat* always makes for a good story if not necessarily for good social planning.

I saw *Pimpernel Smith* again quite recently, through the magic of videotape, which erases time and also makes you recognize, mournfully, that things were never actually exactly what they used to be—that brilliant is often a great deal dimmer than you remembered it. I was pretty close on the general idea of the film's story line at least, which is about an English academic—a man neither as effete nor as absentminded as he appears to the naked eye—who goes to Germany to rescue an antifascist scientist being held by the Nazis. Along the way, of course, he falls in love with the scientist's beautiful daughter, who is soon able to see the heroism hidden behind the mask and to get over her first impression that he's a total dork.

Pimpernel Smith follows one of those enduring archetypes that you can trace back—via the original Pimpernel, Sir Percy Blakeney, and Sydney Carton—to the apparently disengaged misanthrope of Restoration comedy, the hero who pretends to care for nothing but is in fact a passionately moral man. After undergoing a very modest name change and a very slight nudge to the left in academic career from Professor Smith's, the most recent incarnation of the character has been Indiana Jones, the world-weary languor slightly energized and made more muscular—and naturally given a gun—on this side of the Atlantic.

The high point of *Pimpernel Smith*, for me, comes in an interchange between the good professor and a German officer in charge, mainly, of being extremely unpleasant and, incidentally, of catching spies. He is played by the redoubtable Francis X. Sullivan. Black-uniformed, fat, and magisterially stupid, the officer tries to persuade Professor Smith that the best of English literature, including Shakespeare, is actually German—a theory that the Professor counters with a deadpan suggestion of his own. Shakespeare he says has lately been proved—well, almost proved—to have been the Earl of Oxford. Which is odd since Oxford, as far as he knows was until recently still located in England.

I can see now—although I did not see this as a child, of course—that the conflict between the ironic Professor, who understates his position and is always right, and the snarling German officer, who rants and overstates and is always wrong, is peculiarly a conflict of style rather than substance. It is certainly not political or moral since we are given no real sense of the factors that would add up to making England a better place to live in than Germany is. It is largely esthetic, a question of proper conduct and conflicting notions of how to play the game. The Germans apparently play it the wrong way: they play to win, and they are very bad sports as well as being rather slow on the uptake. The English Professor and his following of college students have learned cricket in Public School, and even when they cheat they cheat tongue-in-cheek and therefore, paradoxically, cheat by the rules. They are also all blessed with a sense of humor (apparently God-given to every Englishman, or at least every decently educated Englishman), and they easily stay afloat upon seas of nonsense in which the poor German officer helplessly drowns.

> *Twas brillig and the slithy toves*
> *Did gyre and gimble in the wabe . . .*

He quotes from "Jabberwocky," bewildered, pronouncing it "vah-be." And he ponders fruitlessly over a phrase he has hit on at random in a novel by P. G. Wodehouse—a Nazi collaborator who is said to be funny and who should at the very least be comprehensible: "Down in the forest something stirred."

"Down in the forest something stirred" is, of course, not funny. It is also not particularly comprehensible. In fact, in its utter lack of humor or meaning or anything remotely resembling pith, "Down in the forest something stirred," like "'Twas brillig and the slithy toves," is a triumphant, definitive demonstration of the Absurd.

The Absurd is an environment alien to the German officer, and he is totally lost when confronted with it. Those of us in the audience who understand this know that nothing anyone can do would help him. Even at ten I knew that, like the ability for wiggling your ears, a knack for absurdity is something you are either born with or not born with. And in later life I discovered how futile it was to try to argue with people who are annoyed by Harold Pinter dialogue ("Here's your cornflakes. Are they nice?" "Very nice." "I thought they'd be nice.") The best you can do for them is to suggest that they go see something meaningful by Arthur Miller instead.

✬

It was a shared sense of the Absurd, I think, that I took home with me from *Pimpernel Smith:* a fellow feeling for the quizzical compassion re-siding in Leslie Howard's slightly raised right eyebrow as he tries to ex-plicate the Jabberwocky for Francis Sullivan. It would be years before Sartre would begin writing *L'être et le néant.* But *Pimpernel Smith* intro-duced me early on to the proper conduct for making one's way through the territory of the nameless and the meaningless, which re-mains still largely uncharted now, fifty-some years later at the begin-ning of the twentieth-first century. In retrospect I can see that it is a snobbish and rather silly film, full of clichés and focused as much on a prejudiced view of class as on an equally prejudiced view of nation-ality—but it provided me with an Ariadne's thread to lead me through the labyrinth.

One should also not dismiss, however, the possibility that my sense of kinship with Professor Smith may have come from some deeper, mysterious tribal recognition. That some secret, unacknowl-edged handshake of genes may have informed my inner being that the man was an impostor—though, of course, I wasn't aware of this at the time. It was quite recently, in fact, that I discovered that Leslie Howard, the epitome of the perfect English gentleman had in fact been born Leslie Howard Steiner, the son of Hungarian Jewish immi-grants. And far from being the prototype of insouciant heroism that he portrayed on screen, he had gone into the theater therapeutically, so to speak—as a way to recover from shell shock after a brief tour in the armed forces during the First World War.

The man, in fact, was exactly the sort of sham I was myself—and he was brilliant at it. No wonder he spoke to me! But what this fraud, this charlatan—this *actor*—told me was completely authentic, and it has stayed with me for the whole of my life. Distilled to its essence it was just this, that those who prevail with dignity don't look for meaning where there is none.

It took me decades, of course, to understand that this was almost all of the time. But now when I listen to discussions about gender-neutral pronouns or the just administration of the death penalty; when I hear it said that Hollywood is responsible for sex and violence in our culture, or that every fertilized ovum should be counted as a baby and given its full rights as an American citizen; even when there is serious argument about grave matters, like the existence of God or the definition of a Good Life, I think to myself, "Down in the forest something stirred." And I feel at peace.

☆

The long avenue of horse chestnut trees was the dividing line between Twenty-Three the Towers and the real world of Leeds. If you went from our house all the way down the avenue and crossed through the wide, wrought-iron archway, shadowed and grazed by the branches of the great old trees, you came out onto Armley Road—a blank, cobbled expanse crisscrossed at this point by several tram tracks. We were the last stop at the end of the no. 16 Wingate line, and the tracks were laid so that trams could maneuver to turn around. On the other side of Armley Road, veiled by a black fence, was West Leeds High School's playing field: soccer for the boys (who were contained in one wing of the school) and hockey for the girls (who were contained in the other wing.)

The no. 16 tram connected us to the rest of Leeds and to the rest of life. It must have been Smigs, a swimming enthusiast from infancy, who introduced us to the swimming pool at the Armley Baths—where, if you lived in a house without plumbing, you could also rent an actual bathtub and a hand shower to wash your hair—and once or twice a week, the tram took us there. On Saturday afternoons it often carried us to the movies, while on Wednesdays—which were school half-holidays—it brought us, every month or so, to the Theater Royal to see *Quiet Weekend,* or *The Second Mrs. Tanqueray,* or *The Admirable Chrichton.* Once a year, when Donald Wolfitt was in town, we went to the Grand to see whatever Shakespeare he was up to, and of course we saw *The Mikado, The Gondoliers,* and *The Pirates of Penzance*—which seemed to be the only three Gilbert and Sullivan operettas the D'Oyly Carte did in Leeds—whenever they came our way.

The no. 16 tram also took Uncle Bourke to his job at His Majesty's prison. He would leave the breakfast table every morning at half past eight and walk down for the eight-forty tram which would be there, having turned around, waiting to pick him up. I do not remember that he was ever late. But there were two mornings, a year or two apart, when he was not at breakfast at all. At about eight-thirty on both of these mornings a black car, with H.M. PRISON written on its side in gold letters with a crown above them, drove through the horse chestnuts and let him out by the steps at the bottom of the front lawn. Then the car drove away again while Uncle Bourke walked rather slowly towards the house. He came in and sat down with us at the breakfast table, but before he had eaten anything or even drunk the tea Aunt Helen had poured for him, he got up again and went upstairs. And we did not see him for the rest of the day.

Ruth, who was old enough to be told about such things, confided to me that Uncle Bourke had to be at the prison, officially, as a witness whenever a man was hanged—and on both these mornings the prison car had come before dawn to take him to an execution.

I had got the idea early in life that people responsible for executions were not people I should associate with. In Karlsruhe once, on one of our walks through the Schlossgarten, my nanny, Dada, had bought me a little swastika pin from an S.A. man, and both my mother and Stasie, who had thrown the pin angrily into the trash, had called the man selling the pins a butcher. I had pretty much understood, from their tone of voice, that by the word "butcher" my mother and

Stasie were not implying that he made sausages; they were suggesting that he killed people with the blessing of the state and that the people he killed were, more often than not, our friends and our relations.

His black uniform, though smarter and more becoming, was not unlike the uniform worn by the guards at Uncle Bourke's prison. And as I thought about the two men being hanged and about Uncle Bourke watching them while they died, I could not unravel the tangled puzzle for myself. What sense did it make that my Uncle Bourke—who was responsible for rescuing me from the evil intentions of just such people as this butcher—officiated at executions and directed guards in black uniforms to implement someone's death on the gallows. The men being hanged had, Ruth told me, committed murder themselves—their wives, most likely, or some unlucky friend—but this did not entirely clarify matters.

At least Uncle Bourke had looked miserable about being at an execution. But how was I to know that the man selling swastika pins didn't feel miserable too—perhaps he also lost his appetite after he butchered people.

Under these delicate circumstances, it seemed to me, one should perhaps refrain from taking any part in doing away with people, even for a good cause. Apparently the whole question of who was seen to have committed an offense and who was seen as a fit person to deliver retribution for the offense committed was rather more insecure than it should have been; it seemed to be surprisingly easy to slip from the camp of the executioners into the camp of those to be executed or vice versa. How could you ever be entirely sure that you were going to end up on the correct side, or even know, when you were trying to choose, which the correct side was?

✳

But Leeds did offer me some very clear, distinct, and certain boundaries, and for several of these the archway at the end of the avenue of

horse chestnuts served as a border crossing. It was obviously, for instance, the dividing line between two languages, since at the Towers
end of the avenue everyone spoke what was known as the King's English, while at the Armley Avenue end everyone spoke Yorkshire.

It is difficult to find any American equivalent for the regional dialects of England in those days—what they were and what they
meant. The differences between the many variants of local speech patterns and the single speaking model approved by the BBC were not
just matters of accent and intonation and rhythm. They involved
changes in vocabulary, grammar, and emphasis as well—though these
too were perhaps more incidental than the sheer style of just how a
thing was said. But far more important than any of this—most important of all—was the loyalty that regional speech embodied: a loyalty to place, to class, and to tribe, which was of the soil and in the
blood, far older and deeper than any passing patriotic whim of na-
tionalism could hope to be.

It would presumably have been quite possible for a Cockney or
Lancastrian or Yorkshire-speaking person to learn at the knee of some
rural Professor Higgins how to speak as perfectly as Eliza Doolittle
had. But it was the rare Cockney or Lancastrian or Yorkshire-speaking
person who was willing to sink so low—to say nothing of your Scot
or your Welshman. Like a kid from the South Bronx suddenly cursed
with a Harvard education, anyone from the rich-brogued regions of
the United Kingdom would have felt that he was betraying his people
unless he went on speaking like them. And they would more than have
agreed with him.

Almost everyone at West Leeds High had at least a slight Yorkshire accent. The few whose parents spoke in college-and-peerage approved tones, like Joy Bannisters's, were looked upon with mild disdain—though I suppose if Joy had spoken with a broad Cockney
twang she would probably have been welcomed into the fold. The
point was not that you were supposed to sound as if you belonged in
Leeds, but that you were supposed to sound as if you belonged some-

where. If you talked in the way the teachers talked, the way recommended as respectable by educational authorities throughout England, you simply placed yourself beyond the pale of any local identity, out in a void of genteel nonentity.

This put me in a bit of a quandary. From the time I learned to speak English, I spoke English like the Harveys. Without an accent, Miss Paddington had said, congratulating me. She was my first West Leeds High School teacher and generally unpopular, for no reason I can bring to mind. We called her Paddywack and sneered at her large girth and her propriety, though I remember very pleasantly a spring picnic in her garden at which she gave us currant cake and dandelion burdock tea she had made herself. Her endorsement of my way of speaking, in any case, did not recommend me to my fellow classmates. Nor did the fact, the following year, that I won the annual Shakespeare Speech Competition. The set piece for the occasion was from act 4, scene 1, of *Henry V.*

> *O God of battles, steel my soldiers' hearts!*
> *Possess them not with fear, take from them now*
> *Their sense of reckoning lest the opposed numbers*
> *Pluck their hearts from them.*

Possibly not the most fitting recitation for little girls—but I managed to declaim it in such round and pear-shaped tones that no one else came near me. On Speech Day, the end-of-term awards ceremony, I was called up onto the platform to recite the silly thing all over again. Then the President of the Board of Governors handed me a Complete Works of Shakespeare—bound in blue leather and sporting dramatic illustrations by Henry Fuselli and other nineteenth-century Romantics who did a great deal with thigh muscles and codpieces that was anatomically impossible but of considerable interest to a ten-year-old female child. I still treasure the volume, and I still prefer to read the plays in it rather than in later editions that were far better re-searched and better printed.

I suspect that the main reason I won the Shakespeare Speech Competition was the judging panel's admiration for my flawless, ac-centless English. But by then I already knew something of which the judging panel was still ignorant, that there is no such thing as accent-less English. Any way of speaking is an accent somewhere; in fact any way of speaking is an accent just about everywhere. We are all, ubiq-uitously, aliens, and we may as well try to get used to it.

Still, I suppose by that time I was in the habit of trying to pass whenever and however I best could, and after a few years of going to West Leeds High School I found my words, quite inadvertently, tak-ing on a slightly Yorkshire flavor every morning as I walked down the avenue of horse chestnuts towards the school, while every afternoon, as I walked home again, my tongue would begin to revert to its more genteel mode. I would stop thinking of dinner and start thinking of supper, expect to be greeted not by "hi there, loov," but "hello, dear," and instead of complaining that it was so cold that I was "fairly starv-ing and feeling right poorly," wonder mildly why I was "so cold I was not feeling too well." When you spoke Yorkshire you let yourself go a bit and used larger, broader, and more thumping terms than you did in genteel speech, the whole point of which was to restrain yourself into demure and self-abnegating respectability.

I must have changed over to the local vernacular fairly convinc-ingly: the second time I tried for the Shakespeare Speech Competition, I barely got an honorable mention.

☆

Winning the speech competition had whetted an apparently inborn greed for drama. I was already reading as constantly as the Harvey cul-ture of fresh air and exercise allowed. But I put aside my Enid Blyton and Frances Hodgson Burnett, my J. M. Barrie and Rudyard Kipling, and instead took up the royal blue leather–covered *Complete Works of William Shakespeare*, which, with its illustrations of draped and drooping women confronting undraped and ramrod-rigid men, promised deeper pleasures.

Not, I hasten to say, of the purely esthetic variety. I wouldn't have known a great iambic line if it had climbed in my ear. Nor was there anything particularly seductive about Shakespeare's narratives—and anyway I already knew the plots of many of the plays from Lamb's *Tales from Shakespeare*. It was the theatrical mode that was so attractive: all those characters expressing themselves independently, individually, directly, like the multiple roles that I played for myself in my own head! I suppose that theater was the world as I experienced it, and from the moment I was introduced to the stage I loved it.

It has been, alas, an unrequited passion.

At West Leeds High School, where I was much younger and hence smaller than anyone else in my class, I must have looked a bit of a swarthy dwarf. Yearning to play Prospero or at least to costume myself as Miranda, I was cast as Caliban instead. I did have one brief moment of glory as Hermia in *A Midsummer Night's Dream:*

> *And are you grown so high in his esteem*
> *Because I am so dwarfish and so low?*
> *How low am I, thou painted maypole? Speak—*
> *How low am I?*

But in the end, I only got to wear tights and a green shirt, having been assigned the role of Puck.

Monsters and fairies: aliens. That was me. But at least, I consoled myself, they got a lot of the good lines.

Later, by the time I came to America, my theatrical talents were even less in demand. As far as small, dark girls went I was pretty much in the majority on Long Island; but I had still not managed to lay aside my accentless English accent. Whether I spoke in my Yorkshire or in my BBC mode, I was an oddity for the High School Drama Club and this, in Great Neck, was a far more serious offense than it would have been anywhere in oddity-loving England. I made one feeble attempt at reading for Shaw's *Saint Joan.* Then I gave up acting for life and resigned myself to the lesser and less nerve-racking glories of costumes, properties, and stage-managing.

I know now that I would never have made a good actress—not on stage anyway. To act convincingly for a paying audience you have to lay aside the consciousness of playing a role: you have to be the part. Sorting through the multiple characters I play in my own head makes me far too self-conscious for the theater. For that you need either to play from a single secure identity or to sport a casual attitude about the dangers of floating around on a random series of improvised ones.

MUTTI AND PAPPI

⌒◠◠◠ My mother, meanwhile, was living in
Philadelphia. She had no money and no prospects. Most of her possessions were lying at the bottom of the sea in the hold of the Dutch
ship that the Germans had sunk during their invasion of the Netherlands. And since the American Medical Association had declared all
foreign medical certification to be null and void, her profession was
closed to her. Board exams for recertification in America differed from
state to state, but they were all biased against the incoming tide of
German refugee doctors, who tended at the time to be rather better
educated than their counterparts in the United States and therefore
posed a threat to the prevailing, comfortable mediocrity. In the north-
eastern states in particular—and most of all in New York—recertification for a European physician was considered all but impossible.

So my mother paused briefly after her escape from Karlsruhe to
catch her breath at Aunt Liesel's house in New Jersey and then found
herself a job in Philadelphia. First she cleaned houses for people. This
period of her life was not one she talked about in any detail, but I

imagine that she found the houses to be cleaned advertised through some German-Jewish organization by German Jews who had got out a bit earlier than she had—attached to more of their goods and chattels—who were trying now to show fellowship for their less fortunate brothers and sisters by patronizing them. "Washing the floor on my hands and knees," was her casually caustic description of her work, and it was something she never allowed anyone else to do—not me, not Ruth, not the household help she hired to clean her apartment in later and more affluent times. She acquired an array of mops, most of them with remote-control squeezing mechanisms to keep one as faraway from the dirty business as possible; and if a floor needed to be washed it was washed gingerly, at arm's length and from a respectable distance.

When she had spent a few months, perhaps a year, keeping house for her fellow refugees, she was hired by a young American couple to care for their newborn baby. After that her services were in steady demand by the couple's abundantly pregnant friends and neighbors, until, moving up once again, she was taken on as the medical officer—no certification required—at a summer camp for girls.

From the time she had set up the infirmary and dismantled it again, the job took about five months out of each year, so she made a courageous and somewhat pigheaded decision against the counsel of all conventional wisdom. She had been a doctor. Her life, the cornerstone of who she was, had been medicine. She would become a doctor again. For the seven months of the year when she wasn't in the Adirondacks at the girls' camp, she began to prepare for the impossible New York State Boards. She had to immerse herself not only in medical texts, but in books of American medical usage and colloquial English. The New York State Boards might be given under the legally necessary conditions of anonymity, but they notoriously got around that little problem by including questions phrased so as to be incomprehensible to anyone unfamiliar with local idiom, questions that focused on small eccentricities where American and European practice differed. If you missed such a question, if you were discovered to have a slight foreign edge to your answer, if you gave any hint of having had a European education, you automatically failed.

By then, my mother had moved from Philadelphia to New York. A distant cousin, Fred Reichenberger, had come over early—in 1935 or '36—and he had made good as a stockbroker. He lived in Great Neck with his wife Andrée and their two small daughters, Dorothy and Bernice, and though he knew my mother only slightly he offered her room and board on a sort of au pair basis.

Bonds and shares may have been Fred's bread and butter, and in a good year perhaps even his fillet mignon and béarnaise sauce, but he was hardly your typical stockbroker. His passion was music. He played in the first violin section of the Great Neck Community Orchestra and anywhere else, with anyone else, at any time else they allowed him to. Andrée played the piano. And though Bernice was still just a toddler and too young for scales, Dorothy, at nine, already had a miniature cello on which she joined her parents for nightly, casual family trios, a movement or two of this or that after supper.

✻

To keep us current on the progress of her life, Mother had been writing Ruth and me a letter every week. It was always a joint letter to "Liebe Kinder," which really addressed neither of us, growing up as we were and away from any knowledge she had of us. Every week in return we each dutifully wrote a letter to her, "Liebe Mutti," which also addressed no one of flesh and blood living on this earth. It was a sort of astral projection, directed towards two abstractions: the Children; the Mother.

I had conveniently forgotten what she looked like. Not that she didn't send us ample evidence: photographs arrived four or five times a year of her clutching some anonymous baby, photographs of her standing guard beside prams and strollers, photographs of her in a

white lab coat with a stethoscope swung proudly round her neck, surrounded by assorted little girls in shorts.

All of these photographs agreed: she was a small, slight, dark
haired woman with huge eyes, a considerable nose, and no chin to
speak of. An interesting-looking woman with an intelligent, even a
sensitive face, but no beauty. I put all visual evidence of the existence
of this pleasant odd duck in the back of my sock drawer and substi-
tuted a totally different icon of Motherhood in its place: tall, sweet
faced, with long, light brown hair done in a maternal knot, this phantom creature became the mother of my mind. She baked cookies. She
loved dogs—she probably had several golden retrievers frolicking at
her skirts when she went out to pick beans and vegetable marrows
from her ample and always sunlit garden.

I had no trouble whatever erasing my actual mother from memory nor any hint of unease in addressing the weekly letters I wrote to
"Liebe Mutti" to her absolute antithesis, the phantom woman I had
created for myself.

This spectral invention lasted for seven years, for the duration of
our stay in England. Its ghost was laid only when it was usurped by
the reentry of Mother herself. It was a shocking revelation. Truth usually is. Naturally, I resented the intrusion of this crude reality into my
life, and for a very long time after our reunion I resented my mother
for being so unlike what I thought she should have been and for not
making the slightest attempt to remake herself into my invention.
Good God—this woman had a German accent! And she wouldn't
have known a golden retriever from a herring.

It took me a good twenty years to recover from the disappointment over this disastrous letdown. The shadow image of my fantasy
of what-a-mother-should-be continued to smile sweetly at me over the
shoulder of fact. By the time I was thirty, I began to suspect that what
the woman of flesh and blood lacked in indulgent motherliness and
cookie-baking talent she more than made up for in intelligence, char-

acter, and originality, and another ten years entirely erased the simpering, immaterial substitute from my thoughts. I had come to take my smart, perverse, unflinching little mother to my heart—but by then, of course, we had missed most of our life together. Since her death, my memory of her has become, oddly, more vivid with each year that passes and more affectionate—the recollection of a complex, admirable, and contradictory woman, too prickly to be easily embraced, too intense to be easily forgotten, and far too puzzling to be easily contained.

✶

She was born Helene Heidingsfeld, near Strasbourg in 1894, the daughter of Doctor Wilhelm Heidingsfeld and Henrietta, née Willstätter. The Willstätters were a branch of an old Karlsruhe family that also counted among its members both the chemist Richard Willstätter—who won the Nobel Prize in 1915 for his work on isolating chlorophyll—and the composer Kurt Weill.

I assume that my grandmother moved to Alsace because that is where her new husband had his practice. I assume the family moved back to Karlsruhe again because that was home.

It was a good town for Jews. There were a lot of us in the general area already by the fourteenth century, and when the town itself was founded in 1715 we were ready and waiting. Karlsruhe—which translates roughly as "Charlie's Rest"—was the brainchild of Karl Wilhelm, Margraf von Baden-Durlach, who thought that building a town might be a good excuse for getting away from his wife and spending some quality time with his mistresses. Moral laxity has always been a friend of city planning. Moral laxity suggests to those who practice it that life should be comfortable. And so Karlsruhe was duly built around a very pleasant and pretty palace surrounded by a grand complex of gardens and woods; it rejoiced in museums and public parks built on a city plan rather similar to that of Washington, D.C., though both its climate and its social hierarchies, of course, were considerably more moderate.

And Karlsruhe, born of a liberal attitude towards life, continued through the centuries to reflect the easy-going virtues of its founder. From the first, the town attracted scholars and writers, musicians and artists. It welcomed the odd, the outré, the liberated, and the alien. Many of its governors were Free Masons. Some of its noted citizens were Jews. It is presently the seat of Germany's Supreme Court and the home of one of Germany's more interesting artists, a gay man who signs himself Salome and whose imagery is often sadomasochistic— though more gently so than the Grünewald Crucifixion or the Stations of the Cross two rooms down from it in the Karlsruhe Kunsthalle. It was, and it still is, a town remarkably sophisticated for its size. In the midst of its sophistication, Jewish life flourished.

And my grandmother flourished with it. Not that she was much of a Jew. In fact, she wasn't anything of a Jew, which may be why she did so well in Karlsruhe, which being a freethinking sort of town wasn't all that keen on Judaism either. It was just willing to let you forget about it. She had a salon of sorts, where people came to exercise their wit and to display the latest acquisitions from their dressmakers.

In those days, and in fact until the war put an end to such luxuries, everyone had a dressmaker. My mother had most of her clothes made for her, and so did I. I remember being fitted for a light blue silk dress with tiny black polka dots, the prettiest frock I have ever owned, smocked at the shoulders with a double ruffle at the neck. The fitting was a rather traumatic event: the dressmaker lived in a small apartment that smelled pungently of old cooking, and her two daughters, who were about my age, shouted and hit at each other. They came to visit us to deliver my dress after it was finished and took my favorite doll hostage, tugging her between them until she fell to the floor and cracked open her poor china head. Erika her name was. Her eyes fell out, and though she was operated on at the Doll Hospital, she was never really the same. Her new eyes looked so blankly out from her broken forehead that I did not even care that she was too big to go on the *Kindertransport* with me, and I left her behind in Karlsruhe without a tear.

My mother told us that the dressmaker's husband had been put in prison for being a Communist and that the dressmaker was a Communist too. Her life was therefore very difficult, and this was why we continued to have our dresses made by her, even after Erika's eyes fell out. I wore the adorable ruffled dress to have my picture taken for the *Kindertransport* application, and another tailored tartan frock she'd made for my first passport photo—the one with STATELESS stamped on it. Both pictures came out well; the starched white collar and the ruffled neck both suited my smart new, fashionably shingled haircut.

My grandmother, of course, had a different woman to make her clothes, someone who was not a Communist. Oma was a tiny woman, even in my child's memory of her, but despite this she managed to strike one as somehow regal, with the carefully bouffant arrangement of her fine white hair framing her face as if it were a crown. Style was important to Oma, more I suspect than substance, and I still hold the front room of her and Opa's apartment—the sacred salon where her salons took place—as the measure of Edwardian elegance. It had a parquet floor, and there were potted palms scattered among the oriental rugs. The walls were half-paneled, and three pairs of French windows led out onto a balcony that overlooked the Kaiserstrasse. It was the balcony from which we used to watch the *Fasching* parade on Shrove Tuesday, until the year most of the floats seemed to be about nasty, dirty people with hook noses and yellow stars on their backs and I was taken home early before the parade was even half done. There were pots of geraniums and pansies around the balcony railing in the summer; and everything in the room behind it—everything in my memory of it at least—was multiplied by its reflections in the gilt-framed mirrors that flanked each wall and turned the room's probably quite ordinary upper-middle-class ambience into memorable theater.

Oma herself was somehow theatrical, a presence that filled a room much more authoritatively than its actual cubic measurements should have warranted. She had seen to it that my mother and Aunt Liesel were properly trained in the skills necessary for young ladies: music, embroidery, and enough of the rudiments of cooking to be able to instruct their cooks. The assumption was not only that Helene and Liesel would both be married, but that they would marry well enough to require this particular skill in communication.

For Liesel, the pretty one with a knack for watercolors and the domestic arts, this assumption was reasonable enough. But Helene was another matter entirely. It was not her lack of beauty that went against her—she had quite enough intelligence and verve to make up for that insufficiency. It was her disastrous clarity of mind. She had her own, firm idea of what things were worth, and not only did they disagree with my grandmother's firm idea of what things were worth but they were much stronger, much more enduring, and much more rational than Oma's. My mother used to claim that she had survived her misfortunes because of her sense of humor. In fact she had no sense of humor; what she did have was an ineradicable sense of proportions.

This, of course, was a quality entirely lost on Oma, who made something of a fetish of beauty and had favored pretty Liesel from the day she was born. She would inform my mother sardonically at frequent intervals, "Du bist nicht schön. Du bist nicht mies. Aber du bist shön mies" (You're not pretty. You're not ugly. But you're pretty ugly). Such things rankle. But I suspect that Mother's real conflict with Oma was much more a matter of character and history than a mere failure in esthetics: my mother, born in 1894, could do things with her life that would have been impossible for my grandmother. She was also by nature a courageous woman, which means that she must have been a courageous child. My grandfather adored her. It seems to me highly likely that Oma was simply jealous.

Not someone who liked taking long trips away from herself— nor even short excursions, for that matter—my grandmother, like many people with a selfish disposition, had married a saint. He had been born into a family of religious Jews—his brother, I have been told, was a quite well-known theologian—and though Opa himself was not particularly pious, prevailing opinion held that he deserved beatification.

He also had a reputation as a brilliant diagnostician. He had once identified a case of bubonic plague over the telephone, a diagnosis that had stumped all the attending doctors in a Berlin hospital, no case of the bubonic plague having come their way for some time. I suppose his genius was largely a question of paying attention to the obvious—if it sounded like bubonic plague it probably was bubonic plague, even if this seemed highly unlikely. And no member of my family within memory has ever shirked the opportunity for assuming the worst.

Opa's white beard and whiskers hid three pale blue wens on his cheek and chin, which I once proudly pointed out to a friend I was trying to impress. I was immediately sentenced by my mother to life imprisonment in my room. When the sentence was repealed an hour or so later and I was allowed to come out again, three chocolate cream candies in little gold paper skirts—the chocolates of absolution— had appeared outside my door. Put there by Opa of course. He had very large, very penetrating, very kind, and very blue eyes, and a gentle diffidence of manner that I am startled to recognize, reborn two generations later, in my cousin Kurt.

He also had a weak heart—in more ways than one, I suppose. He died the same year my father did. The story goes that as soon as he became really ill, after the first of his three heart attacks, Oma developed an insatiable need to go to Wiesbaden for the winter. "I can't take this," she is reported to have told my mother—or anyway words to that effect—"You're the doctor. You take care of him." And off she went, returning only in time for his funeral.

✡

Before I go any further, I should note here that what I know about all this is based on rather flimsy, rather unreliable documentation. Our family was scattered and never developed anything even approaching your normal family myth. Family archives—letters, diaries, objects, everything—were swallowed into the great maw of the Third Reich or lost during travel or storage. There were a few stories about my grandfather and grandmother, of course, rumors about my father's flamboyant youth, references to my mother's knitting socks and sweaters to sell during the Great Depression and even Greater Inflation; but these are sporadic and unrelated, and I have had to piece them all together as best I can into a patchwork joined only by my imagination.

An added problem is that my mother herself did not have much faith in the little bits of history that she had collected and then passed on to us. She was dubious both about her own memory and about the truth of the stories that came down to her from other sources. And then in 1939, even these few shards of recollection disappear, as though there were nothing left now to report of her, as if the minor decorations that make up history have disappeared in the great simplicity of just trying to survive.

She rarely talked about the years after she left Germany and she never willingly released details. I don't think that her silence was the result, really, of having been traumatized. Trauma is the wrong word for what she went through; and aside from that business of washing floors, nothing she ever said suggested her days had been virulently unpleasant let alone violently shocking. She was not in Dachau or Buchenwald. She had not been assigned to a Christian Hell of flames and torture and stink and misery. What she endured was a quietly stunned netherworld of some other sort, like Tantalus endlessly thirsty in Tartarus or Sysiphus eternally compelled to roll his rock uphill. Why should she recall a time when there was nothing to recall except infinite stultification and tedium or go through the boredom of remembering the meaningless days that had already bored her to anguish in the event?

And then, besides all this, there was that odd personal trait of hers that seemed to make her unsure of what she was saying in the process of saying it. She was a confirmed and unwavering skeptic of everything, including herself. I suppose if you manage to escape from the whirlwind by clinging to a tuft of grass on the edge of a precipice you will put your survival down to one of two antithetical causes. Either you will be sure that you have a private and intense relationship with your Maker, who miraculously saved you, and you alone, from disaster, and you will gratefully worship Him, or you will dismiss the crisis you have just luckily overcome as example and proof that the universe is uncaring, impersonal, and dismally arbitrary in its workings and conclude that there is no rhyme or reason for anything.

My mother was a doubter by nature, and that quality must have been amplified by the harshness of her life. She has passed her skepticism on in turn to my sister and me. It is something for which we seem to have a familial—possibly a genetic—talent, one that I observe has also been inherited by my own daughter. We doubt everything as a matter of course, from the existence of God to the likelihood of the train's being on time. When circumstances suggest—as they all too frequently do—that our uncertainty is completely warranted, we are not bitter. On the contrary, we tend to be grateful for finding ourselves, inadvertently, once again on the right track.

✳

So when I think about my mother's life, I can only pick out a few sure facts and try to string them together along uncertainties.

I do know, for example, that even when she was a child, her decisions were informed by that firm sense of hers that told her exactly what things were worth. She was quite ready to follow the traditional curriculum in sewing, baking, French, and piano; she learned these things well and easily, and she enjoyed them for life. But she never considered herself particularly brilliant at any of them, and therefore, failing to think that they were of major importance to her existence, she did them rather casually and very pragmatically, using a knack for organization so as to get the best results from the least of her effort.

For instance, in 1955 while she was recovering from a near-fatal heart attack, she liked to watch television and embroider tablecloths in large and handsome patterns of cross-stitching, instead of the usual, meticulously stitched articles that can take one years to finish. At home in her New York apartment she would often knit, duplicating the method she had found for herself to make a bit of extra money during the Depression; she made wonderfully huge sweaters in enormously thick wool on enormously thick needles. An entire sweater took her less than a weekend, and the effect was always highly original and remarkably chic.

As to cooking—a piece of cod or haddock thrown cavalierly into a large pot of boiling water would sit there for a minute and then come out, transformed, to be bathed in a bit of melted butter and a little lemon juice. Her roasted stuffed breast of veal—for which she always used prepared stuffing mixes that any self-respecting German should have scorned—was as good as any I've eaten. And she made an excellent brisket of beef braised with vegetables in less than an hour since she always simmered it in a pressure cooker.

All of which is to say that she was efficient about her daily life and suffered from no compulsion to follow the rules for domestic management. Since her childhood, her innate sense of proportions had guided her to the conclusion that while the feminine arts of sewing and making strudel were all very well, it was the masculine art practiced by her father the doctor that she valued.

She matriculated at Freiburg University, became a doctor, and went on to a specialty in pediatrics. She seems to have sailed through all these studies without difficulty; languages came easily to her, so did medicine. She found the smoothness of her successes unsurprising, accepting her intellectual gifts the same way a beautiful woman accepts her good looks, casually and as a matter of course.

In fact, it was precisely in the realm where beautiful women succeed that my mother had the most trouble. Not that her life was without romance precisely. Pressed for stories about their girlhood, my mother and Aunt Liesel would both volunteer tales about those who had loved them, and it has to be said that though Aunt Liesel's were more varied and also more detailed as to who had said what to whom and what they wore when they said it, it was my mother's stories really that had the ring of truth.

I should say *story* here in the singular, because I can recall only one. It was about a fellow student from Dijon, or Rouen, or Lyon—some French province or other—to whom my mother was briefly engaged just after the First World War. His mother didn't like Germans and put an end to their romance, but he seems to have remained the love of my mother's life. Whenever she got to the part where he went away she said her heart was broken. The trouble is that she said this with a heavily ironic emphasis, as if a broken heart were a rather despicable ailment; she maintained the same tone to report that when she saw him off for the last time on the train back to Dijon or Rouen or Lyon he wept.

My aunt's suitors also tended to weep in various stages of rejection; many of them were army officers or members of the lower aristocracy, and uniforms and white gloves got a great deal of play in my aunt's dramatization of events. It deserves mention, I think, that in these romances my aunt always did the rejecting, whereas it was my mother who was rejected.

But what is truly remarkable and unites their romantic histories is the fact that the men who loved them both were invariably and emphatically gentile.

✶

By the time my mother became a doctor, the First World War was over. Inflation and then Depression followed it. And when she began her practice as *Kinderarzt*—a doctor of children—Karlsruhe needed her.

She married Bruno Cohn in 1924; she was thirty by then and he was forty-five.

✶

Why did my mother marry this man? Why did this man marry my mother? Hardly out of love, I would suppose, nor even friendship. He only liked *Carmen* and *Cavalleria Rusticana* she would complain in a voice that suggested that this was tantamount to a moral failing. She had had a miscarriage three years after Ruth was born; when she called my father for help he was out playing bridge with friends and he told her she could wait till the end of the rubber or take a taxi.

She took a taxi. The miracle is that after that incident I was ever conceived. But she seems to have taken my father's behavior pretty much for granted, with a pinch of contempt for seasoning to help her swallow it as just the sort of behavior one should expect from him. "Pfui" was a syllable she used frequently and well, drawing it out so that it conveyed depths of scorn, amusement, and resignation arranged layer upon layer upon layer, like a *Dobostorte*. I am sure that over the ten years between their wedding and his death she directed many a "pfui" silently toward Pappi. Still, she stayed. I remember seeing her once throw a dinner plate at him. But she stayed. So did he. I suppose they must have served a reasonable purpose in each other's lives.

My sister thinks that the marriage was arranged; that my mother's dowry paid for the Kronenapotheke that my father did buy shortly after their wedding. And though my mother never mentioned a monetary agreement, she did say that she would only have married a man who would let her go on with her medical practice and that he accepted this. For his part, it seems, my father insisted that any wife of his must be a virgin. Indisputably and demonstrably a virgin; the mere flicker of any suspicion on the wedding night—*to be once in doubt is once to be resolved*—would be cause for instant annulment of the nuptials.

None of this, looked at critically, quite adds up. Surely it took a tolerant man in those days to bear with a wife working in a profession a notch or two higher in status than his own. Equally surely, even in 1924, only a sexual bigot would have made such boorish noises about his bride's sexual purity. Given these contradictions, I am inclined to adopt a modified version of my sister's explanation of things: there must have been a definitive transaction, even if it wasn't explicitly an economic one. A bargain was struck in which both parties outlined the outer limits of their tolerance.

Were they ever happy together, the plain young woman, newly a doctor, and the round little man, bald as an egg, already in his mid-forties and on his second marriage? Or have I forgotten to mention that detail? He'd been married before for a couple of years and had a son, but his wife walked out on him because he beat the dog. That at least was the account of things that I had later from Hermann himself, this same son who turned up in Tel Aviv around 1970 or so. Married to a nice woman who'd spent her childhood in Teresienstadt. With children of their own and grandchildren. And he still hadn't forgiven my father—and his—who not once, not one time in all the years of the boy's growing up, had expressed the slightest interest in paying him a visit.

Well—who knows? Maybe the dog-beating story was an invention of the bitter wife or her angry parents. Maybe Pappi did try to visit his son. Maybe, all evidence to the contrary, he was an all-around great, warm, and wonderful guy and my suspicion that it wasn't just the dog who got beaten is baseless.

But the evidence points against him.

There were, it seems, not counting Hermann, four or five other offspring somewhere. Casually conceived during and shortly after the First World War—the same period during which Pappi was also actively acquiring an Iron Cross Second Class and becoming a German patriot. I imagine that in those days—his dark eyes still unspectacled, his head crowned by black curls—he was attractive, even handsome, a small, intent young man with a bit of swashbuckle in his laugh. One of the women was French, according to my mother, who tried to track them down after my father died—possibly at his direction, it should be said—so as to offer them a nominal share in his estate. The others were of unknown nationality. But I have a nagging, unprovable suspicion that, though one of them may have been French and some of them may have been German or Austrian or even Polish, none of them was a Jew.

I have no idea why I believe this to the point of taking it as certainty—or at least as a central tenet of deep faith. I suppose I see him—a practicing Jew raised in Cracow where Jews, even those who spoke German, were not treated well—visiting upon gentile women what gentile men had visited on his relatives for generations. I seem to have made him, holding my nose while I did it, a Hebrew Hero of some sort, reprehensible, nasty, and righteous. A mean-spirited avenger of past wrongs: Reuben Hood got up as the Sheriff of Nottingham.

Which is to say that I am absolutely not to be trusted on the subject of my father. And, after all, whatever way you arrange the numbers—divide them, subtract them, add them, multiply them—the final sum of four or five illegitimate children, one divorce on the grounds of dog abuse, and one small son abandoned permanently before he is even a year old—can amount to only a single conclusion: the man was a son of a bitch.

✲

But wait. Voices contradict me. My aunt's, for instance, telling me in a tone that seems to disapprove of her own testimony that he was generous in his affections and that he had a good nose. My aunt, whose propriety is bulletproof, does not mean by this that he had a good nose for seducible bimbos; she means that he was generous in his affections and his nose was straight. It was. So were his teeth. And his eyes were fine: deep brown and serious, my sister's eyes. And speaking of my sister, there's her voice too, and my cousin Clare's. They say that he liked to play games with them and that he was fun to be with.

Is my memory that has turned him into this comic tyrant, this Humpty Dumpty in a three-piece suit, merely punishing him for leaving me? Or am I getting even, about seventy years too late, for being afraid of him: for the time he swung me too hard in the swing he had put up for me in the kitchen doorway, for yelling and slapping me when I fell off the swing and cried. Do I still resent his anger that time I stood on the kitchen table and proudly, showing off my salivary prowess for him, spat as far as I could. For that innocent demonstration he hit me and locked me in my room.

But yet, even my mother, surely the one who should register the biggest complaints, has little to say against him. She may have her own reasons for restraint, of course: one should take into consideration that when a bully does you the favor of dying you might be inclined to forgive and forget. Her major complaint against him was always that he had bad taste, as proof of which she tended to proffer the bit about *Cavalleria Rusticana* being his favorite opera.

But then, quite out of the blue, she comes up with another piece of information: he was good in bed. Well, and no wonder—by then he must have had enough practice. But this item of news from my mother is astounding. She is not a woman to admit to enjoyment if she can help it: if pleasure, for her, comes hard, owning up to pleasure comes even harder. And though she's open to a fault—a glaring fault—about the sexuality of other people, poking her friends and relatives in the abdomen to inquire after potential pregnancies and their latest menstrual periods, she is entirely silent about her own. So believe me—if she says my father was good in bed, he was good in bed. In fact, he must have been a living, breathing, life-size demonstration of the Kama Sutra.

✳

He was also, by physical fact, a warm man. By this I do not mean that he was affectionate or kindly, but that somehow his mere presence actually raised the temperature of the environment. It wasn't so much that Pappi was friendly, but that the room he sat in became more conducive to friendliness. Perhaps I should say, in fact, not that he was a warm man but that he was a hot man, hot in every sense of the word. He heated the air around him—sometimes to an uncomfortable level by his anger, but more generally to a nice warm coziness that my memory, despite its longing to reject him, often bathes in an ochre light.

It is usually when I am not looking for him that he enters the picture inadvertently at the edge of some scene I am recalling for other reasons. Those are the times he comes surrounded by that aura of warm yellow light, and I see from the corner of one eye a rather jolly fellow in danger of upsetting the Biedermeier demitasse in the gust of his laughter. He has just married me with the paper ring from the big cigar that he is smoking, and as he sits affably among his brothers telling stories about their childhood, he puts me on his knee and holds me tightly against his portly front so I won't slide to the floor under the aegis of his mirth. He is the oldest of twelve children, but these three brothers are the only ones I have met, are the only ones I will ever meet. They are slim and rather handsome—not at all like him—but the laughter of all four, as they tease each other, is identical.

Since I am the youngest at the seder I get to ask the questions and he answers them, and when I begin to look for the hidden matzo, he rolls his eyes for me secretly to show me the cushion where it is buried. He lets me listen to the tick-tock of the seconds on his pocket watch, and I ride on his back while he pretends to be my horse. He is an impatient horse, but when he tires he will hand me over to Ludi Kohn, his assistant in the pharmacy, who will tell me a story to which my father will listen almost as contentedly as I do.

✡

And then he dies.

While he is in the final throes of uremic poisoning from the huge carbuncle at the base of his skull I am told to stay in my room—at the furthest end of the apartment away from his. But I can hear him screaming. Then at last he is quiet. He seems to have disappeared.

He dwindles in my memory into something of a cipher. But now and then I meet his ghost in the hallways of my dreams—a bandage-wrapped creature staggering down the stairs towards me or lurching round the corner at the end of the passage. The experience is an unpleasant one. I do not want to meet this thing again, ghost or no ghost. Even dead, even in memory, even comically reduced to a shorter, rounder version of Frankenstein's monster-in-progress, he is always potently brutish and frighteningly rudimentary.

THE TIGER IN THE ATTIC

❧ By the time I came to England my father had already been replaced by the swaddled, lumbering specter in my dreams.

Luckily, I was still young enough to accept by default that Uncle Bourke, the man of my newfound family, was the prototype of everything manly. Everything fatherly. Above all, I took from him the pattern of those qualities that one should look for in a mate. My romantic and matrimonial history suggests that paramount among these qualities are shaggy eyebrows, a talent for brewing tea, and an absolute, Peter Pan refusal to grow up into anything resembling a serious human being.

I am convinced that it is because I took my Uncle Bourke as the model of what a husband should be that—despite their scarcity in my rather academic circle here in America during my mating years—my most fervent alliances have been with Anglo-Saxon Protestants. I am not suggesting, mind you, that being an Anglo-Saxon Protestant is any sort of romantic advantage: it may on the whole even be rather a disadvantage, considering that the Anglo-Saxon Protestant tendency to emotional chill, depression, alcohol consumption, tightwaddery, and all around cluelessness is probably a fair percentage above that of the general population. But these things are never rational, and I always knew that any serious search for an emotional partner would have to be limited to Anglo-Saxon Protestants. Other ethnicities simply would not have done.

This is because the Anglo-Saxon Protestant qualities exemplified by my Uncle Bourke can only be encompassed—can, indeed, only be approximated—by another Anglo-Saxon Protestant. A Jew couldn't come close. Nor a Greek. Nor a Nigerian, an Indian, a Russian—not even a Dane or a Swede, to say nothing of anyone from Japan or China. I will concede, of course, that it has always been easy to find men from any of these places—men from anywhere on the globe— who, like my Uncle Bourke, are kind, perceptive, humorous. It has always been at least possible to find men who are self-abnegating, reticent, affectionate, other qualities shared by my Uncle Bourke. And as to men who never grew up—I suppose the challenge from time immemorial has always been to find a man anywhere who ever did.

All of which leads one to the complicating conclusion that whatever it was that made my Uncle Bourke so quintessentially an Anglo-Saxon Protestant male had very little to do with the ingredients of his character and a great deal to do with the exact proportions in which these ingredients had been mixed and the means by which they had been cooked into that unique end product, Major George Bourke Harvey himself. Or, to put it another way, I have no idea how to describe for myself, let alone for anyone else, the delicate confluence of characteristics that constitute the Anglo-Saxon Protestant male, nor could I describe those mysterious processes that mold those properties into the Anglo-Saxon Protestant male rather than a Chinese Buddhist male or an Irish Catholic one. But I know the difference.

There is, to begin with, a certain blithe quality among the English, which, when it is translated into any other society, becomes either overbearingly smug or unbearably silly. My Uncle Bourke was blithe. He was never smug; and though he could, on occasion, be very silly, it was in such an innocent way that he became almost poignant: one worried for his safety.

"*The Mikado* is a brilliant satire of English manners," said my sister, who was sixteen at the time and therefore taking seriously her obligation to educate any ignorant masses she happened to come across.

"It's set in Japan," my Uncle Bourke told her kindly. "The Mikado is the Japanese emperor." This was during Sunday dinner and we had all just seen *The Mikado* at the Saturday matinee the day before. My sister was unmoved.

"That's the way you create a satire," she said informatively. "You look at things from a different perspective. Like *Gulliver's Travels.*"

"Is *Gulliver's Travels* set in Japan?" asked my Uncle Bourke. "I don't think it is, is it?"

I still have no idea whether he was being funny. Possibly. You could never tell with my Uncle Bourke. He was not at all a stupid man. But despite his merry eye for human frailty and for the vagaries of society, his native loyalty and decency led him to blind himself to certain possibilities. It is quite likely that he might not allow it to occur to him that English manners—as opposed to French or German or Japanese manners—could become a particularly ripe subject for satire. There were certain treasons he refused entry into his thinking, so that, for instance, he barred himself from even entertaining the notion that any inhabitant of the far-flung colonies and dominions might occasionally legitimately consider the British Empire a complete pain in the neck.

And he assumed—without snobbery because it was an a priori unattached to any other aspect of life—that the Church of England was superior to chapels unblessed by English royalty, accepting on a faith that bypassed history from Anne Boleyn to Wally Simpson that the chemical composition of the royal family itself was something finer than mere flesh and blood.

But he was also essentially a very kind man. A very humble man. And he held his fellow earthlings in such affection that when the delicate and vulnerable assumptions of this whimsical world were shaken by the wind of some rude truth, he did not argue with the facts by becoming pompous or dictatorial or taking refuge in his status as the head of the family. He had grown up being the youngest of several boisterous and, one suspects, bossy siblings, and I suppose he had learned early in life not to take his own opinions too seriously, but also—at least in the privacy of his own soul—not to retreat from them. He protected what he thought in cotton wool and muffled any contradiction to what he said by being vague. Faced with serious challenge, he changed the subject.

"Do we have any of Margaret's Christmas chutney still?" he said. And that was that for Japan and satire. "It would be nice with the beef if we're having it cold tomorrow."

Blessed in his innocence, however, he also sometimes cut through the received ideas and learned responses that muddled the rest of us. Quite often he would give voice to some embarrassing but essential truth we were all politely trying to ignore and lift a shroud of silence from our shoulders.

"Shouldn't she be wearing a dress?" he said as we watched the soon to be made Dame Sybil Thorndike, clad in bloomers, leaping off a parapet. She was playing Prince Arthur in *King John,* to which Uncle Bourke had agreed to take Ruth and me. I think Di and Val were there too, but I remember clearly that it was because of Ruth and me that we had come. I must have been ten or so at the time, and I had been lobbying to go to this Shakespeare play; I had never seen a Shakespeare play and I wanted to be able to say I had seen one. Ruth had been excited because of Sibyl Thorndike—whose performances, especially in male roles, were much praised in the *Guardian* and the *Times* and who now lay before us after her leap, resplendent in olive velvet plus fours and a little squashed hat. Apparently she was at death's door.

> *Oh me! my uncle's spirit is in these stones.*
> *Heaven take my soul, and England keep my bones,*

she said feebly, and expired.

We were sitting in one of the boxes quite close to the stage, but I hadn't understood a word for approximately three hours. Nor, as it turned out in later years, had Ruth. So we were both quite pleased to see the last of Miss Thorndike in the role of this person to whom everyone else in the play kept referring as "boy" and "child," although they were clearly considerably younger than she—he—it—was. Despite the amazing tedium, I was bearing up quite well. I was dressed in my favorite frock just recently handed down from Val; the murk and incomprehensibility of the play reminded me pleasantly of the incense-scented mysteries of a High Church Service we had all attended in Ripon Cathedral; and—precisely because nothing that was going on on stage made any sense—my respect for Shakespeare was increasing by the minute. Besides, my main attention was on the butterscotch balls Uncle Bourke had acquired for us during an intermission, after which, his duty accomplished, he had fallen asleep.

I should make it clear that he had nothing against women in male roles or women wearing pants. We all wore pants, including Aunt Helen. Wearing pants had become, subtly, part of the War Effort. But he was absolutely right; Sybil Thorndike should have been wearing a dress. Or possibly a pair of black slacks and a white shirt, something that demonstrated that she wasn't *really* trying to be Prince Arthur, just reading his lines for him. It would have been far more convincing.

An aggravating aspect of her lack of cogency was that *King John* was being put on at the Grand Theatre, where the last dramatic performance we had seen was the Christmas pantomime. Leeds was a major center for Christmas pantomimes—perhaps *the* major city for Christmas pantomimes—and there were three of them every year, one at each of the three theaters. For most of the year the Grand brought in London plays on tour, the Royal did repertory, and the Majestic was mainly vaudeville; but the pantomime was a very important cultural event and usually lasted from just before Christmas until just before Easter.

Perhaps I should explain that of course English pantomime has nothing to do with classical pantomime and a great deal to do with nineteenth-century music halls. It is always based on a fairy story, preferably one with sound British credentials, like *Babes in the Wood*, which was the absolute Leeds favorite; there are always at least twenty changes of scenery and a vast chorus of dancers, nymphs, mermaids, or flying fairies; the comic lead is always a woman played by a man, and the romantic lead is always a man played by a woman. Those are the rules, and I will firmly resist my strong temptation to go into a sociosexual analysis of what they mean.

The pantomime at the Grand the year of poor Sybil Thorndike had been *Cinderella*. Prince Charming—played by a big-bosomed, long-legged, half-famous movie star considerably shorter in the tooth than Prince Arthur—had thrown jelly babies into the audience. At a time when sweets were rationed, this was excellent. Even more than excellent had been the tall, gangly Yorkshire comedian who had played Cinderella's stepmother and who, dressed in a convoluted wig and an excruciating costume, had poignantly embodied the woes of exuberant nature hobbled by a corset and high heels. The high point of the pantomime had been his orchestration of a fugue of rude noises with a simpering counterpoint of apology as he had lurched daintily into the orchestra pit during the ballroom scene.

Ever since the pantomime, therefore, our standards for crossdressing had been set extremely high.

It was a great relief to find that they were not unreasonable; it made us somehow feel sure of ourselves, validating our tastes and our opinions, to have Uncle Bourke establish on public record what we would have been thinking had we dared, that Sybil Thorndike was not very convincing in drag and that she should have been wearing a dress.

✢

You came into Twenty-Three the Towers by way of a front hall. Through an arched double doorway on the left there was the dining room, and through an arched double doorway on the right there was the drawing room. That was what it was still called, although the ladies had not withdrawn there after dinner—leaving the gentlemen to port and cigars—for more than a generation.

One end of the drawing room was entirely taken up by a wide bay window overlooking the upper garden. There was a marble-mantled fireplace in the center of the long wall (the wall that backed onto Twenty-Five the Towers), and on the wall opposite the bay window there was a glassed-in bookcase that contained most of the better books: leather-bound volumes of Scott and Macaulay and first editions of Ernest Thompson Seton. The ordinary books overflowed bookcases in the upstairs hall and the built-in shelves that lined the room we all still called the nursery—a large back room furnished only with a huge old sofa and the great leather-topped table where we did our schoolwork and painted our pictures and played our games.

The grown-ups now and then had a preprandial glass of sherry in the drawing room or a postprandial glass of brandy and soda. But except to practice the piano very occasionally, and under duress, we children were only there at Christmas or other Official Occasions— which were also the only times that the drawing room fire was lit. The decor was standard for that time and class: there was a baby grand piano that none of us played well and none of us wanted to play at all; there were two slightly frayed chintz-covered sofas and three arm chairs; there was a beautiful eighteenth-century writing desk inlaid with ivory; and a handful of little side tables with ivory-inlaid tops that were burdened with decanters of sherry and brandy, sherry glasses, a soda siphon, and several ashtrays.

The one object in the drawing room that was at all out of the ordinary was a tiger-skin rug. It was replete with a snarling tiger head displaying a full set of tiger teeth. The tiger had been killed by Uncle Bourke while he was on safari in the Sunderbans delta in West Bengal. Most of the safari was spent waiting for the tiger to appear. Uncle Bourke had done this in reasonable comfort and safety up on the tree platform erected by some twenty-odd low-caste Indians before they beat the underbrush so that the tiger would either spring out and maul a few of them or spring out and get shot first by Uncle Bourke and the three gun-bearing cavalry officers by whom the Indians had been hired. The three officers spent the night with Uncle Bourke up on the tree platform, while the twenty-odd Indian bearers slept on the ground. In the morning they got up, made tea for Uncle Bourke and the three officers, beat the underbrush, and made various loud noises approved by tradition for getting tigers to move on. When at last the beast lurking in hiding was driven into the open and to a place where he was clearly visible from the platform, the cavalry officers had simultaneously, all four of them including my Uncle Bourke, shot him.

Well, I am making this up, of course. I only vaguely remember what Uncle Bourke said about hunting tigers, and at the time I took it as one of his amusing but invented stories about India, an amusing but invented place—where shoes were said to grow mold within minutes and trains were reported to travel so slowly that on a trip to the Punjab Uncle Bourke's dog, Demon, got bored two hours north of Madras and jumped out of the train window, only to jump back in— the journey still unfinished—through the same window again three days later.

But the story, in any case, for what it's worth, was that it was Uncle Bourke who shot the tiger. Probably it was his turn to be assigned the honorary shot, to be declared the honorary victor, and to be awarded the honorary pelt. Judging by the hole-riddled tiger-skin, he was certainly not alone in hitting the poor animal, but the receipt of hunting trophies has always, historically, been more a matter of protocol than just desert.

Of eight subspecies of tigers alive a century ago, only five remain, all of them now in danger of extinction. One of the largest extant populations of Bengal tigers is in the tiger reserve in the Sunderbans, Uncle Bourke's old hunting grounds, and their disposition is instructive about survival in a hostile world. A couple of years ago the naturalist, Sy Montgomery, who lives near us in New Hampshire and is the source of much of my tiger information, traveled to West Bengal several times to research her book, *The Spell of the Tiger*. For about ten seconds on one of these expeditions Sy did, definitively, see a tiger and one of her photographers did, definitively, take its photograph—which disappeared along with the rest of the luggage later in the trip. For Eleanor Briggs—another of the book's photographers and also our friend and neighbor—no tiger made even a brief appearance. Which was, by and large, just as well. Though tigers are known generally to disdain human flesh, those which survive in the Sunderbans are voracious man-eaters.

The Raj is finished; the cavalry has retreated. For centuries, the Sunderbans tigers have had a reputation as man-eaters, but I am sure that both their appetites and their brilliant hunting skills were sharpened in the contests with my Uncle Bourke and his trophy-seeking friends, those poachers noisily invading their sacred territories. Now, according to Sy, the tigers' hunger is insatiable: they roam the shores of the delta formed by the mouths of the Ganges and remain hidden in the dense overgrowth along the banks. Formidable swimmers and ferociously strong, they leap from the water onto the riverboats with astonishing agility. Once they have seized their prey, they swim back to shore and in the blink of an eye disappear once more into the forest. They have been known to swim for miles in pursuit of a likely meal, and since unlike their old foes, the Indian Cavalry, they can do without sleep and without their wake-up tea, they most often hunt at night. The boatmen are often not even aware that one of their crew has been taken into the darkness until, with the morning light, they find him gone.

The tiger on our drawing room floor, flattened and bullet scarred, looked far too humble to have been such a radical terrorist. Perhaps, after all, he was the meekest among the fierce, a moderate from the old school of Bengal tiger and therefore, naturally, the one who got caught. I think of him as a Raj tiger, lying there, the helpless victim of British imperialism, while the two Welsh terriers, drawn by his lingering feline scent, peed on him and gave him fleas. The lacunae on the stripes of his handsome coat became more and more apparent, while the odor of dog pee took over the once-august ambience of the drawing room.

Finally, he was banished to a far corner of the attic—to the delight of Lassie and Vixen who could now have their way with him uninterrupted. After a year or two of massive dog abuse, you began to smell the poor thing from the bottom of the attic stairs. And he was thrown out.

After he was exiled from it, the drawing room never really recovered its old cachet for me. Not that it smelled or that any fleas remained. But the ghostly aura of defeat, the sense of an absence where a rug should have been, stamped this haven of chintz and leather-bound classics with a reminder that redness in tooth and claw—fierceness, bloodiness, and general mayhem—are not by a long shot the worst that nature has to offer. The space from which the tiger skin had vanished conspired with the flowers fading on the sofas, with the untuned piano and the cracked wood in the beautifully inlaid desk, to bear witness that everything that the drawing room encompassed was on its way to the attic and out—including the rule of Empire and the herds of elephants who had so generously contributed all that ivory, including also and emphatically every civilized opinion offered by the venerable and deceased gentlemen, bound in leather.

✳

Beside the defunct tiger, the Empire had contributed another gift to the household, bestowed on a quite astonishing number of the Harveys' relations and friends. "A touch of malaria" was the inevitable diagnosis when Uncle Clyde or cousin James failed to appear at breakfast. It was always said in a voice that suggested that "a touch of malaria," was roughly equivalent to "a drop of brandy" or "a pinch of salt" or "a hint of color," that it defined the delicate application of something of which too much would have been unfortunate, but which, in small supply, was rather to be desired. "A touch of malaria," they said as Uncle Clyde or cousin James was found shivering uncontrollably, unable to stand up or leave his bed, his temperature having hit 105.

As touches went, in short, malaria tended to be a bit of a whopper. But since it was a gift from the Empire it was perhaps natural to refer to it with imperial understatement. Besides, unlike the drug-resistant strains of today, the malaria of the 1940s, properly treated, was seldom fatal. It was like our drawing room tiger a relic of the old school, not yet rampaging into deadly mutations of postimperial anarchy. I think you might say that in those days it was quite a reasonable disease: chronic but not overly demanding, it became, with luck, milder over the years, and the administration of quinine soaked into lumps of sugar usually limited the bouts of fever to one or two days. Occasional flaring up of the disease would continue throughout one's lifetime, of course, and return at unpredictable intervals with random fierceness every few months or every few years; but I suppose, objectively looked at, it could be construed by an optimist as being no worse than a tendency to catch cold or a predisposition to stomach flu.

It was the men who were mainly infected—they were the ones who had frolicked with tigers and stalked antelope in colonial jungles while the ladies had stayed sensibly in fan-cooled, netting-protected houses back in Nairobi or Poonah or Capetown. And though I imagine that ordinary soldiers must have been bitten by just as many mosquitoes as their officers, perhaps most of the ordinary soldiers were native to India or Burma or Uganda and therefore not much in evidence in Leeds; whatever the reason, I formed the firm idea in my childhood that malaria was yet another badge of class.

It was at least a clear emblem of participation in British rule. Uncle Bourke's malaria was well tamed and made itself known perhaps once or twice a year as a day of mild chills and slight fever. But Uncle Clyde, who had joined an order of Anglican monks and hitched up his long black robe over his trousers whenever he was in motion, had been infected more seriously while converting the unconverted in Rhodesia. He was a naturally gloomy man, and I suspect that he found both Africa and Africans so depressingly sunny that he had failed to take proper precautions. Young Major James Vickers, Aunt Helen's cousin and movie star handsome, had contracted it while supervising the planting of tea on his tea plantation in Ceylon, and he stayed with us, shaking and out of his mind with fever, for a week. It seems to me that Dickon too came back at the end of the war in the uniform of an R.A.F. officer and mildly infected with something that kept him in bed for days. I am sure that Aunt Helen's half-brother, Uncle Max, had it and so did Uncle Lionel. They were identical twins—now clearly distinguishable because Uncle Lionel was in a wheelchair while Uncle Max wasn't. I think their infection had something to do with the Suez Canal.

I went to stay with Uncle Lionel once, in his country house in a place my memory labels Appleby, though I'm no longer sure about its actual name or that of any of its inhabitants. It was near Gloucester, a wonderful house of ancient brick built at a time when Chaucer was still alive. There wasn't a straight line in it: the walls were bowed with age, the floors sagged, the ceilings above them had curved with the weight of the centuries. But one sensed no danger in this decline—the process of decay had been going on so gently and for so long that it had achieved a sort of stasis, a constant state of mellowing and fading that was altogether beautiful. The house seemed mature rather than decrepit. It was set among orchards, and from my bedroom window I could see, in the distance, the blue outline of the Malvern Hills.

I had gone there toward the end of May in 1944 to convalesce after some plebeian illness. Nothing romantic like malaria—mumps, I think. Country air was thought to be good for recovery, and Leeds air was known to be bad.

Uncle Lionel almost always stayed home, wrapped neatly in brown wool so one could only guess at the mysterious vacancy where his legs had been—where they probably still were, useless and invisible. In fine weather he ventured now and then to roll his wheelchair into the garden, but no further. So it was Aunt Betty who came to collect me from the train at the Gloucester station. She was driving the smallest car I have ever seen: a tiny green tin toy that had been custom built for the racetrack and probably could have circumnavigated England, Scotland, and Wales on a single squirt of lighter fluid. That was the point of having it I suppose—saving petrol. I was in terror. The car, if you could call it that, lacked doors and floors and every other amenity not essential to motion. It had metal seats and bars to keep your feet up, and it rattled ominously even when standing still; clearly, contact with even small and feeble alien objects would cause it to crumple instantly and enfold you in a fatal embrace.

Aunt Betty blithely drove us around the scenic highlights, pointing them out. I had my eyes shut. She was one of those women who see themselves as cheerful and sensible, though what they are, in fact, is out of their minds. Aunt Betty spent a great deal of time away from home, doing good things, like running church bazaars and distributing clothes and books among the parishioners or to needy natives in African missions. She was energetic about educating those who stayed still long enough to let her do it, and her two children, Heather and Georgie, had been brought up on extremely healthy food, processed as little as possible between its natural state and its digestion; its natural state was, of course, exceedingly natural, which rendered its digestion somewhat arduous.

At the time of my visit, Uncle Lionel had been persuaded that it would be practical to raise rabbits for meat, meat being scarce and strictly rationed. So there were five or six rabbits in wire cages on the back lawn when I got there. They were fed great quantities of the very healthy carrots and lettuces from Aunt Betty's garden. By the time I left Appleby only four or five rabbits remained—the biggest one,

Chuckle, had given up and died of old age. The other rabbits were also antique and unlikely to be an addition to anyone's dinner menu. Rabbits are cute and fuzzy and look you in the eye, squeaking, as you advance upon them with a butcher knife. The ones at Appleby had all been given names by Georgie, and no one, not even Uncle Lionel who was known to be a hero of the First World War, was capable of translating them from their vegetable paradise on the back lawn into the oven.

I helped Georgie bury Chuckle's remains behind the spinach bed, and we marked his grave with a rosemary wreath. Then we went for a bicycle ride.

Georgie and I had been bicycling together every day. Our first day out we had brought lunch with us. We had ridden westward towards the distant Malvern Hills, turned left just after a little stone bridge across a stone-filled stream, and trudged up a hill steep enough so I had to get off and push my borrowed bicycle—an old one of Heather's—for the last few yards. There was a view from the top, Georgie said.

And there was.

A city of tents lay below us. Camouflaged tents in rows, hundreds of them, tent pavilions, tent palaces with small tent houses and tent cottages spaced neatly between them like pieces on a Monopoly board. At the center, where the rows of tents seemed to converge, there was a large American flag blowing in the wind.

"That wasn't exactly the view I thought it was going to be," Georgie said.

After that, we came back every day to check on what the Americans were doing. Whatever it was, there was a great deal of it: comings and goings of trucks and jeeps, marchings back and forth of men in columns and men alone, shouting and blowing of whistles and horns.

"That's a bloody tank," said Georgie, awestruck. "That's a bloody American tank." It was not, we found out, the only one.

So from our distant hill we supervised the bustling about of the Americans. Until one day, at the beginning of June, they bustled no longer. The encampment stood there still; but it was silent and deserted, the tanks gone, the columns of soldiers shrunk to a disorderly handful of men who moved among the canvas rows doing something to the tents that seemed to fold behind them as they passed through.

"They're leaving. They're bloody leaving," Georgie said. "What're they bloody leaving for?" He liked to say "bloody" and took the opportunity whenever his parents weren't around.

I had been at Appleby for three weeks by then; I was supposed to be back in Leeds, my convalescence long since finished. But mysteriously, a few days earlier, the trains had stopped running. No one said why, just that there were no trains from Gloucester to Leeds. No one said when, if ever, they would start running again. Their dysfunction was entirely unexplained, and the only thing clear was that there were no trains. I was seized by such a dire case of homesickness that I could concentrate on nothing but my state of exile. Terror that I was doomed to live in Appleby for life knotted my stomach and drove all other thoughts away. I didn't care about the Americans and their tanks and their tents. I left Georgie to his bloody exclamations over their departure and began to bicycle back towards the house to see what the trains were doing.

I was halfway down the hill towards the little bridge when a man exploded from the bushes. That, at least, was how I experienced it. He was huge and dark, his stubble-chinned face shadowed under a helmet, and he was clothed in the khaki-and-brown splotched garments of war. Pistols and knives and other bellicose objects hung from him, and I saw a gun slung from his shoulder. He burst at me from behind a bush just as I was about to pedal past it; and he roared at me in a deep baritone so foreign that I could distinguish not one word.

It was the first American I had ever seen close up. He was warlike, brutish, and horrible. The terror of never getting home to Leeds was suddenly driven out by a newer and greater fear, and I pedaled more and more furiously towards safety, while the American waved his arms from the roadside bushes and bellowed after me.

"You should have stopped and talked; he's nice," Georgie said when he came back to Appleby—a half-hour after me. "Look, he gave me a Hershey's bar. He says he's from Alabama and he misses his mum's cooking. He calls her 'ma.'"

"He's a walking arsenal," I said coldly. "He's ready to kill people."

"Of course he is; he's a soldier," Georgie said reasonably. "He likes Gloucestershire: he says it reminds him of Alabama."

As mysteriously as they had stopped it seemed that the trains had started running again. That was what Aunt Betty told me as soon as I was back in Appleby, breathless, leaning Heather's old bike against the wall. She also told me that the Allied Forces had landed on the beaches of Normandy.

I went back to Leeds the next morning.

✫

It was in Appleby too that I was introduced to what, for want of a better excuse, I will call my vocation.

One of Aunt Betty's projects was a performance of *Ladies in Retirement*. She was directing it, and a group of parish women was staging it in the parish hall. For some reason Aunt Betty had told me to come to the dress rehearsal to render my opinion.

"Well," Aunt Betty said when it was over, "so what do you think of our play?" She was standing in the glow of the footlights, and the ladies of the title had gathered around her, holding up their Edwardian skirts and staring out into the blackness at the back of the parish hall where I was sitting in judgment.

I have recently looked through an old copy of *Ladies in Retirement* to check whether my memory of it—that you could easily confuse it with *Arsenic and Old Lace*—was at all close to the facts. Like *Arsenic and*

Old Lace it does, in fact, revolve around several somewhat dotty old ladies, one of whom does, indeed, go counter to one's expectations by committing a murder rather early on in the proceedings, which take place in the late eighteen hundreds and in the standard upper-middle-class environment in which such things happen on the English stage. Three of the dotty old ladies are highly respectable old ladies—impoverished but sufficiently refined to consider murder rather more to be accepted than taking a job—and only the fourth, the victim, is of dubious social standing: a demimondaine retired from the demi-monde.

As I watched Aunt Betty's dress rehearsal it struck me that the woman who played the leading respectable old lady, as well as those who played her two respectable sisters, spoke with a very broad Gloucestershire twang—as, of course, did the ex-demimondaine and the girl who played the incidental maid. Since the play is set on the Thames and nowhere near Gloucester, and since money and class are central to its plot, this unvaried way of speaking seemed to me to make rather a hash of the play.

I had been highly sensitized to accents, to their meaning and to their power. But if I had become a snob, I had become an inverse sort of snob. I knew my place, after all, defined for me by Uncle Bourke when, recalling his years in India, he occasionally alluded to "coolies." I had asked him once what the word meant, and he had told me that a coolie was someone who did odd jobs for people for very little money because he had no exactly defined place or function in society. He looked surprised when I asked whether coolies were usually darker than other Indians, but yes, he said, by and large he thought they were.

"I am a coolie," I thought, dark and without any exactly defined place or function in society. No one in England knew it, of course; no one even suspected it. But if they had thought about it, they would have seen at once that a coolie is what I was. I had felt at the time a slight indignation on behalf of all the coolies of the world, a slight annoyance at the dismissive tone in which even my Uncle Bourke, respectful of almost everyone, allowed himself to speak of them. It was apparently a lack of definition that made one vulnerable to such indifference; and one became a coolie because no one had any regard for you.

When I browsed through *Ladies in Retirement* again a year or so ago it became clear to me that its authors, Edward Percy and Reginald Denham, intended it to dramatize the violent center of social inequity. The chief retired lady of the play—she was first played in New York by Flora Robson—is warm, responsible, intelligent, and also, as it turns out, pushed by poverty, capable of cold-blooded murder. The play, which weighs the helplessness of being born poor but genteel against the vulgar power granted by money, begins in offstage and almost off-hand violence and ends on a strange note of moral equivocation.

But of course if everyone speaks in the same broad Gloucestershire dialect, the delicate balances of money and class are rather blurred. In that late spring of 1944, watching it from the back of the parish hall, I found the whole thing embarrassing and excruciatingly pointless. Aunt Betty's actors, disastrously cast, had been left looking ridiculous. Pale-skinned though they were, on that stage they too had been deprived of their true character and function and turned into a species of stage-coolie.

"Well, so what do you think of our play?" Aunt Betty asked perkily of the darkness in the back of the hall where I was sitting.

"Why don't Ellen, Louisa, and Emily talk properly?" I said. "They've got the wrong accents for ladies."

It was the closest I have ever come to being an actual revolutionary. I could feel from the shock on Aunt Betty's face and from the sudden silence of the ladies that a bomb had been dropped. And since I was the only other person in the hall, I knew I must have been the one who had dropped it. The ladies began to chat with each other again almost immediately—perhaps assuming they had misheard and most probably, anyway, not caring. They were happy with the way they sounded. But Aunt Betty remained silent for most of the drive home in the horrible little green tin monster. Then she outlined for me, briefly and much more gently than I deserved, the shameful social solecism of which I had been guilty. For weeks, for years afterwards, I was smitten with inward embarrassment whenever I thought of Appleby. It still makes me uneasy to remember it. And until this moment I have never told anyone what I did.

But it was, in fact, my first outing in the disreputable profession to which I have been doomed: I had become a critic.

✧

"He wants to see you," Georgie said.

Aunt Betty was at the front door waiting to drive me to the station, and for a moment I thought I might ignore Georgie's summons and carry my suitcase straight out to the green monster without going to see Uncle Lionel first. He frightened me: a cool, dry man, aquiline in feature and scornful in temperament, ramrod stiff above the waist and hidden in brown wool below it. I think he frightened Georgie too, and perhaps he even frightened Aunt Betty. We all tended to fall silent at his approach, announced from a fair distance away by the rolling of wheels over rough floors.

But I went out obediently if fearfully to see him, in back by the rabbit cages.

He gestured me to come nearer, and I did come nearer, gingerly; but he waved me to come nearer still until he could reach me and take hold of my arm. I had become rigid with terror, my eyes fixed on the brown wool shadow of the blanket, where he was not.

He pulled me close and gave a cool, dry terrifying kiss on my cheek. "Thank you, my dear, for coming to stay with us," he said. "It was a joy to have you here," and he brushed a gentle hand against my hair. With his other hand I felt him reach into my skirt and leave something in the pocket.

I waited until I was safe in the train and halfway to Leeds to find out what unpleasant thing he had put there. It was customary in those days to give money to children when they left your house or, if you yourself were leaving a house where there were children, to give them a parting gift of cash. You tipped the valet and the maids and you slipped the kids a half a crown or maybe even ten bob when you were saying good-bye. But in my pocket I found a five-pound note. It was more money than I had ever had in my life.

I sat there, grasping the treasure in my hand and looking out at the passing landscape. And then I remembered a detail I had quite forgotten, something I had disdained to file in my memory: that as the American soldier, warlike and bellowing, had waved at me as I bicycled furiously away from him, he too had held something in his hand. He had waved and waved at me and gestured at what he was holding, and suddenly, thinking back on it, I remembered that it was nothing horrible or belligerent after all, but a bouquet of bright blue, newly picked harebells that he was holding out to me.

JESUS AND ME

⌒⌒ I think both Valerie and Diana were
reasonably content at West Leeds High School, and I know that Aunt
Helen and Uncle Bourke were happy to have them there, at home, living with them at Twenty-Three the Towers. But in 1943, despite
parental qualms, both girls were sent away to boarding school; probably, I suspect, through the grace and generosity of some high-minded
relative who had faith in the value of a proper education. In England
in those days a proper education meant spending quite a lot of money
to sleep in a chilly dormitory, eat bad food, and receive rather unin-
spired instruction. The point, a rite of passage and a ritual of caste,
was simply to have left home, and so Valerie and Diana duly left to go
to Queen Margaret's.

Ruth was also gone most of the time. She had won a scholarship
in physics to Leeds University and she was on the University fencing
team as well as being the cox of the rowing crew. She came home every
evening, but she came home later and later. Sometimes when she
waltzed into our shared bedroom and it was after midnight she would

be wearing the cast-off taffeta dress my cousin Clare had sent her for dances. Usually, on these occasions she would be humming to herself and I would throw a pillow at her.

When Val and Di were still there we had said morning prayers together every day, kneeling around the big bed where Uncle Bourke and Aunt Helen slept. One of us read aloud the short passage from the Bible assigned to that day and we recited the Lord's Prayer and the Apostles' Creed. And even after Val and Di were gone, I continued to go with Aunt Helen and Uncle Bourke every Sunday, following Mr. Hutchins, the vicar at Christ Church, as he led us through matins in his comfortable Yorkshire-tinged voice. Uncle Bourke and Aunt Helen genuflected as they came into church, crossed themselves whenever the word "Christ" was said, and would not, I think, have objected to a hint of incense now and then. They were somewhat discomfited by the plainness of Mr. Hutchins's approach—but in Leeds Mr. Hutchins was as High as the Church could be persuaded to go.

There was also a Mrs. Hutchins, who wore a pale blue shiny costume—one would call it a suit in America, but there was something a bit unsuitable about it and I have continued to think of it as a costume. With it she wore a matching hat with pale blue paper hydrangeas arranged in a rather salad-like fashion around its brim. Even at the time, although I am sure no one actually came out and said as much, I saw that both the blue costume and the matching hydrangeas were not considered de rigueur. Nor was Mr. Ramsgate, the curate, who occasionally attempted to bring a welcome bit of popish decoration to the show but who had made the fatal mistake of rejecting an offer of salt—he had brought his mother over to Twenty-Three the Towers for lunch—with the words, "Mother and I require no condiments, thank you."

Nowadays the Harvey's frequent and regular observance of Christian ritual would suggest a depth of devotion the Harveys, in fact, entirely lacked. Their sense of morality was intrinsic, intense, and passionate, but it was totally unrelated to their adherence to Anglican lore, whose very Anglicanism inclined towards the avoidance of passion and intensity. Their piety sprang from cultural habit not spiritual need; it was a matter of daily custom, pretty much on a par with putting on their shoes. And it would have seemed as inappropriate to them to wax ardent about saying their prayers as it would have been to be extravagant about tying their laces. It was simply what you did because it was practical and because it was what was done.

But though their faith was not notably metaphysical, it was in no way shallow. In fact it was profound and underlay not only their own lives, but their whole history. Spreading down through the generations and through centuries it had become an innate attribute, an inalienable, unthinking, and essential part of who they were.

Accordingly, they naturally assumed that some sort of religious observance was an essential part of who everyone was—and they had no impulse to load their own beliefs onto anyone else; people are allowed to tie their own shoelaces, after all, in any way they please. But since Aunt Helen had a high regard for regular exercise, whether of body or soul, she got in touch with a local rabbi very soon after we had arrived in England. It was arranged that Ruth and I would attend Saturday service at the only synagogue that was close by. An Orthodox congregation, as it happened. The rabbi suggested that on the Shabbas no one from his congregation would be able to pick us up. Could Aunt Helen herself deliver us?

Somewhat bemused, Aunt Helen drives us to the synagogue on the following Saturday. We are taken upstairs by a guide—the rabbi's wife, I believe—and we observe the Shabbas service from the gallery where we have been seated with other females of varying ages—who seem to be passing their time in diverse relaxing pursuits of a fairly secular nature while the men do their weekly, energetic, necessary business with God downstairs.

Brought up in the cool, egalitarian customs of the Reform tradition, Ruth and I find everything entirely foreign. I was too young to go to services more than two or three times with Pappi, and after he died we all stopped going altogether, so I can take all the davening and shawl kissing and randomly syncopated Hebrew chanting pretty much in stride—though after an hour of it, I'm painfully bored. Ruth, however, already has convictions and strong political principles that do not sit well with such Orthodoxy. She is immediately outraged by the placement of women here. It is barbaric, debased, and humiliating, she announces to Aunt Helen, who is waiting outside to pick us up after the service. She refuses to go back to the synagogue next week and is unenthusiastic about looking for another one more to her liking.

Aunt Helen must have been rather dismayed by this apostasy. And as soon as Mother has arrived in America and has settled in enough to receive mail, Aunt Helen writes to ask her for guidance as to our spiritual upbringing.

✡

Poor Mother! She must have wondered what Aunt Helen meant by "spiritual." My mother greatly respected Plato and Hegel and Schopenhauer, and she also admired Nietzsche—whose complete writings, bound in gold-embossed leather I recall as having always held a central position in her bookcase. But it was unlikely that Aunt Helen's dilemma about our spiritual education would be solved by telling her to make us read *The Republic* or *The Phenomenology of Mind*, let alone *Thus Spake Zarathustra*.

Nor would the situation have been helped by a discussion of my mother's own spirituality—which she herself probably didn't recognize as such, but dismissed, instead, as having everything to do with an enjoyment of the senses and nothing whatever to do with the satisfaction of the soul. She had severe doubts about the soul anyway—in its existence, I mean, and in what people meant when they talked about it. What her deepest feelings were involved with was music. And her most profound response was to opera—to Mozart's *Die Zauberflöte* and to Wagner. She particularly loved *Parsifal*, and in later years, in

New York, she went to hear it every year at Easter, not because she was engaging in a specifically paschal ritual herself, but because that was when it happened always to be performed at the Met. All her life she was moved to her most profound depths by *Parsifal*.

But of course it never even occurred to her to advise an English lady raised on *The Pirates of Penzance* that a five-hour opera by a Nazi-friendly composer could be just the ticket for our spiritual fulfillment.

What she did, in fact, was to write Aunt Helen to thank her for her concern and to say that she trusted her to do what was best for us, in this and all other things. She was enormously grateful for Aunt Helen's tact and her care of us, and she was sure that Aunt Helen would know much better than she herself could now guess—far away as she was from us—what would be the right thing to do for our spiritual well-being.

✡

So Ruth, who had chosen a set of religious beliefs years ago in Germany, was left to follow the direction she had already taken. She remained, and still remains, more or less Jewish in her culture and in her faith—or at least her lack of it, Judaism being admirable in its tolerance of heterodoxies, including agnosticism. She never looked for another temple in Swansea, nor did she go in search of a synagogue in Leeds. Later, in America, of course, she did attend services—but that was to please her husband and her son and to observe the major rites of passage of their more pious friends.

No one from the Swansea congregation ever came to inquire after us. No one from the much larger congregations in Leeds ever came to inquire after us. And even in America we remained untroubled by any attempts to gather us into the fold. Christians of all varieties, Baptists, Papists, Presbyterians, Lutherans, are eager to persuade one to believe as they believe. Mormons and Jehovah's Witnesses drop by daily to urge one to salvation. But Judaism is passive and exclusionary.

And why not? What would be the point of Jewish evangelism? You can become an Episcopalian and you can get over being an Episcopalian. You can become and get over being a Quaker or a Methodist or, with effort, even a Roman Catholic. But Judaism is a history written in the blood of your forefathers and passed down from generation to generation. If you're a Jew you'll always be a Jew no matter how much you convert to something else; and if you're not a Jew you probably never will be.

Still, one would have thought that somewhere over the last sixty-odd years some local leader of my tribe might have been moved to remind me whence I came. I suppose perhaps on the whole—given an acute distrust of classification—I'm quite grateful for the oversight. Besides, how should I respond to an invitation to join an organization to which I've already had a lifetime membership since birth when I know I'm unlikely ever to go to a meeting?

Despite all this, however, I must admit that often over the years I've missed the comfort of wrapping myself in a sustaining history and yearned for the support of the ritual that expresses it. Wonderfully rich in anecdote, magnificent in the depths of its narrative detail, and filled with pride for triumphs over adversity, Judaism seems to me a surprisingly upbeat institution. Those of its champions I can most easily call to mind—Abraham and Isaac, David and Saul, Esther and Judith—prevail with remarkable, if occasionally bloody, practicality. Whatever needs doing they seem to get it done.

This is a comforting message.

Of course, in counterpoint to their triumphant pragmatism, one can also hear a gloomy muttering from the Prophets, and what has needed doing most often, what has needed to be done again and again, is to get us the hell out—away from Egyptians, Babylonians, Persians, Romans. Our history is one long, ineluctable flight from bondage—into which, equally inexorably though without quite the same enthusiastic documentation, we are then, at some later time and in some other place, eternally returned.

We are a culture of Houdinis—and he was Jewish, of course—brilliant practitioners of escape from everything and everyone but ourselves and the fatal pull back into captivity.

☆

Even at thirteen Ruth had enough integrity to determine to go on being simply herself. But I was made of feebler stuff. I just wanted to be like everyone else. So every morning I knelt with the others by the big bed for morning prayers, and every Sunday I went with them to church. In winter I wore my felt hat with the rolled up brim; in summer I wore the straw hat cast off by Valerie the previous year and trimmed with new ribbon.

After following these exercises for several years, I found that I was in love with the naked young man nailed to the cross. By the time I was twelve I worshipped everything about him: his elegant, bare body, the poignant fact that he was a heroic victim, the delicious sense of his suffering need for my sympathy. Above all, I was intrigued that he was a Jew—a fact to which no one else seemed to pay much attention, but which struck me as singular and extraordinary. In a complex and paradoxical sleight of hand, I tried to use his Judaism to obliterate my own. I suppose it was my one last oblique and desperate attempt to become a real little English girl, combined with an onset of adolescent hormones that attached themselves to various Freudian implications of the Crucifixion. To my credit, I should say that there was an undeniable impetus of some inchoate spiritual impulse that also urged me towards conversion—but that was secondary. It was my romantic yearnings, really, that turned me into a Christian.

Unfortunately, if it was an Episcopalian English schoolgirl I was trying to become, I had turned into the wrong sort of Christian. I might have made a go of it in medieval France or maybe Renaissance Italy—but the passionate conviction and inventive masochism of my prepubescent spiritual fever were entirely foreign to the Church of England in the 1940s, which was as uneasy with adoration as English cuisine was with garlic. And besides, there was something a little askew in my approach—I not only yearned to convert people to Jesus's cause, whatever that was, but I also thought a great deal about nails and crosses and crowns of thorn and I had daydreams about Christ coming to claim me just as they were strapping me down on the pyre for an auto da fe. In these fantasies, the image of Jesus often melted into the character of another one of my frequent rescuers, the Handsome Captain, who intervened as I was about to be put to the torture, or encased in the Iron Maiden, or raped by the entire, unshaven, unattractive company of his own men. I was not entirely clear on what "rape" was, but in retrospect I seem to have got the main points pretty close to right.

✦

Some years ago, when Val was visiting me here in New Hampshire, she asked me why I no longer went to church. "You were so keen on it. Don't you miss it?" she said.

Her question was echoed by the one Helen Westheimer asked me a bit later. Helen had been born in Karlsruhe, left it on the *Kindertransport,* and now lives in Andover, quite nearby. She saw my name in the *Kindertransport* newsletter and called me, astonished that a fellow Karlsruhe refugee might be living in such an unlikely spot as New Hampshire. We met for lunch in Manchester—an uncomfortable lunch during which we both contemplated the deep chasms between our surface similarities. Her mother had known and admired my mother; she herself had been in the class below mine at the Jewish School.

"You don't observe anything Jewish any more at all," she said. "Doesn't that bother you?"

I had no answer for that question to deflect its implicit disapproval. I give presents at Christmas. I cook turkey at Thanksgiving. I

set off fireworks on the Fourth of July. I go through the normal ges-
tures expected by society, partly to assert that I belong to it, partly because in fact I recognize that I do belong to it, and largely because
these rituals of solstice celebration and national triumph, happily per-
fected over centuries, embrace everyone with mindless enthusiasm and
require no enrollment or registration; they come, as it were, with the
territory. Religion is quite another matter: you have to choose. My
love affair with Jesus is long in the past, and while the Passover seder
still touches me, I also feel that there is something a bit paradoxical in
that inflexible litany of rather ambiguous triumph.

And then, I have had trouble with God for a long time now, the
word, I mean, the deconstruction of a concept that suggests something entirely different to every person who uses it.

Twenty years ago or so I saw a short film about the solar system.
It began with a description of the planet Mercury and headed outward
into the void. By the time we got to Saturn, I was beginning to feel
giddy. By Uranus I had entirely lost my sense of reality. And when the
narrator came to the dead, dense chill that is Pluto I felt something
very close to terror. My mind could simply not accommodate what it
was he was talking about—the words and the numbers were clear
enough, but the concept of what they implied was unthinkable.

If my intellect cannot even entertain the more remote reaches of
our nine-planet solar system, how can it be expected to stretch to the
galaxy—to the universe, eternity, ubiquity, infinity? To the infinitesi-
mal worlds within the atom and the immeasurable vastness of the ex-
ploding cosmos? There are no terms one can use even to approach
such unimaginable territory; we can consider it only mathematically
because any other language for its consideration is not within the limits of our intelligence.

I suppose there is no real harm in giving a name to the huge
paradoxes our minds are too small to reach for; we may as well call
them God as anything else. But it seems to me that it would be highly
self-deluding to suppose that baptizing the void in our own heads had

magically endowed the ineffable and unthinkable with any meaning we are capable of understanding.

✵

Trumpets, please. A small fanfare to decorate that grand agnostic declaration.

But can that same ineffable and unthinkable whatsis that I have just set so majestically beyond my reach in the preceding paragraphs be the same whatsis with whom I catch myself trying to bargain when I'm not paying careful attention? God, let the day go well and I will contribute an extra $100 to a cause of your choosing. God, don't let the engine stall and I will be good and call poor lonely Elmira as soon as I get home and endure a half-hour of her narcissistic ravings. God, let me not be sick. God, let me not be pregnant. God, don't let Dubya win the election.

A year or so ago, I heard a reporter interviewing a woman wrestler who had just won a gold medal in the Gay Olympics. She was proudly African-American, almost forty years old, and she claimed to weigh a good three hundred pounds. The woman she had defeated was also African-American, also nearly forty, also in the same weight class. "God be praised," the winner proclaimed to her radio interviewer; she was still a bit breathless from her victory. "The Lord found me worthy today and blessed me. He did not despise me for being a fat, black, old lesbian." Apparently, however, he despised her rival for being a fat black old lesbian, or why had she lost? Naturally, in my superior mode of noncontention, I thought this was very funny. But I make exactly the same sort of inferences myself when I'm under pressure and so does everyone who has ever played for a baseball team or a football team or anyone who has ever rooted for one.

On occasion—and with excellent results—I have been known to bribe Saint Anthony into finding things for me. When I was six, in the months after my father died and Stasie, our Catholic housekeeper, was taking care of me, I went to low mass with her every Sunday. Some

Sundays she would put a pfennig or two in the church's poor box as we were leaving: for Saint Anthony, she told me, because last week he had found the scarf she'd lost—or the comb, or the eggbeater, or her sister's shawl. I have followed her example ever since, though not being within easy reach of a poor box I think I must now owe the Church at least twenty thousand dollars—not counting interest. I have been thinking that I am pretty much honor bound, in fact, to mention Catholic Charities generously in my will, to the astonishment, no doubt, of anyone who thinks they know me.

I pray, quite often and quite deeply. I converse intently and at length with my Creator—with the same God I dismiss as being the creation of my own abject neediness. I tell him what I think he should do, though I despair of his willingness to take my advice.

I suppose I should be embarrassed by this discrepancy between serious thought and mere superstition, but in fact I hold it in high esteem. There seems to be an innate compulsion, hard-wired into the human psyche and certainly into mine, to be familiar with celestial beings on a daily basis, and it seems wise to give in to it. I take my communications with the whatsis in my own head very seriously, not only as revelatory of my deepest needs, but also as a poignant attempt to reach beyond the wall of my human limitations. Despite their abjectness, my prayers and curses have a transcendent aspect to them. But the thing to be avoided at all costs is to mistake these chats with God as having any connection to the divine truth.

✡

I could have suggested to Helen Westheimer that perhaps there were more ways of being an observant Jew than she might be aware of, but I didn't say anything, of course.

I did answer Valerie's question, though, whether I missed my old keen enthusiasm for going to church. I told her, yes, I did miss it, very much.

1. Mutti

2. Pappi

3. In the Black Forest (me in 1937)

4. My favorite dress

5. Ruth at thirteen

6. Aunt Helen

7. Uncle Bourke

8. Aunt Liesel, seaside near Swansea

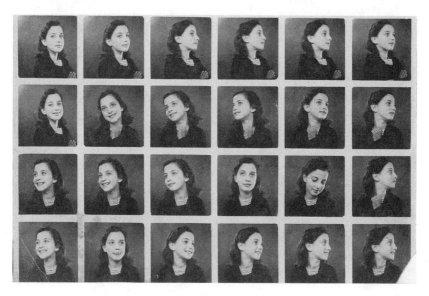

9. Multiple me (1941)

10. Me on the farm (1942)

11. Twenty-three the Towers

12. Picnic (unknown gent with Val, Ruth, and Uncle Bourke)

13. Val (ca. 1946)

14. Aunt Helen, Aunt Margaret, Uncle Bourke, and Aunt Violet

DRIED EGGS AND PUBERTY

⟋⟍ The war had been going on too long. Or perhaps it was just that I was beginning to suffer from an onset of adolescence; a sort of boredom had taken me over, a sense that the days were not light enough, the air not warm enough, the news not exciting enough. My sister navigated her way home at night with her blackout torch, creeping in by the back door long after the rest of us were in bed. She would sing to herself, sotto voce, and dance softly round our bedroom, reliving her evening with Laurence and Tibby and the men on the Leeds University fencing team. I hid my head under the pillow, trying to go back to sleep, or threw it at her when I couldn't. I wished I were as grown up as she was so that I could do something worthwhile at last. In winter, when it was dark long before teatime and when a dirty drizzle fell upon Leeds almost constantly, I thought that I might be doomed to this gray, damp, nowhere world forever. Ruth was dancing and fencing and rowing, and possibly kissing Laurence. Valerie and Diana were away winning lacrosse games and jumping horses over varied colorful obstacles—and perhaps even meeting boys and other strangers in a place where the sun shone (I assumed) and the sky was blue. But I was here. Nothing would ever happen to me.

In the late autumn and winter of those last years of the war the world seemed to be always dark. And perhaps, quite literally, it was; at night the blackout wrapped itself around us. During the day the windows of our classrooms were covered with yellow mesh so that if a bomb blew them out we would not be cut by flying glass. We carried our gasmasks everywhere in square little cartons like lunch boxes always by our side, and one Saturday morning when I was in City Square on my own there was a gas drill. The sirens sounded their special alert to tell us that it was a gas raid. Everyone slammed on their gasmasks, and the whole square, an alien landscape to begin with, with its walls of sandbags piled damply around the dirty gray statue of the Black Prince, began to resemble some place in another galaxy: the habitat of monsters with rubber snouts, snorting heavily and walking slow motion away from the clouds of gas that blossomed at our center. From above, if there had been in fact a plane that had in fact dropped a gas bomb, we would have looked like an exfoliating flower, blowing away.

I could hear my own difficult breath; it was far noisier than anything outside the mask. But I was getting no air. It was appallingly hot inside my rubber prison and impossible to see much through its small, scratched, steamed-up visor. Apparently I was not alone in my discomfort: one by one people had started taking their masks off, chancing death by poison rather than suffocation.

But it was, after all, just a little teargas; and in time, in a few hours, it had quite evaporated. It was only a drill. Nothing serious; nothing to worry about.

The rocket bombs, on the other hand, were something to worry about. The V-1's didn't reach as far north as Leeds, but the V-2's did, and by the summer of 1944 they were on their way. V-2's were ballistic missiles, the first ballistic missiles, and since you couldn't hear them coming there was not much you could do about them. They hit you and killed you before you knew it, and though their effect on morale was depressing it was also somewhat abstract.

The V-1's, however, made a loud racket, a noise rather like a moving hydraulic drill. You could hear them coming closer and the noise growing louder, and as you stopped doing whatever you were doing you would wonder when it would stop. If it grew very loud and then stopped, it meant the V-1 was overhead and was about to land and explode—but it might come down either at a straight 90 degrees or float down at a gentle slant to detonate miles from where you were. It was pretty even odds.

In the autumn of 1944 I must have been away from Leeds somewhere in the south, somewhere within rocket range, because I once heard one of the monsters' raucous approach and then, suddenly, silence. I remember waiting, terrified, for what seemed like a very long time, for an explosion that never came.

Meat had been rationed since the beginning; so had butter and petrol and coal. In the course of time eggs and milk and sugar were rationed. Clothes were rationed. Shoes were rationed. And by the end you needed coupons for just about everything except mackerel and vegetables. Greengrocers hadn't seen an orange or a banana since 1940, and when a shipment of fish arrived at the fishmonger's, housewives from up and down the neighborhood called their friends and rushed to stand in line and buy some before it ran out. Even bread became scarce, and we needed to queue up for it two or three times a week.

And so on Wednesdays, which were school half-holidays, I would often find myself waiting in the bakery queue. It was an amiable experience; the women waiting to be served chatted with each other about the past week's hardships, about ways to make a coal fire last longer, and about their children and brothers and nieces in the armed forces, off fighting in places no one had heard of until yesterday. But their gossip, full as it was of war and shortages, was also oddly comforting, the communication of people with a purpose in life which, far beyond picking up bread, stretched to winning the war; indeed, to saving civilization.

One Wednesday—but that was later, in 1945—I noticed that the woman two or three places in front of me was looking at me intently. Then she whispered something to the woman in front of *her* who turned and looked at me too. What had I done? Did I have a hole in my tunic or a stain, or some secret mark of shame they saw which was invisible to me?

"She does, and all," the second woman said, adjusting her glasses more firmly on her nose.

"Remarkable is what I think," said the first.

My perennial terror of being discovered as an enemy alien and a spy began to reach panic proportions. I contemplated the distance between me and the door and the number of kerchiefed ladies in woolen coats and baggy lisle stockings whom I would have to knock down before I made my way through it.

And it turned out that, indeed, I had been discovered for the outlander I was. *A Song to Remember* had just been released and was being shown at the Odeon: I had seen it myself, though unlike the ladies in the bread queue, I hadn't been struck by my apparently amazing resemblance to the young Chopin. "It's an incredible coincidence, really," the first woman announced, and as the other women began to gather round me and to coo in appreciation of my twinhood with little Frederic, she insisted I should get ahead of her in the queue. I demurred—breaking a queue would certainly mark me as even more foreign than looking like a baby genius from Poland—but she would brook no denial.

By the time I got home with my two loaves of white and one of Hovis, I had pretty much resolved to eschew celebrity as one of my life's goals.

✡

The war ground on. The size of the weekly allotments from ration coupons became less and less while the few things still unrationed were daily harder to come by.

Aunt Helen kept all our ration books in the kitchen, in a tin nicely decorated with green and pink roses and the portraits of the princesses, Elizabeth and Margaret Rose, garlanded in a halo of gold swirls. Sometimes Ruth would take her book so that she could go to a restaurant with friends and have the waitress clip the necessary coupons for a meal out. And I got a coupon or two every Friday so I could buy my week's ration of sweets, an essential part of any English diet even in times of want.

Choosing what sweets to buy was a serious and complex decision: you got quite a lot of bulls-eyes or licorice allsorts or jelly babies per coupon and you got very little chocolate. But then of course a two-ounce Cadbury's fruit and nuts bar was a lot more satisfying than a pound of bulls-eyes or licorice allsorts or jelly babies could ever hope to be. Buying sweets, in fact, was an excellent lesson in basic economics, and our lengthy deliberation as to exactly what to buy must have driven the poor lady in the sweet shop out of her mind. Usually, as soon as school was out, I went there either with Smigs or Pauline Mole, who would then come back for tea with me at Twenty-Three the Towers. Most often we compromised on sourballs; and before we went in for tea, we would sit on the steps leading up to the front door and we would arrange the sourballs neatly in front of us by color. Then we would lick each candy in turn before putting it back again in its paper bag. We would repeat this procedure two or three times a day until, towards the end of the week, the remains of the sourballs had become pretty disgusting. At which point we ate them.

✫

There was still tea—though coffee, which no one at the Harveys ever drank anyway, was scarce. There was mutton. There were beets and cabbage and cauliflower and mangel wurzels and vegetable marrows—quaintly known across the Atlantic as rutabagas and zucchinis. There was margarine. There were dried eggs.

There were, in fact, a lot of dried eggs. Drying eggs is a criminal activity from any esthetic viewpoint. Undoubtedly they provide all sorts of health benefits and supply the body with necessary protein and heaven knows what else. But they do not smell like eggs, nor taste like eggs, nor look like eggs. Dry, they are a hellish yellow not much improved by adding water; and unless you sneak them into things like sauces or puddings, their texture, which is somewhere between old glue and young cement, is nothing you would obviously think of putting in your mouth.

But we were at a point where shortages had become dire enough to put dried eggs to the forefront of nutrition as a dietary staple. The only way to cook them on their own was to scramble them. And they therefore appeared, scrambled, not only at breakfast and lunch, but at tea, between slices of bread, pretending to be a sandwich.

It was with dried egg sandwiches, wrapped in waxed paper and stowed in a brown paper bag, that Aunt Helen sent Ruth and me off one Saturday afternoon to see *This Is the Army* at the Odeon. And it was dried eggs that I threw up at the movie's climactic chorus of the title song. I think this set me up rather badly for America, where it was now established I was to go to rejoin my mother after the war. It disposed me badly towards America and Americans in general: somehow dried eggs had got into the whole idea that the Yanks were coming— that the Yanks, in fact, were already quite palpably here—and lent a somewhat jaundiced tinge to American military savoir fair and joie de vivre.

A Yank had come to West Leeds High School one afternoon, and we had all marched into the auditorium, two by two and class by class, to sit on the floor as we listened to his description of the New World. He was a nice American. He told us about soda fountains and drug stores, about the coeducational system of public education, about dating, about the A&P and Sears, Roebuck and driving on the other side of the road. I don't know what he saw, looking down from above from his platform onto a scene of many little girls of assorted sizes, all wearing pleated navy blue gym tunics and all staring up at him. But I know that what we saw was a man who, despite his officer's uniform and display of medals, was entirely innocent of war. He didn't seem to realize there was one going on.

✡

I was not in good shape. Val and Di seemed to flourish amid food shortages and lack of heat. I felt that Queen Margaret's had changed them and raised them to a higher level of existence than the one to which I was doomed. They had both cut off the long blond braids I so admired, but the arrangement of their hair was now still more to be envied: Di's hung in long waves not quite to her shoulders, while Val's was done in a short, obedient pageboy that bounced as she walked. I could see, when they came home on holidays and weekends, that they thrived, pink-cheeked and bright-eyed, despite their tales of ghastly food and boring schoolwork.

I, on the other hand, was wilting, a constant victim to any flu or cold or random germ that happened to be available. Probably dried eggs disagree with the onset of puberty. I was almost never free of a sty, and often—on days when I had one or two on each eyelid—though I could still read, I couldn't open my eyes enough to walk to school. I had to stay home for other reasons too: mainly for chilblains, a mild form of frostbite, which I would get on the toes of both feet and the heels as well. My feet became so swollen I couldn't put my shoes on and had to hobble around the house in bedroom slippers. "Poor Granny," Uncle Bourke would say indulgently, and Aunt Helen nightly put a hot water bottle in my bed.

I had started to have my period, a sign of adulthood for which I had been eagerly waiting but one which turned out, in actuality, to be quite tedious. Aunt Helen had tried to tell me about the facts of life ahead of time. She had come in delicately one night while I was taking my nightly bath—the three-inch lukewarm variety advertised as favored by King George himself as the perfect compromise between keeping clean and helping the War Effort—and she had sat down gingerly on the edge of the bathtub.

"Now that you're almost thirteen," she had said, "there are some things I should tell you." And she had started, hesitantly, to evoke the birds and the bees.

"We were taught about that at school," I said. Three-inch tepid baths are not conducive to being educated, and I was eager to get dried out and climb into bed. "They had a film about it."

"Thank God," said Aunt Helen, and left.

The film, unfortunately, had presented its message by way of diagrams, which were not entirely explicit or easy for the uneducated eye to interpret. I got the general idea more or less all right, but since the entire process—egg dropping, nest cleaning, fertilizing, and fetus growing—would have struck any sane person as hopelessly repulsive, I had changed a few of the grosser details for myself to make them more acceptable. For instance, I'd heard some of the older girls snickering about someone's sister having bought some "French letters" at Boots—the pharmacy, lending library, and backbone of British Empire. I'd never heard of a French letter, but when I asked Ruth what a French letter was she told me that it was a rubber thing that a man wore during sexual intercourse. "Aha," I thought, hugely relieved. You didn't, after all, have to go through the disgusting ritual involved in conceiving babies in close proximity to a male; you could stay on your side of the door, and he could stay on his side of the door, and you could run this French letter thing between you, like a hose, through the keyhole, while the conceiving process was in progress.

There was a problem also with menstruation; it was considered as pretty much equivalent to any other form of bodily elimination, and you were supposed to be embarrassed by it and enormously discreet. I got the idea, although no one said as much, that for someone to know that you were menstruating would be tantamount to public defecation; if a man found out, your chances of ever being married would be reduced to nil. Ruth, arriving from Germany where attitudes were sturdier, had come fully equipped for puberty. She had brought with her a dozen big fat woolen sanitary pads that could be washed out as need arose. But by 1944 Kotex had come to England. We burned the used ones in the backyard in a tin bucket provided for the purpose. I don't know why we didn't just throw them out, there seemed to be a faintly sinister, magical quality attached to menstrual blood, and it had to be destroyed by fire and in secret. And with difficulty—a used sanitary napkin not really being in any hurry to burn, especially on your usual, damp Yorkshire day.

☆

I was not alone in being overwhelmed by puberty that year. One morning, during school assembly, something struck my shoulder with a soft thud. I swiveled around to see what it was and came face to face with poor Irene, who had been standing behind me. She had gone a nasty shade of yellow as she fainted onto me—and subsequently, when I turned and dislodged her, slid very slowly down to the floor. Her eyes seemed to have risen toward heaven inside her eyelids, and only the whites were showing; she looked ghastly. She looked, in fact, as if she had been dead for some time.

She stopped the show, of course. We all crowded round her to admire her color and artistically morbid effect, all in a heap and with her tunic hiked up above her stockings, until we were sent back to our classes, the final assembly announcements and closing prayer left unsaid. Irene, meanwhile, was carried to the headmistress's office to regain consciousness.

I didn't know anyone else who was driven by menarche to such a public display of delicacy, but then Irene was, in general, an extreme case. All of us were uneasy about our budding sexuality and mortified by its more conspicuous manifestations—breasts, pimples, pubic hair. We hadn't even known we had vaginas until the damn things started leaking! But our nascent shame at the arrival of this sudden, surprising fleshliness was on a different scale from Irene's, whom the smallest whiff of carnality could reduce to a state of bewildered terror. The mere sight of a boy caused her alarm—and the thought that one might actually speak to her was enough to put her to flight.

Her name, pronounced in the usual English way, with three syllables—Eireenee—had a sort of ululating quality that went rather well with her generally terrorized state of mind. She was with us for two weeks of volunteer work during the harvest of 1944: late August or September, it must have been. A lot of the girls in our class had signed up to pick potatoes and apples, to help the War Effort, which was in dire need of us. There was a desperate shortage of farmhands because it seemed that everyone who wasn't in the army or the navy or the R.A.F. was off making munitions. Even prisoners of war were being allowed to leave their camps to help with the crops, and appeals had been sent out to all the secondary schools.

Aunt Helen said it would be a healthy thing for me to do, Uncle Bourke said it would be a help to the county, and I was delighted to escape the damp embrace of Leeds for a while. I had always enjoyed our little victory garden, the square of vegetables and herbs next to the lower lawn. I had done my share of weeding and hoeing between the rows of spinach and gathered beans and peas for supper. On our summer holidays we usually went to a farm near Scarborough, and now I was old enough—and strong enough, finally—to join in when the others raked hay and stooked the corn.

So when all the girls who had signed up for farmwork collected one Saturday morning in the front hall of West Leeds High School, I was there. So were Joy Bannisters and the Bristow twins as well as a dozen or so others I didn't know so well. And Irene. A bus was waiting for us, and it drove us off—westwards and southwards. Somewhere, anywhere, different.

I never knew precisely to what county it was we went. Our lodgings were in a long, cinderblock structure, a section of a Land Army camp, probably, reserved for the temporary help. There were four or five of us to each of the rooms, which were furnished only with straw palliasses, which we stuffed ourselves, and shelves on which to stack our clothes. It wasn't exactly what I had been expecting, but then the fact that it wasn't exactly what I had been expecting was just what I was hoping for. A new experience.

I was sharing a room with the four girls from my class whom I knew best—Joy and Irene and the two Bristows. After a tea of bread and margarine and some awful cake that was served in the bleak cafeteria as soon as we arrived, it seemed time to go for a walk and check the lay of the land. It was rather nice country, wherever it was, with pebbled lanes bordered by thick, wild hedgerows that also framed the misty fields beyond, where sheep were grazing.

"If they come any closer, we can always scream," Irene said.

I was puzzled since I thought she meant the sheep, but Joy and the Bristows had started to giggle.

"If they try to rape us," Irene clarified.

Not, it seemed, the sheep. Possibly the three young men in the distance, far behind us, sauntering back from work along the same road we were on.

"Shouldn't we start running?" Irene asked.

"No," Beryl said. "We shouldn't." And her sister Joyce, who had a wicked streak, added, "It might give them ideas."

So we walked on, followed in a casual way by the three young men. Irene turned to look every few steps, to check up on their dangerous progress. And probably, if they had been paying the slightest attention to us, she might, in fact, have given them ideas.

✳

Irene, in her constant condition of alarm and agitation, may have misdiagnosed the specific dangers of our new environment, but her intuition about its essence was pretty much on the mark. I got something of an education during those two weeks, an illumination, at least, of a couple of areas that had been dark before.

The first was a vivid demonstration of the abuse of masculine power, and my epiphany came on our first working day. We were picking potatoes, which is dirty, difficult, and quite backbreaking labor. We were at it all morning, following the tractor that ran through the mounds of tubers and uprooted them in rows for us to gather into large sacks. Every hour or so we were given a few minutes to straighten up, drink some water, and stretch our backs, until we headed into a new row. After two hours we were already exhausted.

"The girl in red. You, the girl in red," the farmer yelled at regular intervals. He was a big, beefy, florid man, probably in his late fifties or early sixties, and he was not happy. Particularly, he was not happy with me. I was the girl in red, having tied a bright red patterned kerchief round my hair to keep it out of my eyes. It was a cotton kerchief that Ruth had brought from Germany and that she still liked to wear when she was doing fieldwork on our farm holidays. She had lent it to me, and I had put it on, I suppose, for luck, as a sort of talisman.

It was distinctly not working.

The farmer had started, reasonably enough, telling us that we had to rake our way carefully through the loosened dirt to make sure that we picked up every single potato. Then he had added, rather less reasonably, that we were not to talk to each other while we were doing this. He had singled me out, almost from the start, and used me as a potent demonstration of what not to do.

"Girl in red, you're lagging."

"You, girl, you've left half your row behind. Go back and do it over." There was no pleasing him.

"You're wasting time. You're wasting time. We haven't got all week."

"No talking, I told you, no talking, you, the girl in red."

And, finally, "If the girl in red doesn't pay attention to what she's doing, I'll come over and pay attention to her myself." The man did none of the work. He only supervised. Or, more exactly, he only found fault, largely with me; and as the morning wore on, his faultfinding became threatening. We had started soon after seven. By eleven I was quite frightened and near tears.

But by five after eleven I had inadvertently found the solution. I had taken off the red kerchief and put it in my pocket.

Silence. Without my insignia, the scarlet badge by which to identify me, the man hadn't a clue which one of these girls he should be shouting at. I think, with the red kerchief gone, he doled out his anathema rather equally, having plenty of it to share, but I know that not one more wretched word from him was directed at me.

From that day forward I have had a deep appreciation of the power of symbols and even more of the power of avoiding them.

✳

We stayed with the ogreish farmer only two days. It was after we had moved from picking potatoes to picking apples, from scrabbling at the dirt beneath us to reaching for the sky above, that I was enlightened again on another subject about which I had been dismally ignorant.

The apple orchard was a jolly place. There were some local lads around, still in their middle teens and too young for war, and they had the idea that they were under obligation to entertain us, especially to entertain Eileen Halliday, who was in our class but a bit older than most of us. She was tall and buxom and laughed with energetic, bosom-shaking glee. Naturally the boys did their utmost to get her to laugh—and to set her bosom to jiggling. They were only restrained by adolescent shyness and inexperience—and the inconvenience of their all being very nice boys. But there is no getting around the fact that the jokes they told and the songs they sang became more and more ribald as the day progressed and that by quitting time the air was filled with something I had never experienced before but which I now recognize as lechery.

And, astonishing even myself, I found that I knew things I hadn't known I knew. I sang the songs with gusto. I laughed at the jokes with genuine mirth. I inhaled the bawdy atmosphere in happy gulps as if I'd been starved for oxygen—as perhaps I had been. In a few months—between the springtime of my brilliant reinterpretation of French letters and the autumn of my coming here to pick apples—I had ineffably, without any special instruction or added experience, come to some sort of mysterious understanding. I suppose I had simply and naturally ripened through time—and a very short time at that—to a point where what had once seemed disgusting had become enchanting and desirable. And since it was enchanting and desirable I had already thought about it at length for some months and luxuriated, in my imagination, in vague but intense fantasies. They came to me unwilled and without my permission, and they were filled with suggestions I made no attempt to understand. But I could see that the suggestions were the pale shadows of the substance that these boys now rollicked in—that they were muted echoes of their loud, jolly singing.

I suppose it could be said, in fact, that the farm lads' raunchy renditions of "Mademoiselle from Armentiers" and "Roll Me Over" didn't really teach me anything. What they did was to demonstrate for me exactly what it was that I already knew. They revealed the crude details with which, from now on, I could furnish my dreams and gave my hazy yearnings something solid to chew on.

✿

Not that I had ever been altogether innocent of sex: I'd been falling in love for years with every male presence, every whisper of masculinity, which crossed my path. But those passions had been abstract, surrounding me in a sort of formless longing that I inhaled like air but that lacked substance. It was an atmosphere that emanated, obviously, from some deep emotional need, and it was pretty potent. But it was totally divorced from the flesh and devoid of physical particulars.

Until now. Yearning removed itself from my head and clamped itself firmly onto my body.

At ten every morning one of the farm women would bring out a great laundry basket filled with sweet, flat cakes, which she would pour onto a tablecloth laid down on the ground at the entrance to the orchard. Next to it someone had already put some jugs full of water, a keg of cider, and a few tin cups—though after the first day we all learned to bring our own. Whenever we got hungry or thirsty we needed only to help ourselves, and we could embellish the sandwich lunch that we had brought with us from our camp with as many apples as we liked as well as more flat cakes and cider.

The cider, it should be noted, was well on its way to being hard—though being unacquainted with alcohol we didn't know that at the time. After several applications through the morning and a good glass at lunch, we were a happy lot. Even Irene had a slight flush on her pale face, and she could be seen smiling upon the farm youths sprawled on the ground around Eileen Halliday in hope of a better view. Occasionally, one of the younger boys would wander off into the hedgerow on his own; more occasionally, an older boy would wander off to the haystack in the adjoining field, where one of the farm girls would join him. It was probably the same boys with the same girls each time, but in my memory their coupling is random, casual, and swift— and they emerge from it tousled and laughing. Once a couple stumbled out from behind the nearest hedgerow—arms still entwined, heads, red faced, bent toward each other's shoulders—and we all applauded, though I have no idea why.

We went back to Leeds, burned golden in the sun, happier than we had been.

And the war had turned around: the desert was ours, and the Allied Forces that had landed in Normandy in June were beginning to make headway.

WAR AND PEACE

    I think it was early October of 1945, a month or so after VJ Day, when we moved to Princetown. It should be noted, however, that VJ Day, the day which, according to history books, at last finished the war, is inscribed largely in American and Asian memory; for me, as for most Europeans, it was a minor event, a moment almost of anticlimax.

The real victory, for us, had already been won a few months earlier—on May 8, 1945, the day that the German surrender was made official. That was the end of it, as far as we were concerned. The end of bombings and blackouts and gasmasks. The end of anxiety. We could expect butter and oranges any day now and as much chocolate as we could eat—or so, at least, we imagined. On May 8, 1945, the war became somebody else's war: it now belonged to the Americans, who had had it easy until now, so it was really their turn for it. We, however, were finally free to celebrate, to dance in the streets, and to kiss, in public, everyone within reach.

In Leeds, May 8, 1945, was a bright, warm day full of sunshine.

Uncle Bourke and Aunt Helen, in the spirit of the occasion that had been proclaimed a national holiday, declared it was time for the first picnic of spring. We got out the bicycles, and we pedaled down the drive where the horse chestnuts were in bud, across Armley Road, and down the lane where the sheep lived. Beyond the sheep there were only open fields, which stretched into the wooded hills of the countryside. We had brought along sausage rolls and real hard-boiled eggs—prodigal with what would soon, we thought, be plentiful—and jam tarts and a thermos of sweet tea, and we spread it all out on a nest of rocks.

We were high up, on a little bluff overlooking the outskirts of the city, faraway from the crowds and the happy madness down below, but even so the clamor of victory was loud in our ears. During the war, the church bells had been altogether silent—had they rung, it would have been to announce a German invasion. But now they had been set free again and finally, given back their voices, they were all going mad. Every church bell in town, every church bell in England, was ringing victory, declaring its joy in a great cacophony of jubilation.

Diana was away, training to become an occupational therapist, and Valerie was still at Queen Margaret's. But since Leeds University had closed for the day Ruth was with us; so was Robin. He had come back to England to go to Oxford. Naturally, given his penchant for peculiar names, it was to Brasenose College that he had decided to go.

I had fallen in love with him. In his absence, which is by far the most intelligent way to fall in love when you're first starting out, giving you the chance to get in a good bit of practice without having to handle the more awkward aspects of passion caused by the beloved's actually being there. When I had first heard Robin was coming Home from India and that he was going to stay with us I had immediately been swept off into an absolute and abstract fondness. I doubt if I had any real memory still of how he looked or sounded or behaved. I hadn't seen him since he was thirteen, after all, and that was five years ago. But I did recall, in some subliminal pocket of recollection, that he was kind and tolerant of little girls and that a lock of dark brown hair fell perpetually out of its place and swung down towards his dark brown eyes. That was enough.

So I was already in love with him by the time he actually appeared and, appearing, seared my entirely theoretical affection deeply and truly into my soul. It stayed there for years. It stayed there, I suppose, more or less for a lifetime, as these things do, as a sort of blueprint, fading through time, against which to measure all later loves. It was, inadvertently, a brilliant choice, because as it turned out Robin was an extraordinarily decent human being, appealingly adventurous, and far more easily affectionate than most boys are at eighteen. I don't suppose he had the slightest idea that I had a crush on him, or, if he did, that he would have looked at it with anything but faintly amused tolerance. I was quite the wrong age to be noticed by him—let alone to have my feelings taken into account.

Still, when I came to America, Robin wrote to me now and then. He was teaching in Ghana by then—it was still called the Gold Coast in those days—and he sent me a snapshot of himself in his exotic new environment. The photograph shows a small, bright Englishman in shorts standing between two huge Africans who are shading him with palm leaves. They are satirizing the Rule of Empire and their own places within it. I know it is satire because the palm leaves are held in such an exaggerated pantomime of taking care of the master and also because all three of them are grinning from ear to ear.

And since it was the only picture of Robin I had, and since, when I got it, I still thought of him often and with great fondness, I put the photograph in my wallet where it stayed for several years, nestled among a growing collection of other snapshots: of the Harveys, of my mother, my sister Ruth, my husband, our children. Then one afternoon in Baltimore a man snatched my purse off my arm as I was walking home with a bag of groceries. The man who snatched it was certainly in far greater terror than I was, but in such desperate need of money—for drugs, I suppose, or drink—that he seemed to have no choice in the matter. I have always wondered what he thought, if he thought anything, a black man rifling through my white lady's collection of keys and checkbook and comb and lipstick and photographs, when he came across the one of Robin flanked by his two African giants, all of them grinning hilariously as though the world promised nothing but good.

I heard that after years of teaching in England, after a reasonable marriage and two or three reasonable children, Robin turned his back on convention, that his wife divorced him, and that he returned to Ghana. By now, I suppose he's retired. I imagine him as headmaster emeritus of his African school, traveling between London and Accra, stopping at Woolworths now and then to get his bearings. That seems the perfect destination for the boy of my fantasies and just where he belongs.

But before all that I saw him again; when he was still being properly English and still married, at least a quarter of a century ago it must be now. Uncle Bourke had recently died and my husband, our children, and I were visiting Aunt Helen in her little house in Felsted. It happened that this was right next to the Public School where Robin taught. We all had lunch together. And it struck me that quite possibly my crush on him might be the exact reflection of his crush on my sister Ruth. Something about the way he talked about her. Something about the way he remembered the week when the Leeds transportation union called a strike and he and Ruth joined up as volunteers and ran the no. 16 Wingate tram from the center of town to its terminus at Armley Road at the end of our avenue of horse chestnuts. Robin drove the tram; Ruth was the conductor and sold tickets. He spoke of that week as if running the tram were a magic enterprise. And of course it was in fact an enchanted time—with the war in Europe just ended and the tedium of peace not yet quite settled in.

I think it was a matter merely of weeks before we all recovered from the first dizzy moment of euphoria when we basked in that instant of triumph; a matter merely of weeks when it began to occur to people that their personal rights had been neglected for a very long time and that they would no longer be counted traitors for making a few, simple demands—that it may have become permissible, in fact, to go on strike. It will take no more than a couple of months, after that 8th of May in 1945 when our war has finally ended, to prepare for all the quarrels of a world at peace. But the victory bells' loud assertion of triumph and relief echoing up from the town are still innocent of such concerns, and at our tranquil distance, the five of us and the two dogs, dozing after our picnic in the hills above Armley, believe unequivocally in their ecstatic promise.

✧

Princetown is on Dartmoor—the Devonshire moors named for the river that runs through them—which in turn gives its name to Dartmoor Prison.

The little town came into being in service to the prison, which was built during the Napoleonic Wars in 1802 but not much used until ten years later—during the War of 1812, when the unfortunate Americans incarcerated there staged a bloody rebellion in protest against their terrible ill treatment. The prison structure does not suggest such horrors. It is a tidy, stone, Georgian building with tidy, stone, Georgian mansions at either side of it for the prison's governor and his deputy, and tidy, stone, Georgian cottages spread below it for the rest of the staff. I assume that it was built where it was built because that was close enough to the major port of Plymouth to have made it possible to transport prisoners by ship and because it was also high enough up in the middle of the moorland to have made the prisoners' escape close to impossible.

Escaping is still close to impossible. The Devonshire moors are pathless and as lacking in landmarks as a desert. The heather scrub and broom, which are the moors' major vegetation, make walking difficult and exhausting. Then too, there are bogs studded through the whole area, which, like quicksand, trap you and pull you in if you set foot on them—and which you can't see because they are hidden under broom and heather scrub.

Nestled in this little Siberia, Princetown can look quite charming. But from its beginning the prison has been notorious and for more than a century its notoriety has been nurtured in fiction and in reportage: the bleakness of its location and the reputed viciousness of its inmates has made it an enduring icon of desolation and a symbol of stern, punitive justice.

But when we arrived in the late fall of 1945 it had become the gentlest of penitentiaries having just been turned into a first offenders' prison for nonviolent crimes and a Borstal—an institution long established in Great Britain for boys who are considered too old for reform school and too young for jail. Since Uncle Bourke had earned a reputation as a kindly and progressive sort of governor, he was called in to look after the place in its new, rehabilitative mode.

By then Ruth had left the University, but she stayed on in Leeds where she had a job with a research laboratory. And since Di was in training and Val in school, I was by myself in Princetown, alone with Aunt Helen and Uncle Bourke.

✼

The last time I saw it, in 1975, the prison, back in the business of locking up convicts, had grown huge and had overwhelmed the town, turning it into a sprawling complex of barracks and tenements to house its growing population of felons and the men to guard them. But in the late autumn of 1945 both prison and town were small and still quite beautiful, plain and strangely elegant in the pure simplicity of their native stone buildings. They were of another time: a hundred years away from Leeds, a century away from the war we had all just finished fighting. The streets—the cobbled road to the prison and the small alleys between the officers' cottages—were lit by gas; two of the Borstal boys came round to light each of the gas jets at sunset every evening, and as the dark came on the town began to shine. Our house was lit by gas as well, and so was the prison itself; as the evening fell and the boys lit the street lamps, everyone in town followed their joyful lead—for now, of course, there was no more blackout—and the whole of Princetown shimmered. It was as if we had all gone back in time, to some golden age before there was electricity, or bombs, or gasmasks, or rationing.

At least that is how I remember it. In my memory, even the Borstal boys and the first offenders are happy. The Borstal boys wore brown uniforms, and the first offenders wore green ones, and they did most of the work of the town. They collected garbage and fixed the roads. They ran the prison farm and milked the prison cows; and then they drove whatever the farm yielded to the Tavistock market. They delivered the prison cows' milk to our house twice a week, rich, wonderful milk that arrived in a big canister straight from the milking. Aunt Helen would pour it into the largest cauldron we owned, a five-gallon monster big enough to cook soup for an army, and we would allow it to settle for the whole day on the cold stone floor of the pantry. The next day, after the cream had risen to the top Aunt Helen would put the cauldron very carefully onto the old gas stove in the stone kitchen. It stayed there all day on a flame so low you could hardly see it. By night, the milk was pasteurized, while the cream had wrinkled and buckled and turned a soft, pale ochre. It had, in short, become Devonshire cream.

We went to church every Sunday. In Leeds we had always gone to matins; but now that the war was over, now that the blackout was over, we could safely attend vespers instead, walking through the softly gas-lit streets to the old stone church, whose vicar also served as the prison chaplain. Fifteen or twenty of the most favored of the prisoners were allowed to join us for the service. The first few rows of pews had been reserved for them, and they would arrive just before the processional—the last to come—and leave just before the recessional—

the first to go. Two prison guards, who did their best to look wor-
shipful during the service while keeping a weather eye out for their
charges, walked with them—one in front and one behind.

They pretended to be a solemn lot, trying to keep their eyes to
the ground. But even during the service they would cast quick, subversive glances at the congregation on either side; and on their way in
and out they stared at the passing scene pretty boldly. Handsome fel-
lows they were, dressed in their brown and green like Merry Men, and
now and then, when I caught the eye of one of them and he grinned
at me, my heart would skip a beat.

I had found a new purpose in life: it seemed to me that if only
these boys would escape in my direction I could give them all the
money I had, and my bank book too, and I could steal clothes for
them from Uncle Bourke's dresser; then they could escape and go
home to their mothers in Ireland or Wales and love me from afar forever.

✴

Prisoners did occasionally manage to run away. Two I remember were
friends of the boy who usually came round with our milk. The boy
with the milk had a wide grin and crooked teeth—most of the prisoners had crooked teeth—and a head of curly brown hair with more
than a touch of red to it.

"Marnin', Missy," he would say, carefully putting the canister
down on the stone floor of the pantry. "This where you want it today?"

He always put it down in the same corner, out of the way, but
he asked the same question every time, taking nothing for granted.
Though the conversational range was minimal, there was such bright-
ness in his face, such a combination of good cheer and quick wit, it
made one like him. The chaplain's favorite, Uncle Bourke said, and
most of the guards' as well. He was always among those who came to

church, and he sang the hymns with tremendous gusto; you could tell, even from five rows back, that he was having a good time.

Of course, he was the one I most hoped would escape in my direction. But in fact it was his two friends who got away instead. One morning, just after Uncle Bourke had left for his office, the prison siren went off—a sinister sound that we hadn't heard since VE Day. And there were barricades on the road out of Princetown when Aunt Helen and I drove to get groceries in Tavistock in the little Austin 6— back to its prewar glory, recommissioned and with its wheels back on. The guards on either side of the barricade looked us over critically and then recognizing Aunt Helen, tipped their hats.

"Sorry, mum," the guard on Aunt Helen's side told her as he waved us through. "One of them's got out."

But he didn't get far; he was back by midnight. He'd got lost on the moor, fallen into a bog, and almost drowned before he made his way back to the road, where a prison officer on his way home from the pub had seen him and picked him up. He offered no resistance. He seemed, by and large, grateful to be back in civilization—even if he was on the wrong end of it.

The other escape followed in less than a week. After a few days it was decided that this one had probably made it safely out of town and the barricades were lifted again while the search was expanded, rather casually, to Plymouth, London, and Southampton. In a few more days the escaped prisoner would have been safe—free for the rest of his life because by then the powers that be would have grown tired of looking for him. But a Tavistock constable, passing by the milk truck during its rounds one morning, heard stentorian snoring coming from the back. A brief inspection revealed the unfortunate escapee asleep behind the canisters. Apparently the boy who delivered the milk had started a budding taxi service for those wishing to break away from prison—a rather expensive taxi service. When Uncle Bourke questioned him, he admitted, quite cheerfully, that he was hoping to run a regular route for the runaways, hiding them in the truck until the road was clear. He had even supplied a bottomless canister for his clients to hide in in an emergency. For this enterprise he was charging enough so that, with luck, he had hoped to make a down payment for a business by the time he got out himself in a couple of years—a shop or a restaurant maybe. He seemed to see nothing whatever wrong with his plan, except, of course, having been found out.

I never saw him again—his days of delivering milk were over, and he was no longer let out on Sundays to sing hymns lustily in church.

✫

In the few months after the war ended, the world had changed beyond recognition. It had become, in an instant, enormously more complex. The war had made things coherent; it established a single goal—winning—and a single moral design that made it clear to everyone that what was good was Us and that what was bad was Them. With victory, all such simplicity vanished.

It was certainly not that they, the enemy, appeared any more ambiguous. On the contrary, it seemed that they had been even worse than we could have imagined. More crimes and atrocities, newly discovered to have been committed by them, were daily enumerated in the newspapers and actual pictures of horrors, undreamable in the worst of our nightmares, proved that what would at one time have been unthinkable to us had actually happened. It had, we began to discover—reluctantly, hardly believing what we read—happened to people Ruth and I had known, to our neighbors, to our relatives. They had been victims of an outrage—an outrage exponentially worse than any we could have invented as an accusation against our foes, who had done in fact, in daylight, unashamed, these things that were even beyond fantasy.

And that was where the trouble lay. During the war, evil had been inflated beyond our comprehension; and now peace was conflating the distance between that evil and ourselves. The end of the war had allowed two processes moving counter to each other to come together. The sense of the horror that had been committed was escalating; the distance between those who had committed that horror and ourselves was dwindling. Without their helmets, their swastikas, and their weapons, they turned out to be merely human after all. Détente required us to understand that our enemies were probably pretty much like us—and if that were true, we were forced to redefine humanity.

I am speaking generally here, of course, not about myself. I was barely fourteen and struggling with sties, chilblains, and pimples rather than with some ultimate moral vision. But I suppose one's basic way of thinking is probably formed in those early years of adolescence, and while my thoughts might not have had the wisdom or judgment of Albert Camus' thoughts, the world I was looking out upon was pretty much the same as his.

War, we all know, is hell, but from a philosophical viewpoint, and for the general population not immediately involved in killing or being killed, the state of being at war can be remarkably comforting. It certainly makes the world a neater place. In the absence of armed conflict, boundaries tend to become porous. And the nastiness one thought safely contained on the other side leaks inexorably through to your own. It corrupts everything. It becomes a universal condition.

✻

During the war, the papers had reported news that was clean and purposeful: victories, defeats, advances, retreats. The statistics were crisp and packaged in large, coherent round numbers: the thousands wounded, the hundreds killed, the square miles of landscape turned to rubble. Meanwhile, the unfortunate details of unpleasant human behavior, the things that happened at home by ones and twos and threes, were either omitted or left for the back pages.

But once the peace set in it was exactly these minutiae of beastliness that made up the headlines. The petty atrocities of daily life were everywhere.

They stared at me from the front page every day. A farmer was on trial, in Manchester, I think, or maybe Coventry—somewhere in the Midlands—for the murder of his foster children, two young boys whom he had exploited, tortured, and abused. Who knows why: possibly for pleasure, very likely because he had been raised to see exploitation, torture, and abuse as constituting a proper upbringing. He and his wife had taken in the boys when they were little—five and six—and now they were both dead. One had been beaten and burned and finally bound and gagged and locked inside a small cupboard where he had either suffocated or starved to death. The other, younger boy had been punished by being lowered into the well, where he drowned.

The trial lasted for weeks. I forget what the defense was or whether the farmer's wife was still alive—and if she was, what part she played in this catastrophe. I only remember that during the last months of the war I had picked up the afternoon paper at the back door to read how Monty was getting on in the desert or how Ike was progressing through France and now, with the same eagerness with which I had looked for public triumph, I scanned the afternoon headlines for yet another sickening revelation of private shame.

Uncle Bourke observed my growing obsession with this nastiness. If he happened to pick up the paper before I did he would carefully look through it for news of the trial and hand that section over to me. "What do you think, Granny?" he asked on the day the jury delivered its verdict. We were both in the kitchen, reading the different pages from our shared paper. "How would you deal with someone who does something like that?"

I said I didn't know. I said that nothing I could think of would be adequate.

"Not even hanging? Or a whole life in solitary confinement—no sun, no work, no company?"

"Nothing," I said.

"And I suppose you wouldn't consider the possibility that being a brute who kills children is pretty much punishment enough."

"What do you mean?" I said.

But I knew what he meant. It would be a terrible thing—a terrifying thing—to be one of the poor, tortured boys; but I could see that to be trapped inside the hideous spirit of their torturer—stripped of humanity, impelled by the disgusting essence of what one was to debased and sickening actions—would be a great deal worse. To be a monster, to forego one's soul, in effect, was in some ineffable way even more horrendous than to suffer at the monster's hand.

Given the choice in some celestial, prenatal waiting room between a brief and wretched existence as an abused child or a long life as the child's depraved abuser, we'd most of us choose, reluctantly, to be born the victim after all. Better to be Ludi Kohn, my father's assistant, than to be the SS guards who killed him.

Uncle Bourke, smoking his pipe, was looking at me quizzically as for the first time in my life, though certainly not for the last, I understood what astonishing luck it is for anyone to have escaped the need to make any such choice. To be neither predator nor prey—to be safe, one of the impartial, unofficial, unimpaneled jury, merely looking on—is, indeed, to have been blessed.

"Aren't we all lucky!" said Uncle Bourke, as if he'd read my mind. "Good old Granny." And he went back to reading his part of the paper.

✵

Even during the winter we went for walks every day on the moor. It often snowed, and the brown heath and gray stone would be outlined by a rim of white. The two little terriers, Lassie and Vixen, grown old and rather stiff, were no longer a threat to ovines or bovines—these days they had difficulty even seeing a rabbit let alone chasing one. On the moor, set free from their leashes, they would run about in genteel, arthritic circles.

Our destination was always one of the tors—those outcroppings of granite set on top of Devonshire's ancient hills. They seemed like the bones of the earth, formed in fire and ice, exposed by eons of shifting tectonic plates and by frost, erosion, and flood. Poised a little above the rolling level of the moorland these tors dot Dartmoor like natural temples: around them you will often find the stone circles left by prehistoric tribes, and dolmens, the remains of Druid worship, mark the enduring reverence of man.

It was after we came back from walking the dogs across the snow-flecked heath one late, cold morning that Robin told me why "Tintern Abbey" was his favorite poem. He had come down to Princetown for a long winter weekend, and we were huddled, trying to get warm by the fire he had just lit in the second-best sitting room, which we now refrained from calling the nursery but used just the same as if we still did.

I had read "Tintern Abbey"; it was, however, not my favorite poem.

"'... The sounding cataract,'" Robin read, having found a complete Wordsworth on one of the shelves, "'... haunted me like a passion ... / The mountain, and the deep and gloomy wood, / Their colours and their forms, were then to me / An appetite. ...'"

It sounded considerably more convincing coming from Robin than it had on the stumbling tongue of poor Brenda Thistlethwaite trying to make her way through "hedge-rows, hardly hedge-rows, little lines / Of sportive wood run wild."

I read the rest with him, silently over his shoulder: "That time is past, / And all its aching joys are now no more, / And all its dizzy raptures. ..."

✫

The farmer, I would like to remember, I would like at least to hope, received a life sentence in an institution for the criminally insane.

And Robin, before he went back to Brasenose, told me that I was clever. I was standing by the cold radiator in our Wordsworth-reading room, and the fire in the fireplace was almost out. By then I had read "Tintern Abbey" three times.

> *. . . I have learned*
> *To look on nature, not as in the hour*
> *Of thoughtless youth; but hearing oftentimes*
> *The still, sad music of humanity.*

"You know, you're amazingly bright," Robin said. And with his hands on the radiator to either side of me, he rubbed his nose against mine as though we were Eskimos, kissing.

SAINT BRIDE'S

⌒ Since its only significant population of high school age was in prison, Princetown had no need for a secondary school. I am not sure what the occasional officer's child in search of an education could do: take a bus to Tavistock, I suppose, or live with relatives in Plymouth.

I was expecting to take School Certificate in a year or so. I was also expecting passage to America within a few months. No one, given this dilemma, could decide what should be done with me, and from the time we came to Princetown until after the Christmas holidays I simply stayed home with Aunt Helen and Uncle Bourke.

For the first time in my life I had my own room. It was a tiny room at the far end of the bathroom corridor, but it had two major assets: it was utterly private and it was the only room in the house from which you could look down into the prison yard and watch the young men in brown and green do their morning calisthenics every day. An advantage of which I made full use. To remind myself of higher things I had hung the famous profile portrait of Byron over my bed and next to him another, smaller picture of Shelley looking soulfully into the middle distance. On the dresser, to balance these inspiring decorations, I had put the china doggy that I'd won at penny toss at last year's Armley Fair. It was definitely a doggy and not merely a dog; it had a pink and green china bow and a look of extreme yearning—rather like Shelley's—in its big china-brown eyes.

The expression in the eyes of the china doggy is emblematic of my memory of Devonshire during that winter. That time and place come back to me wreathed in an aura of something painfully desired and painfully out of reach, the very paradox, I suppose, which is the essence of romance. Attached to the recollection there seems to be a faint scent—like violets, perhaps, or perhaps jasmine or honeysuckle—so transient and fragile that the wind has blown it away before you can say, "there it is. That's what I meant."

✳

Most probably, however, the scent of flowers that nudges at my memory of Dartmoor does not rise out of the stark, flowerless beauty of Princetown, but from Saint Bride's, where flowers filled the garden and the wood beyond it. Masses of them grew wild from the walls of the school all the way down to the river. I should admit that I cannot remember Saint Bride's exactly—I was only there a few months from January to mid-April of 1946—and the names I vaguely recall here, the details of architecture and chronology, should be taken more as fiction than as fact. Nothing I can retrieve now is exact except an atmosphere of ubiquitous, mellow beauty and of regret, a sense of sorrow close to grief that had no conscious cause. Perhaps it was just adolescence, a time of such sudden and radical change that you tend to mourn your childhood as you feel it slipping away. Perhaps it was the shadow of leaving England. Or perhaps it was that the ancient stones and timbers of Saint Bride's in that timeless landscape brought the past so vividly to life that it constantly brushed against one's present, making so palpable a time that was no more that the view onto the here and now was smudged by a history of things long gone.

I do remember the garden. There were no violets while I was there or jasmine or honeysuckle. The earliest flowers were primroses; then came daffodils, which transformed the spring grass into a field of green-flecked yellow. By late March, the spectrum changed; yellow began to fade and the lawn became green again. But in the wood across the little bridge the ground under the trees had turned into a carpet of bluebells. We would gather armfuls of them during walks and bring them back to the school for Cook or Matron to put into jugs and vases. First daffodils filled the halls and the dining room, and then bluebells, and I always had a glass of flowers on my own little dressing table next to my bed.

It had been decided that I was to go to Saint Bride's after Christmas while I waited for my passage to America to come through. Saint Bride's had originally been a London school, but during the Blitz it had moved to Chagford, away from the bombs. Like many such institutions it was run by two women: Miss Thompson was the headmistress and taught the older girls; "Auntie" Vera was in charge of the younger children. I think the school had bloomed happily in its West End setting, but in Devonshire it dwindled. It dwindled even further once the war was over and its exile into the West Country no longer had a purpose. By the time I arrived it had become an oddity. Most of its students were children whose families, for one reason or another, deemed them undesirable—or children who were, at least, undesired. Most of us were damaged in some way, victims of chronic ailments, offspring of broken marriages or of dysfunctional homes.

I felt, even at the time, that being nothing more exotic than a refugee—an easy enough state to explain even in polite society—made me, in that ambience, enviable, fortunate, even perhaps blessed. I was there for simple and practical reasons: because the school could take me on midyear; because it was close to Princetown; because I was about to leave, within a few weeks or a few months, for America.

I only realized long afterwards that the Harveys, who were not at all rich, had paid for my tuition and board out of their own pocket without even mentioning this fact to my mother, who could certainly not have afforded to offer any help. When I tried later to thank them for that particular piece of generosity, among so many others, they brushed my gratitude aside quite casually. My education was too important to be interrupted, they said—and besides, Saint Bride's was so wonderfully and so luckily convenient that it almost seemed, didn't it, as if it had been put there quite on purpose.

☆

There were a few day students at Saint Bride's, from Chagford and Moretonhampstead. But there were only six of us in the upper school who were boarders. We slept in the two rooms up on the third floor, which had once been the servants' quarters. From the casement by my bed I could look down onto the river, and beyond the river, the woods, through the thick, leaded panes that had not been reglazed since Charles I was king. But then, by the time Charles I was king, the house was already ancient.

Like many of the big houses of its day, it had started out as a monastery. It had been built soon after Bad King John signed the Magna Carta, around the middle of the thirteenth century. But after 1534, when Henry VIII implemented Cardinal Wolsey's brilliant recognition that you could get rich and divorced simultaneously by simply coopting the papacy, after he had pillaged the monasteries and then razed them to destroy the evidence, the only part of the original structure left standing was a single arched stone passageway. It led from the kitchen to nowhere in particular and was the favorite haunt of Cook's nasty little Pekingese, sniffing out ghosts and rats.

Having stashed the booty and destroyed the buildings, Henry generously gave the ruins to one of his loyal retainers—along with a good amount of acreage, a suitable title, but one assumes no money.

It therefore took some years for the loyal retainer to build himself a new house, far more modest than the monastery, rather more comfortable, and, as it turned out, a great deal more enduring. The school's kitchen and dining hall had been left largely unchanged for four hundred years. They were oak beamed, dark, and massively handsome, while the common rooms—now turned into studies and schoolrooms—had been altered by very little more than the addition of floor-to-ceiling bookcases that matched the original wainscoting lining the walls under the extraordinarily long sweep of mullioned windows. Even a loyal retainer of Henry VIII is apparently not immune to a charming view of lawns and stream.

The bedrooms were low ceilinged but pretty, and several of them opened onto balconies invaded by ivy whose roots undoubtedly reached back to the Middle Ages. The younger pupils slept on the second story; we older ones were above them in two large dormer rooms. On the same floor, far in the back, was a tiny space that was still more an attic than a bedroom. That was Desirée's little lair. She had been orphaned as a small child, a foundling straight out of Dickens, and she had been taken in by Miss Thompson. Plain and a little lopsided, she always listed slightly to the left. Abstractions of the simplest sort entirely eluded her, and she understood things so literally that she hardly understood them at all. "Throw me some bread, would you?" I said at tea one day. Unfazed and unquestioning, she took the bread from its basket and threw it.

She stayed on at the school, not a student and not really part of the staff, although she helped Matron with housework and Cook with chopping and peeling for the meals. She stayed on, having nowhere else to go, and lived on in that small attic room. There, sound asleep, she talked and moaned to herself all night.

*

At the end of the eighteenth century, one of the house's owners got rich enough to indulge in some architectural ambitions and he added on a large wing. It was, in fact, noticeably bigger than the house to which it was added, and its rooms were large and bright, with French doors leading out into the garden or onto balconies. Later, around 1918, when the aftereffects of the First World War may have suggested a pressing need for prayer, one of the smaller rooms on the second floor was turned into a chapel. It was the only ugly room in the building. Despite being consecrated, despite a lavish application of brass and red plush, it remained a charmless space, quite unevocative of any spiritual dimension. Miss Thompson did her best there to uplift our souls when she led us in the required daily morning ritual of prayer—although in her mouth this often veered disturbingly towards pantheism, and even, I see now in retrospect, occasionally, in moments of lyrical despair, converged on the atheistic.

The pièce de résistance of the new wing, intended to be the center of the house, was a great, sweeping staircase where the two sets of stairs from opposites sides of the second floor met each other on a splendid oval landing, and then, having become one, fanned out again into a sort of delta, an alluvial deposit of steps into the elegant oak entrance hall at the wide, double front doors. I used to dream about coming down those stairs, dressed in flowing green velvet and celebrating some unspecified global triumph, while a crowd of my admirers stood at the bottom and applauded softly at my descent.

Matron had her own room in the new wing, where Miss Thompson and Auntie Vera also shared a small suite. Cook lived above the old, disused stables, and so did Mrs. Beaty, who taught gym and math. The rest of the staff lived in Chagford and came only for the day.

✳

I have been back to Chagford twice. There was a tour bus on the main street the first time; the second time there were five tour buses clustered in a new parking lot, all with their engines running, while the tourists they had contained, Germans and Italians and Japanese and Americans, were let loose for an hour to graze among the gifte shoppes and picture postcard emporiums. But even in its degraded condition and overflowing with far too many people, Chagford is beautiful—filled with flowers in window boxes and in tubs that line the cobbled streets. I doubt if there is a building in town that is a day younger than Hampton Court, and the place wraps you, as soon as you arrive, in that sort of mellow effluence that old buildings and old books exude. You take a breath of air and know that time is unimportant; that time is not at all what you thought it was.

There are in fact two sorts of time in Devonshire, neither of which is the present. One time belongs to the sun-drenched valley stretching, green and fertile, from the moors to the cliff-rimmed seacoast; the soil here is the deep pink of very old terracotta and the grass that grows on it is so rich that it produces the richest milk in all of England—the only milk that can be persuaded to turn itself into Devonshire cream. The other time belongs to the moorland itself: stark and beautiful, handsome but forbidding, the moors produce only granite and heather. The sheep that graze there on the sparse vegetation among forlorn crags are often lured by winter desperation into bogs, where they drown. In summer the sun reveals a muted, gentle landscape of softly varied blue and gray: stone, heather, sky. But the moonlight reminds you that even summer nights are darkened by Druid shadows and the memory of blood spilled on those ancient, sacred rocks.

Chagford is at the dividing edge between these two Devonshires, and Saint Bride's School, which looked out in one direction at the wood and the river, looked, in the other direction, at a desolate expanse of hillside stretching as far as you could see into nothing, into the sky. On Sunday morning after breakfast we would walk onto the moors, cold, barren, and majestic: a landscape without comfort. Our fingers stiff with cold, we would look down at the green world we had left behind us and hurry back to it gratefully. On Sunday evening after tea we would walk into Chagford for vespers. In the old church, as we came in, one of the acolytes swinging a censer had already turned the air into incense. The priest—he was so High Church that we were told to call him "Father" Smiley—was hidden by a stone scrim, and he performed his mysteries in a singsong that might as well have been Latin. We were caught in Devonshire's strange, temporal dichotomy: the wild, Stone Age moor countered the cozy Tudor town; pagan, moonlit dolmens opposed Christian incense and candles. And two histories, impelled in rather antithetical directions—one back to primal simplicity, the other towards those elaborate concealments necessary to being civilized—became the warp and woof of a thick temporal tapestry, a texture of the past so tightly woven that it refused to let the present through. We were as out of Time, somehow, as if we had been cloistered.

Miss Thompson, who had a stern haircut and a serious misalignment of her lower jaw, which gave an unalterable grimness to her expression, had told me before she led me upstairs to the dormitory that there were no rules at Saint Bride's. By which, quite unfairly—prejudiced no doubt by the severity of her hair and teeth—I supposed her to mean that of course there were rules but she wasn't about to tell me what they were: if I broke one I would know soon enough, probably by finding myself in front of a firing squad.

And then, as soon as we were upstairs, as she was showing me my bed next to the casement window—difficult to close because of the ivy vines trying to push their way through it—she did pronounce a rule after all. "I should tell you, that you must never get into another girl's bed," she said. "That is something Auntie Vera and I will not permit here. Ever."

Why on earth, I wondered, would I want to get into another girl's bed? And if I was weird enough to want to, why would Miss Thompson get her knickers in a knot trying to stop me?

It goes without saying that before I left Saint Bride's I did get into another girl's bed. And that Miss Thompson found me there.

✶

It was Moira's bed.

I was in it, for one thing, because most nights, instead of going to sleep after lights out, I got out of bed again to play Truth, Dare, Kiss, or Promise in the other room. I remember only slightly the two girls who shared the room I was in, and mostly what I remember about them is that they didn't play Truth, Dare, Kiss, or Promise but went to sleep as they were supposed to. The other room was where the action was. Rosemary, a plump, dark, merry girl, who suffered from frequent and violent seizures of epilepsy, was an enthusiastic player. Sallow, fearful, myopic Hazel was a reluctant one. She usually agreed to join us, however, grumbling that we were keeping her awake. Her only relatives were some ancient and distant cousins she seldom saw, and grumbling was her most reliable pleasure; she went on about it expertly, routinely, and with a considerable amount of satisfaction. It was Moira, however, who was the true organizer of the game, and I was her lieutenant.

In any other atmosphere, in any other time and place, Moira and I would have had little to do with each other. She was an athletic sort of girl, a horse-riding sort of girl, blonde, tanned, compact. Flanked by the rest of us five weedy adolescents her physical well-being must have seemed almost aggressive to the casual observer, although she herself, of course, was quite unaware of it. She had parents—in Bovey Tracey, I think, or Totnes; she had brothers; she had an abundance of energy, which made it almost impossible for her to go to sleep when Matron came round at ten to turn off the lights.

I had my own trouble sleeping, though not because of excessive energy. Insomnia was something I took for granted, and it is only in retrospect that my bouts of sleeplessness through the decades suggest a definitive pattern—a pattern of increased anxiety that I certainly never recognized as such when my wakefulness occurred. At Saint Bride's I thought I was quite contented to be going to America in a month or two or three or ten. I would have told you that I was looking forward to it. Meanwhile, I couldn't sleep.

We played Truth, Dare, Kiss or Promise perhaps two or three times a week—just a single round, usually, each night. The way the game goes—or at least the way it went when we played it—is that one of you gets to be "it," while the people who aren't "it" decide on a question to ask. If "it" answers it correctly (which happened rarely since our questions were totally unfair), the next player becomes "it." If the answer is incorrect, "it" chooses as a punishment whether to tell the truth, to take a dare, to kiss someone, or to promise something. Then the other players decide what the truth or dare or kiss or promise will be. Rosemary always chose a dare. Hazel always chose the truth. Moira and I tended to stick with promise, which deferred the need for action. No one, ever, chose kiss.

Our sessions were becoming rather more risky as time went on. At first our challenges were quite tentative: making Hazel show us what was in the trunk she kept under the bed, for instance. A teddy bear, she told us, a few other old toys, a picture of her long-dead mother. Then, though we hadn't asked her to, she pulled the trunk out and showed us everything in it: sweaters, several tubes of toothpaste, shoes, and a small flowered hatbox, which, when opened, revealed an assortment of baby and infant clothes that for some arcane reason she had kept, wrapped in tissue and tied nicely in pink ribbon.

No one said anything about the baby clothes, and we soon went on to more interesting things—which culminated after a few weeks in daring Rosemary to pee out of the window. It was the third floor window. Despite her epilepsy, she performed brilliantly from her precarious position perched on the window ledge, achieving Niagaran grandeur and defoliating several of Auntie Vera's window-box geraniums. Luckily she was not seized by one of her grand mal episodes during the process.

✳

The other factor that caused me to be in Moira's bed when Miss Thompson discovered me there, was Anne. Anne was twelve, which was an awkward age for Saint Bride's, not quite old enough for the upper school nor quite young enough for the lower—to which, however, she had been assigned and where she was patently bored.

Even without the tedium of being stuck in classes too elementary for her Anne would have been a rebel. The intensity and purity of her rebellion, in fact, were extraordinary, and more so because she always acted alone, entirely without allies, without consultation, without support. Also without apology. When the still-rationed sugar was found one day at tea to have a rather piquant, marine flavor to it, she volunteered to Matron, who was conducting the inquisition, that during kitchen duty the night before she had mixed five pounds of salt into the sugar barrel. Out of curiosity, she said, when hauled off for questioning, to see what it tasted like. And her confessions to other crimes of which she stood accused were always without shame and without subterfuge.

I think we were a bit in awe of her. In fact, we may even have been frightened of her. We tacitly recognized that her naughtiness was a reaction to an imbalanced and infuriating aspect of the universe from which we consciously protected ourselves. She knew something we wouldn't let ourselves know. We suspected that by her rebellion she was implementing ideals of justice and retribution that we should certainly have admired and would have supported if we had only allowed ourselves to accept the need for them. But we did not allow ourselves to accept the need for them. And inevitably, comparing ourselves to her, we were deeply and secretly ashamed of the terror that caused us

156 • THE TIGER IN THE ATTIC

to be lazy and apathetic and that prevented us from joining Anne in the fight.

She had been born to be a conscience rouser. Given enough time and a few explosives she could have become a highly successful terrorist. Perhaps she did.

One morning, during a composition class, Auntie Vera told her to stop daydreaming and she threw an inkwell in Auntie Vera's face. The inkwell, which was full, broke, turning Auntie Vera into a dripping black blob, like one of the ink-dipped boys in *Der Struwwelpeter.* The little boys and girls in the composition class giggled joyously, and Auntie Vera, who had something of a concussion and was bleeding feebly into the ink, sank weeping to the ground.

It was Matron on her way to instruct Cook about lunch who finally heard all the giggling and sobbing and went in to reestablish order. Holding Anne firmly by her left ear she expelled her from the classroom and delivered her into Miss Thompson's study.

You may recall that Miss Thompson made a point about the school's not having rules, and one assumes that she had therefore never really considered what the appropriate punishment should be for breaking them. Still, it must have been clear, even to Miss Thompson, that physical assault resulting in a concussion and a face full of permanent ink demanded some sort of reprimand. Today your average headmistress would probably ship Anne off to the nearest psychiatrist; in the 1940s a more likely reaction would have been to expel her. But Miss Thompson had a better idea.

Anne emerged from the study looking uncharacteristically gloomy. She was a lithe and energetic little girl, with an irrepressible smile that she usually shone promiscuously upon the whole world around her. In retrospect, it seems probable that that same smile covered a smoldering resentment, a tinderbox of anger waiting to combust into full rebellion—but to us, her innocent schoolfellows, the bright expression simply indicated an inner glow.

There was no glow when she came out of Miss Thompson's

room. Silent and looking downward, avoiding the eye of anyone she met, she hurried to her room and did not emerge from it until suppertime. In the great, Tudor dining hall with its great old oak tables and ancient benches there were two new pieces of furniture: a card table and a folding metal chair had been put up in the farthest corner and the table was set with a single place setting.

With the end of the war, rationing had become more stringent than ever and Saint Bride's menus frequently included the unnamed and the unnamable. As we helped ourselves to the boiled potatoes and the awful and probably equine stew in front of us, we saw that Anne had sat down in the far corner and that Cook was bringing in a plate filled with the evening's mess. A sort of uncomfortable silence fell over the meal—until, at last, Miss Thompson got up to make an announcement. Anne, she said, had behaved in a discourteous manner; she had not behaved as one belonging to the social unit that was Saint Bride's. Miss Thompson—who kept her tone even and her language mild, exercising civility during this discourse on incivility—had therefore decreed that for the time being Anne was to be put in a sort of quarantine so that the rest of us would be protected from catching her disruptive disorder. She must of course be allowed to eat still, to study still, to walk in the halls and gardens of Saint Bride's still. But until she could be seen to have recovered from her affliction of unsociability— until she had convinced Miss Thompson and Auntie Vera that she was repentant and reformed—she had been directed to keep her distance from us. We, in turn, must feel in duty bound to keep ours. Anne was not to speak to us, and we were enjoined not to speak to her. Aside from that—aside from being banished—she was free to do absolutely anything she wanted.

We filed out from the dining hall in silence, mulling over the strange harshness of this sentence. Next morning we watched mutely as Anne sat in her perch of exile while we ate breakfast, as she read her lessons at the desk slightly removed from the others, as she prayed in chapel in the corner by the furthest window. Her bed had been taken

from the dormitory and put up in a tiny room down the hall next to
the rooms shared by Auntie Vera and Miss Thompson. It was not
much more than a closet, and Anne now slept there, as she lived, in
isolation.

This went on for about a week. Apparently Anne had not yet
convinced Miss Thompson and Auntie Vera that she was penitent
enough. I assume that she never even tried to convince them. And
then, shortly before lunch one Thursday, Anne disappeared. So did
the cash from the Aid to African Missions box in the chapel, which
had been accruing capital over some months and was almost ready to
be turned over to "Father" Smiley. Anne reappeared at supper, grinning widely and carrying under her arm a leather-encased first aid kit
that she had much admired in Boots's window during a school outing to Exeter some weeks before. It was soon known throughout the
school that the African Missions fund had been just enough to buy a
return bus ticket to Exeter, the elegant first aid kit, and a splendid
lunch.

So Anne came in to supper, late and triumphant. Cook, bringing out the junket for dessert, escaped straight back into the kitchen,
while Mme. Vronsky, who taught music and French on the curriculum
and basic sophistication off it, turned her face to the wall in order not
to be observed smirking. Matron, Auntie Vera, and Miss Thompson
rose from their places and stood, appalled.

Anne and the first aid kit were removed and locked, supperless,
in her little room.

That was when Moira and I became true allies. Hazel didn't
much care; Rosemary didn't much care; but Moira and I were both
deeply offended by what seemed to us Miss Thompson's injustice—
or, at the very least, her exercise in illogic. We felt betrayed. After all,
Anne had been told that she could do whatever she wanted to—except to make contact with anyone at school. Why would you tell
someone they can do anything they like and then lock them in a cell
for doing it? It was an outrage!

We also had some unsupported notion that Anne had been sentenced to her prison term on a diet of bread and water. So after a brief round of Truth, Dare, Kiss, or Promise, after Hazel and Rosemary were both asleep, Moira and I, by common agreement, stole down to the kitchen and, whispering to each other and feeling our way in the almost total darkness, managed to put together a rather hearty sandwich of bread, cheese, and tomatoes. This did not, however, fit easily under Anne's door and came apart while we were trying to push it through.

"Looks rather messy," said Miss Thompson behind us. "Goodnight, girls," and she walked on by.

We were crushed. Our support of rebellion was crushed. We cleaned up the deconstructed sandwich from the carpet and crept back to our beds.

But by then we were agreed: Miss Thompson had implicitly confirmed herself Our Enemy. Not that she said a word, next day or any day, about discovering us in the process of smuggling ploughman's lunch under Anne's door; but her mysterious silence only made us feel guilty, and to protect ourselves from guiltiness we formed a tacit alliance. Night after night, once the lights were out, once the last truth had been revealed or the last dare accomplished, after Hazel and Rosemary had fallen asleep, Moira and I would slide under her blanket and discuss Life, Justice, and why we didn't like Miss Thompson. From the window facing us we could see the window of the little flat above the horse stalls where Mrs. Beaty had once lived alone and lived alone no longer. Her husband had just been demobbed from the army and had joined her—and naturally one night Moira and I began to fantasize about what married life must be like. What married life with a man recently demobbed from the army must be like. We slurped kisses on each other's shoulders and called each other "sugar popsum" and "plum dumpling" until, still giggling, we fell asleep.

As an introduction to lesbian love it left something to be desired. But then it wasn't an introduction to lesbian love. It wasn't much of anything except a pathetic, embarrassed, and futile attempt to dramatize our impacted and impossible longings for something ineffable—which neither of us had ever seen, which neither of us was ever likely to find, which we could imagine only dimly, and for which we could find no expression except in the crudest caricature.

Miss Thompson woke me gently. She had the cat in her arms. Probably she had come to look for the cat and then had inadvertently found me in Moira's bed.

"Shssh," she said as I stared at her, still half asleep, not believing what I saw. "Shssh." And she led me carefully to my own bed and tucked the sheet around me. Then she was gone.

I assumed that I must have been dreaming. Paradoxically, I also assumed that Moira and I would be expelled immediately. When Moira and I met at breakfast next morning we sat by mutual, unspoken consent at opposite ends of the table reserved for older students. In Mme. Vronsky's class, forced to claim our usual places next to each other, we avoided each other's eyes and stared either into the middle distance or at *le Cid*:

L'amour n'est q'un plaisir, l'honneur est un devoir.

We expected, at any moment, to be summoned before Miss Thompson.

But Miss Thompson gave no sign, no hint, that I had been caught in flagrante, disobeying The Rule. I waited in vain for weeks, my apprehension growing less and less with every day, until finally I forgot myself that anything had happened. The only thing to suggest that, after all, it had was that by then, driven asunder by an obscure and tacit shame, Moira and I hardly spoke to each other.

✳

Soon after I came to Saint Bride's Miss Thompson had asked whether I would like to have some private tutorial time with her—writing short essays, perhaps, and reading poetry. It sounded dismal, but it would have been too embarrassing to say no.

So on Tuesdays and Fridays at three I went to Miss Thompson's oak-lined study. We were reading the people you read in those days: Robert Bridges, John Masefield, James Elroy Flecker, none of them now highly regarded, but all of them at least easy to understand. I was reluctant and resistant at the beginning, but Miss Thompson, who always had a pot of tea and a plate of toast or biscuits waiting for me, greeted me and my ideas with such respect that I began to take myself seriously and to enjoy not simply the reading but talking about what we read. I am not the first person to be nurtured by an ambience of old wood and buttered toast to develop a high regard for their own opinions. A sense of academic achievement resides in old wood and buttered toast. For a few days after the sandwich disaster and after being discovered in Moira's bed I was, I suppose, a bit hangdog, even perhaps surly, defending myself against the anticipated reprimand. But when no reprimand materialized, I settled back again into the nest Miss Thompson had provided for me.

Anne's father had come briefly, to see Anne and to talk to Miss Thompson. He looked like a film star, tanned and with perfect teeth, and he was driven to the door by a chauffeur who then waited in his big black car so as to take him back again, as soon as possible, to wherever it was he had come from. After he left, Anne was restored to her rightful place among us.

She appeared untouched by her three weeks of shame; she glowed again with mischief and revolution. It was Miss Thompson who seemed to have been transformed. She had become something softer and gentler than I had thought her to be. She was especially kind to Anne, often stopping to talk to her as she passed the table where Anne was eating or taking a place by Anne's side when we were walking on the moor or to church. Meanwhile, Anne's smile, her teeth as white and even as her father's, shone on unaltered upon Miss Thompson as it shone upon us all.

I suppose to be a revolutionary it helps to be impervious.

It was Miss Thompson who now seemed to me unsure of herself. In our sessions in her study our former, cheerful reading, with its moral certainty and its muscular view of nature, had been set aside. We turned to darker things. We started with Houseman and Rupert Brooke; soon we were reading Siegfried Sassoon, Wilfred Owen, and Isaac Rosenberg. Miss Thompson's study filled with a tender sorrow; the death of young men at war mingles in my memory with the apple wood smoke from the fire warming the chill of those spring afternoons. A heady sort of melancholy wrapped itself around us, a sense of lives needlessly, bitterly ended—but so poignantly remembered that death became more sensual, more evocative, than life can hope to be.

✳

My nights, however, were restless: I was dreaming vividly. Often I had nightmares. One night I dreamed that a ghost waited in the dark wood, hid under the bridge, or lurked in the school's passageways. He had been waiting for centuries for the unwary, the unsuspecting, to drag them with him into his ghostly world. In my dream he was called Willie the Wailer, and I saw him, a thin white wraith with a white beard that trailed behind him like smoke. But seeing him was not dangerous. It was hearing him that paralyzed you and put you in his power. He had a whistle, and when he blew on it, it gave a high, long, hollow shriek: the sound of a steam engine letting off steam, the sound of a train departing. Willie the Wailer could blow his whistle and hold that single screech of lament for long minutes on end. If you heard it, you were dead.

I woke up, terrified, with the sound of the whistle in my ears.

Or perhaps it was a scream. It seems likely, in fact, that what I was hearing—and there was actually a very shrill ululation coming from somewhere—was poor Desirée screaming during one of her nocturnal fits. It must have been her I heard. But the dream stayed with me through the night and for days—in fact for years—to come: Willie the Wailer summoning me into the unknown.

Next morning Miss Thompson called me to her office. Aunt Helen had phoned, she told me, to say that I was to go back to Prince-town at the end of the week. My passage to America had come through.

LEAVING

When the train that would take Ruth and me to London pulled away from the Plymouth station, Aunt Helen and Uncle Bourke were standing on the platform, still waving. It was like one of those sentimental scenes in old movies, where the train draws away carrying the hero to war or the heroine back to her dull husband and those left behind on the platform grow smaller and smaller.

These days no one much leaves by train—not if they're going any distance, anyway—and airplanes are totally inept for conveying that essential image of diminution and parting. Airplanes are in a contemporary mode that disdains the dominance of time and space, that divides time and space into discrete, sequential modules, through which you move as if transiting from airlock to airlock, from unit to unit, from segment to segment, until you finally get to wherever it is you're going. And when you do arrive, it's without really having been anywhere else since you left. Between the entrance of the departure airport and the exit of the arrival airport you have traversed merely a series of quasi places—security, gate, plane, baggage claim—and a series of quasi events—boarding, waiting, takeoff, landing—without traveling through any palpable space.

Whenever I deplane and, coming to earth again, reenter the present, the last few hours spent in getting there seem completely unreal. In part that's due, of course, to the plastic meal and the multi-movies on their teeny little screens; their piquant impalpability seems the product of an alien technology that is attempting, rather sweetly, to approximate earthly food and entertainment so as to make me feel at home. It's far more disconcerting, though, that the airplane has transported me between here and there by way of a vacuum through which I have been transferred in an inchoate approximation of Star Trek, beam-me-up-Scottie techniques.

But a train is different. A train, despite its rather crude function as an early icon of the Industrial Revolution, is also a powerful image of transience and tragedy. It connects motion and emotion. It moves through time and space with poignant effort, pulling away gently at first, slowly, and gathering speed with inexorable cruelty as it leaves the known world behind. My favorite scene in *Jane Eyre* is the one in which Mr. Rochester tells Jane that he feels that a string attached to him somewhere under his left ribs is firmly knotted to a string attached to her somewhere under her left ribs. If a large distance were to come between them, he says, "I am afraid that cord of communion will be snapt; and then I've a nervous notion I should take to bleeding inwardly." I have always pictured one of them—sometimes Jane, sometimes Mr. Rochester—standing on the heath near Thornfield Hall, while the other sits in a train and is drawn away to heartbreak. There is nothing in *Jane Eyre* to suggest that anyone ever gets on a train—they are still in the horse and carriage mode. So I suppose the reason for my railway imaginings is an imposition from my own leave-takings— first from my mother in Karlsruhe and then from the Harveys on the edge of Dartmoor.

I did not recognize it as heartbreak at the time, of course. But as the train moved along the platform and away I saw that Uncle Bourke was weeping. Tears had run from his eyes and were coursing down his cheeks. I had never seen him cry. I had never seen any man cry. And his embrace and Aunt Helen's kiss had been more ardent than the delicacy in which they normally restrained their affection.

"They will miss me," I thought with astonishment. I thought it all the way to London, where I'd been only once before, all the way to the adventure of collecting visas and passports and paraphernalia and staying with Ruth in a bed-and-breakfast. It was not until we were well embarked on the ship, the SS *Gripsholm*, and already halfway across the Atlantic that I could even begin to say to myself, "I will miss them."

I think I marked down in memory, as something important to be considered later and at leisure, the fact that Uncle Bourke got out his clean white handkerchief—most probably ironed by me, handkerchiefs being the only article I have ever been capable of ironing without making worse creases in them than existed in their nonironed state. I marked down that he waved it as the train began to move, after he'd wiped his eyes and blown his nose. The moment was much too disturbed—all that packing, the thought of time in London, of time without grown-ups, the prospect of a week's voyage at sea—to consider properly the serious things that needed to be considered: leaving England, going to America, meeting the stranger who was my mother. It was quite the wrong time, certainly, to contemplate Uncle's Bourke's tears. So I put them away for the time being for later use.

✸

The same strange amnesia that afflicts my memory of the journey to England has riddled my journey from England and filled it with holes. A year or so ago I called my sister Ruth to see what she knows. "Where did we stay in London?" I ask her. "How long? What did we do while we were there?"

But my sister allows very little from before 1950 to enter her house. She fills it with photographs of her beautiful grandson, Max, from birth to present, with pictures of her son and his wife, an extraordinarily handsome pair, at their wedding, on vacation, at play, at work, dancing, swimming, smiling. She has a wall of snapshots commemorating moments of a long married life only recently ended by her husband's death: Ruth and Harry with tennis rackets, in formal attire at Dickie's Bar Mitzvah, at their twenty-fifth anniversary, their thirtieth, their fortieth. Harry's parents, however, who used to sit, still youthful and grimly formal, on the buffet, were put away soon after Harry died, and it takes a long search until I finally discover Mother and me and Oma lurking in a single photograph taken at Ruth and Harry's wedding in 1951. It is the earliest photograph on display.

It occurs to me that Ruth's done to the past in general what I did to an unpleasant boyfriend or two, what one does to one's ex-husband as soon as the divorce comes through. Editing one's life is anybody's prerogative, after all.

"Damned if I know," Ruth says. "I think we must have stayed in a hotel. Or a B and B. Weren't we taking the boat train to Southampton?"

"Liverpool," I tell her. "It was Liverpool." I know it was Liverpool because it annoyed me that it was Liverpool. Liverpool seemed to me a ridiculously tacky town from which to embark on an ocean voyage.

✶

Memory, as we all know, is a fickle tool—made even more unreliable by the very instruments we use to secure it, to hold the evidence in place for future use when we write the reports and histories and biographies that document the past. Though I've never kept a regular journal, I usually do keep a diary when I'm traveling, which I can then reread two or five or ten or twenty years later, as I try to relive the events of some journey that is steadily receding into oblivion. The written word certainly does recall the trip, but it seems to recall it somewhat differently with each reading. The shading from pleasant to unpleasant changes subtly; the cast of characters appears to shuffle roles.

For instance, the afternoon in Paris in 1995 when I watched from the balcony of my hotel room while a crowd began to gather on the Pont Royal. For an hour people collected there until they finally overflowed the bridge and covered the entire left bank of the Seine as far as I could see. They seemed to be listening to an undecipherable message that wafted towards me from loudspeakers on the far side of the bridge. Not until the sun started to sink and twilight cast a warm wash over the still water did the crowd move again, streaming across the Seine into the Tuilleries and out of sight.

It was so oddly moving, all those people gathering by the river at sunset, that I wrote three pages about it in my journal. But I had no idea why they were there. That night when I came back from dinner the hotel concierge told me that a week earlier a young African had been killed on the Pont Royal by right-wing thugs. The crowd had met that afternoon to hear François Mitterand speak at the place where the young man had been attacked and to follow the president on a march through Paris to protest intolerance.

By the time I knew all this it was too late to write in my journal, so I added the concierge's information a day or so later as a separate entry on a facing page and I drew a black ink border around it to show that it was out of place.

In the nine years since then, for a variety of reasons, I've reread this part of the journal several times. The initial three-page section poignantly evokes Paris as the city of Romantic passion and of student unrest; it brings to mind the barricades of 1848; it is the city of Delacroix, Berlioz, and Victor Hugo where I yearned to live long before I'd ever seen it. But the odd placement and the emphasis of the black outline have led me more than once to read the concierge's explanation first before I get to the original entry. Taken in that order,

Romantic passion tends to evaporate from my Paris memories and politics takes its place. The city in my mind loses its twilight glow and becomes a sober place, liberal, socially responsible, and addicted to interminable shouted discussions in noisy outdoor cafés.

And then on another visit to France three years ago I took a walk through the cemetery in Montmartre and found several graves in its Jewish section badly damaged: possibly by nature, possibly by age, probably, as I chose to believe, by vandals. And—for a while, at least, for the next rereading of my journal—that pretty much killed the sunset city I had looked on from my balcony. This was Paris, after all, city of revolutions, home of the guillotine. The crowd surging across the Pont Royal, despite its benign and moral objectives, developed, for me, an uncomfortable resemblance to the mob storming the Bastille; and the people gathered to protest bigotry that afternoon on the Pont Royal were overshadowed by bigotry itself, the xenophobia and anti-semitism of France's divided soul.

That will all change again, of course, the next time I'm in Paris, or even the next time I read my journal. It will change because what I write will support whatever reading I'm inclined to make of it. And who knows what evasions and subterfuges deflected the daily entries I made in the first place, what shame or self-deception, long forgotten, nudged what I wrote in this direction or that.

Even photographs can betray you. Pictures you clearly remember pasting in the album are nowhere to be found, while those that have found the way to take their place show scenes completely unfamiliar to you. Consider, for example, the snapshot of me at the age of six, taken soon after my father died, on a sunny spring day in the Black Forest. I have on a Black Forest costume and I am standing under a tree, smiling brilliantly because I have just captured the baby goat that used to butt me and gambol around me as I ran across the fields. It is among the handful of vivid memories I have of Germany: the delight of catching the little goat, the feel of its squirming as it tries to wriggle out of my arms. And yes, there indeed, where I know it must be, is the photograph of me in my Black Forest outfit. But something's amiss: in this picture, instead of the goat, I am holding an entirely un-memorable kitten, and instead of smiling, I am scowling unhappily down at the grass.

Should I ignore the photograph that I remember but that prob-ably doesn't exist and embrace this photograph that exists but that I can't remember? Perhaps a middle course may be best. I will try to strike a balance and reach a compromise between what is clearly here, in front of my eyes, and what my memory still maintains should be there instead. One must, of course, acknowledge the concrete and ir-refutable evidence of snapshots, of news accounts, and of other peo-ple's recollections—but they should take their place humbly in the framework of whatever fiction memory insists on.

✵

We stayed in a bed-and-breakfast, Ruth and I, in a big room that over-looked Hyde Park Corner. There was a sign, I think, LYON'S TEA, or perhaps CADBURY'S CHOCOLATE, which stared at us across from our window. Around lunchtime, and then again when it was time for tea, we could watch men putting up their box platforms to stand on and begin to lecture passersby on the uses of socialism, or the hor-rors of war, or the evils of imperialism. Though, of course, what I may be remembering is the room I was in the next time I was in London, and that was ten years later.

We made the crossing on the SS *Gripsholm*—that much is true—a fine, stately ship on the Swedish-American line, newly rededicated to passenger service after her wartime vocation as a transport ship. And we sailed from Liverpool. ¯

It rained all the way up from London. I couldn't see much through the streaked windows of the train except a generalized gray landscape flattened by rain. I seem to remember that I was excited about traveling by myself with only Ruth for company, though it took me years to see that journey of ours, two sisters traveling together to an alien world, as a sort of parenthesis, one of a pair, which bracketed our life in England. I remember that I was aggrieved because Ruth's attention had been preempted by a gentleman in a corduroy jacket. He was ancient, thirty-five or forty at least, much too old, I thought, for my twenty-year-old sister. And he was not merely flirting with her but making a great show of paying no attention to me at all, my first experience of that peculiar and unfortunately common male stratagem: the exhibition of not listening as a lively act of aggression.

It was still raining when the train pulled up in Liverpool. As we walked from the train platform to the dock, the ancient gentleman in corduroy produced an umbrella that he raised protectively over Ruth's head, leaving mine to be dripped on. I have no idea what his name was. Nor does Ruth. But in the week of our voyage to America he behaved so strangely towards me that I can only assume he had a loathsome younger sister of whom I reminded him.

It was something of an embarrassment for me—not just then, but many years later when I wrote a short story about the journey on the *Gripsholm*, "Coming Over," and realized that his actions were rather too far-fetched to be included in fiction where, after all, you are supposed to aim for cogency rather than truth, an awkward necessity that makes the need to prune a story remarkably common. To be convincing when you base fiction on fact you almost never have to put in something that's untrue but you very often have to take out something that's true—it is astonishing, in fact, how much you have to omit so that people will believe you, though you know that what you're subtracting is entirely factual.

Verisimilitude, as someone must have said somewhere, precludes veracity. And so, for instance, my first husband, Jack, had to be tossed from a story, "Codes of Honor," though by all measures, thematic and narrative, he belonged there. He'd come with me on my first trip back to England in 1956, and he was sitting next to me while a bunch of earnest American penologists asked awkward questions about the in-

cidence of homosexuality at Dartmoor Prison. They were embarrassing the hell out of Uncle Bourke, who only wanted to give all of us a
nice Devonshire tea at Twin Brooks Farm—the penologists and me
and poor Jack, who happened to be having his own incidence of homosexuality at about that time and who was considerably more embarrassed even than Uncle Bourke. It was a piquant study in coincidence and contrast: the truth-questing Americans doing battle with
Uncle Bourke's restraint and, entirely inadvertently, putting English
tact and good manners to the sword. It might have made a rather nice
theatrical scene. But in an autobiography or a novel it could only be
read as a crass exploitation of a minor theme and would simply
muddy the narrative.

But let me return to the man who'd been on the train with us,
the man who'd raised his umbrella over my sister and allowed me to be
dripped upon. What he did that needed to be expunged from my biography as far as any future literary use was concerned was to lock me
inside our cabin on the *Gripsholm*. It had to be discarded as a useless incident without any social or artistic promise since it wasn't even something I could offer up as an amusing anecdote in casual conversation:
no one would ever believe I wasn't making it up.

I have no idea how he managed to lock me in. Cabin doors, like
doors in hotels, can usually be opened from the inside without a key,
so I suppose what he did was to bribe a steward to bolt it, somehow,
from the outside. However he managed it, it made no sense to me at
the time and it makes even less sense now. I suppose he thought that
he would be seen as attempting to preserve my chastity from corrup-
tion and thus acquire points with my sister whose chastity he himself
was eager to corrupt. But locking Rapunzel in her tower was a case of
failed logic even in the Middle Ages. Locking me in my cabin in 1946
smacks of insanity—in fact, it is so unreasonable that even writing
about it evokes uneasiness. So, as I say, it had to be left out of "Coming Over;" and until now it has remained unrecorded in the published
annals of my life. Chaotic motivation and general imbecility do not

make for coherent literary structures and must be ditched from the
narrative.

✻

But I will come back to that later.

Meanwhile, it was on the SS *Gripsholm*, mid-Atlantic that I began
to think about Uncle Bourke and to marvel at his weeping. It was a
fine, sun-filled afternoon, I remember, and, having overcome the malaise of the first day or so of an ocean crossing, I was standing looking
out to sea, enjoying the movement of the ship under my feet, when I
suddenly recalled Aunt Helen's firm injunction that I must on no account sit on the ship's railing, not even—indeed, especially not—if
someone dared me to do it. She had emphasized this warning several
times in the last week and finally repeated it again when we were already
in the car, driving to Plymouth for the train for London. I had dismissed it at the time as something grown-ups probably said to everyone about to embark on a ship much as they would say bon voyage.

But standing where I was, at the very place where danger was said
to lurk for those foolish enough to heed the—totally obscure—en-
ticement of climbing onto the railing, it came to me that it was bizarre
for Aunt Helen to have warned me against it. Whatever had put such
a notion in her mind, so far from her usual, sanguine assumption that
the world, by and large, was safe and sane and so removed from any
possibility of danger into which my cautious and sedentary habits
were likely to lead me? What Aunt Helen usually worried about, in my
case, was that I didn't get enough fresh air, and what one might have
expected her to tell me was to climb as high on the railing as my lazy
bones would take me and then to inhale as deeply as I could, throwing my arms wide in the process.

Exceedingly weird, I thought; and on its own, unbidden, the even
stranger image came to me of Uncle Bourke on the station platform,
waving his handkerchief and not succeeding in holding back his tears.

It would be impossible to define the importance those tears have held for me over the years without getting all Dickensian and mawkish about it—although I suppose what I'd be getting would be more in the Leigh Hunt style of mawkish than in the Dickensian. A sort of "Jenny kiss'd me when we met" variety of self-puffery, which turns a brief moment of sadness or of delight into the measure of one's own worth. But Leigh Hunt notwithstanding, it is a fact that if Uncle Bourke had waved me off cheerfully, if Aunt Helen hadn't uncharacteristically worried aloud about my safety, I would have made a great many more mistakes than the many I did make in later life.

As it was, the train left Plymouth, and Aunt Helen and Uncle Bourke waved and waved and grew smaller and smaller. And I transformed the image of them standing there into a kind of amulet, which protected me, which protects me still, from the onslaught of insignificance and the ever-lurking conviction of worthlessness. They were astonishingly useful to me over the years, that advice, those tears.

✡

I wonder, now and then, why I never thought about my mother crying when we left Karlsruhe. I know she did; I suspect that she wept passionately. But I buried that detail in a vague and generalized image of loudly wailing adults, an image that evokes no emotion, merely a slight sense of discomfort.

I tell myself that I may have been too young, at seven, to process the meaning of leave-taking, which I could, however, understand at fourteen. I tell myself that perhaps one takes passion and grief from one's parents more as a matter of course than from borrowed relatives and then too that a man in tears is more disturbing than a woman in tears.

But I am not convinced.

OCEAN CROSSING

〜〜 Like most ocean liners, the *Gripsholm* had been put into the service of the war, but she was a Swedish ship, and Sweden was neutral, so she had been chartered by the U.S. State Department and put under the auspices of the Red Cross for the exchange and return of prisoners of war and other nonbelligerent purposes. At the time of our crossing in the spring of 1946 she had just been refitted as a passenger liner. Though I have no hard evidence to offer in support of my sense that we were in fact on the maiden voyage of the *Gripsholm*'s return to civilian life, there was an awkwardness about the crossing, a slight air of disarray and inexperience that spoke of virginity.

I suppose that no one had traveled for pleasure and not many people had traveled at all during the seven years that Ruth and I had spent in England. Few of the passengers had ever crossed the Atlantic; those who had, had done so in a troop ship or a long time ago, when things were different. As for the members of the crew, they were either new to the sea or newly back to it after a long absence: stewards had been recruited from factories, cooks from army messes, sailors taken from fishing trawlers and destroyers, mine sweepers, and aircraft carriers that no longer needed them. The staff displayed a sort of uneasiness, as if the routines of transatlantic travel were as new to them as to us, the passengers. A feeling of amiable chaos pervaded the ship and lurked in the corners like a young cat lying in wait to practice its mischievous surprises.

I think the plan most of us had in mind that first evening on board was something glamorous, possibly involving the Duke and Duchess of Windsor, icons of sophistication before the war whom no one had yet replaced. The tall, slender person of Mrs. Simpson was reflected in my mind's eye leaning towards the water and smoking a long brown cigarette in a long gold cigarette holder. She would be wearing something backless and shining, tight to the torso but flowing toward the floor, a pool of silver lamé around the silver, stiletto heels.

Last year I took a tour of the old *Queen Mary*, which is no longer an ocean-going liner but a landlocked museum of her own past, in dock at Long Beach. In the refurbished lounge there were pictures of movie stars who had sailed on her and who presumably had had their martinis and manhattans and whiskey sours in that very lounge—actresses with marcelled hair bleached almost white and actors and dukes and princes with natty little mustaches covering the polite smiles they had readied for the camera. And not even the scandals that have come to light in the decades between now and the days of their glory, the sorrows and failures laid bare in magazines or revealed in later biographies, could mitigate the glow of enchantment that lit that life. Glamour is a potent hallucinogenic, and its effects can last a lifetime.

So when I walked through the *Queen Mary* a year ago it was the models of the first-class staterooms—the glassed-in displays of the ship's most luxurious cabins—that sent me spinning into nostalgia. The twin beds with their inlaid headboards, the shining bathroom fixtures, nautical and elegant at the same time, the ivory telephone beside the delicate glasses on the nightstand, the paisley-covered armchair and the maroon love seat—with a velvet bathrobe thrown casually over one, a silk nightgown over the other—were intensely familiar: not because I'd ever seen them before, or seen anything like them, but precisely because I hadn't. What they exemplified was the *Gripsholm* of my expectations: they were the transatlantic crossing as I imagined it.

The glamorous fantasy has stayed with me, in fact; the boring reality has been discarded—not from my memory, exactly, but from any emotional recall. In my mental scrapbook I seem to have pasted images from movies and magazines rather than the record of my experience. And when I'm reminded of the facts, they interest me because they are facts, but they fail to move me.

I know this is so because next to those models of the staterooms there was one fine replica of an economy-class cabin. Its cramped, utilitarian efficiency—four to a cabin in two sets of narrow two-tiered bunks with storage underneath—evoked in me no nostalgia whatever. I recognized without a pang that this was pretty close to what Ruth and I occupied during the crossing. But I failed to register any feeling to accompany the recognition. It may have been more than merely the drabness of the environment that numbed me. The voyage on the *Gripsholm* was my first real exposure to the crass, biased, prurient atmosphere that surrounded the snug and protective English nest I had just left, and I suppose I needed every emotional cap and shawl and muffler I could find to wrap around my perceptions so as to keep the cold blast of it all from chilling me to the bone.

✳

Ruth and I were the first to arrive in our cabin, and we took the two bunks on the left of the door. Two sisters from the Continent were to be our cabinmates. They came in rather timidly after we'd already put out our pajamas and hung our bags of toiletries next to the tiny sink. I forget the sisters' names now; when they appear in my fiction I have called them Rosa and Bruna, and that may as well do here. They were

Orthodox Jews, the older, Rosa, told us in schoolgirl English; until a
year ago, since the time when they were still children, they had been in
one concentration camp and then another and another. Their imme-
diate family was gone. They were going to America to live with relatives, an aunt, I think, and cousins, somewhere in New England.

Rosa was small, almost pretty, and oddly, ungrammatically ar-
ticulate when she spoke this recently acquired language she was trying
out on us. She had springy brown hair with a good deal of red to it
and a lively authority of manner that gave not the smallest whisper of
a clue about her recent internment. Bruna, on the other hand, was pale
despite her dark hair, and she kept the brown eyes through which she
could not see very well always turned toward the floor. She seemed to
have taken in all their sorrow, absorbed it and become heavy with it,
while Rosa kicked it aside, out of her way.

"Tomorrow is Friday," Rosa said.

Ruth agreed. Tomorrow was Friday.

"We do not turn on or off the lights on the Sabbath," Rosa said.
"Would you mind. . . ?"

Ruth was briefly flummoxed. "Oh," she said, suddenly compre-
hending. "Not at all."

✶

On the first night out the charts for who would have the early and who
the second seating had not yet been posted, so everyone went to the
dining room when they pleased, sat where they could, and helped
themselves to the buffet of salads and meats provided. Ruth and I were
scooped up by the man from the boat train and carried off to a central table reserved for him by a friend of his: a friend of his whose acquaintance he'd made ten minutes earlier and who now also cast an eye
of speculative interest upon my sister. He was in uniform, a sergeant I
think he was, in the American army, and he rushed off as soon as we
arrived to muster up provisions for the table. They were intended for

my sister, obviously: although he delivered his plates of pâté and bread and marinated vegetables to the middle of the table, it was Ruth at whom he was looking.

She told me recently when last we spoke about that time that the boat train man was actually a male war bride: he'd married a woman in the American armed services so as to get entry to the United States, and on his way to joining her in New York he was trying to seduce every female who happened to cross his path. The sergeant, also married, was rather more judicious—or perhaps merely less successful—but distinctly on the lookout for whatever made itself available.

Something was in the air here. Something strange and as unbalancing as the gently swaying, sea-tossed floors under our feet.

"Cheers!" Ruth said, solemnly, raising her glass of wine in my direction; the male war bride had managed to organize a carafe of red for our table and to my amazement Ruth made no objection when the sergeant poured some into the tumbler I'd innocently intended for lemonade. Apparently I had slipped into the realm of adults, unaware. There was no end to what I might be able to accomplish in the next few days if I put my mind to it!

"Bottoms up!" I agreed.

The world, it seemed, was undergoing a sea change.

✡

After a night of queasiness and disorientation from the gentle heaving of the ship amplified by my first taste of wine, I spent the morning recuperating on deck, lying in the sun next to Rosa and Bruna. One of the deck stewards, a blond, blue-eyed, beautiful young Swede, seemed to have taken Rosa under his special care, and he rushed up with blankets for us as soon as we appeared.

We were by no means the only refugees aboard. A committee had arranged this crossing for twenty or thirty others, putting us all up in the lowest and smallest of the cabins at a bargain group rate.

Basking in the sun, their eyes blissfully closed against the spray from the glittering sea, there were young men and women barely a year out of Treblinka or Dachau, people whose childhood had passed in hiding, survivors of ghettos who had managed to find, among the records in their Displaced Persons Center, the address of some distant relative in Chicago or New York. One of them particularly had caught my eye, a boy of eighteen perhaps, or perhaps even younger, who was trying to get around on a pair of crutches. He was doing rather well, in fact, negotiating the perimeter of the deck, clutching for the railing whenever the ship lurched, but there was something very wrong with him. The hands in which he held his crutches were gnarled, and he was an odd color, a nasty, mottled red. He seemed, sporadically, to have trouble catching his breath. He lowered himself gingerly into the chair next to mine. "Aah," he said to no one in particular. "Wonderful!"

My sister, however, was nowhere to be found. She had gone off immediately after breakfast with the war bride or the sergeant or with one of the other men who cast admiring looks at her wherever she went. She would be doing something dashing, probably, playing poker or deck tennis or perhaps learning to rhumba in the class advertised among the notices by the lounge. She was certainly with people whose cabins, while not in first class, were larger and airier than ours and whose condition, however modest, was a good ten steps above Refugee. I was certain that she was having fun.

It had occurred to me that this week at sea might provide the perfect opportunity to be kissed. Ruth had been kissed. Di and Val had probably been kissed. Half the people I knew must have been kissed, and so had all the people I'd read about. It was high time for me to try it out myself—experimentally, as an experience providing empirical data to support my research into life and literature. I noted a group of three or four young sailors contemplating our bodies laid out in the sun: Rosa's, Bruna's, and mine. Particularly, it should be said, Rosa's and Bruna's. But one of the sailors, a medium-sized, blue-eyed sort of lad, an ideal type for gathering evidence, caught my eye and winked at me.

✵

It's been noted, often enough, that people pair off with extraordinary rapidity on board an ocean liner. Sea air and isolation, I suppose, which combine in a chemistry whose potency is astonishing.

By the end of the first day my sister was waltzing alternately with Mr. War Bride and the sergeant. The wire-headed, muscular young American, whom she'd beaten three times running at pool, had, however, deserted her for a honey-haired, pastel-skirted Southern girl whom we were calling Sweetie-Dahlin'. The two of them were inhaling each other and continued to do so until the end of the voyage. Rosa, breathless with anticipation, was to meet the deck steward for dancing after dinner. He was bringing a friend along to dance with Bruna.

And I, to my total amazement, had a date. The blue-eyed sailor who had winked at me had actually come over to my deck chair and asked me to have a drink with him at the bar at nine o'clock the following night. Or, to be more precise, since he spoke no English, one of the other sailors who was with him had asked me out on his behalf: an older man, with a gray, acne-scarred face and a dramatic manner that suggested that what he was offering was something clandestine—something a bit nasty one only did in the dark. He made me uncomfortable; a breath of the unspeakable seemed to wrap everything he said.

But who was I to quibble with this brilliant chance to carry out my experiment? Without hesitation, I said yes.

✵

Ruth had come in from dancing with her two suitors well before midnight. I was already in my bunk but not yet asleep.

"How are things?" Ruth asked me.

"Brilliant," I said, pretty much meaning it.

"Am I neglecting you?"

I was too astonished by the question to answer right away. And before I had time to pull myself together and tell her that if this was neglect it was fine with me, Rosa and Bruna tiptoed in. They seemed to have put on perfume: a heavy wind of *muguet du bois* came in with them.

"Are you awake?" Rosa whispered. Her voice was hushed but happy, filled with repressed excitement. Ruth and I admitted to being awake.

"The lights," Rosa hissed. "Could you turn on the lights?"

"Jesus," Ruth said and turned on the lights, which revealed Rosa turning slowly to stare at Ruth's toothbrush standing upright in the single mug provided by the management.

"I don't think that's kosher," Rosa said to the mug.

"Ah," said Ruth. "You don't think it's kosher? As far as I know my toothbrush is Jewish too. And who did you say you were dancing with?"

"Sven," said Rosa.

"Sven," said Ruth. "Blue-eyed Sven, the gorgeous deck steward?"

"Yes," Rosa admitted. Joy had left her, and she sounded suddenly wary.

"And I suppose you think Sven is kosher? At least you think he's more kosher than my goddamn toothbrush."

"I didn't think," said Rosa, drooping. She was close to tears. "He's so nice. It's all so difficult out here." Clearly she was offering an apology—to God, perhaps, or perhaps to Ruth. But my sister had turned her face to the wall and heard no more.

✧

For the first time in my life I found myself in a wardrobe quandary. For seven years I'd been secure, wearing the school uniform on weekdays, my Sunday dress on Sundays: navy blue gym tunic and striped blouse in winter, gingham checked cotton dress in summer. The occasional skirt and blouse or slacks and pullover passed down from Valerie made do for Saturdays and holidays. Ruth had acquired a few party dresses over the years; there was the yellow taffeta dance gown sent to her from America by our cousin Clare as well two or three other articles of festive apparel. Perhaps I could borrow something from her.

"Sure," she said. "Help yourself!" And she was off for a game of deck tennis with the sergeant.

Helping myself would have been easier if I had had an idea of what you were supposed to wear on a Saturday night shipboard date. Taking my template from Hollywood I assumed that a little black frock accessorized with high-heeled pumps and a scarf would be the acceptable thing—if either Ruth or I had had a little black frock, high-heeled pumps, and a scarf. And even then there would be the remaining problem of underwear: I possessed a half-dozen cotton vests and matching cotton bottoms as well as three pairs of dark blue gym knickers which no one in Hollywood, on or off screen, would have been caught dead in.

I had lunch on deck with Ruth and her retinue. The war bride was extremely negative about my projected plans for the evening and rolled out stories about unpleasant things that sailors had done to female members of his family. He kept looking at Ruth, presumably checking if she approved of his disapproval; as far as I could tell, she was just faintly amused by his tales of cataclysm. "You do what you want," Ruth said to me, over his warnings. "You're old enough to make up your own mind." But her eager swain—most probably, I would presume in retrospect, because he never listened to women anyway—didn't hear her.

And the funny thing is that if he hadn't been so pompous about it all I probably would have decided, entirely on my own, not to meet my sailor. I was not looking forward to the evening, which was beginning to strike me as having the potential to become quite sleazy. I was worried about the older man—the man with the bad skin and the slimy manner who had proposed the date to me in his friend's name. He seemed more suitable for a character in *Rain* than one in *Lorna Doone*. But with the war bride nattering away with his warnings there was nothing for it but to ignore them and try my luck with sleaze.

So a few minutes before nine I was ready to go. I can't remember which of my sister's dresses I had decided to borrow; what do you wear to a tawdry rendezvous? In those days of rationing, even my sister's wardrobe was quite minimal, and I think I chose something undistinguished and unemphatic, something that expressed my general yearning to disappear until tomorrow, at which time, my date having already taken place, I could simply recall what it had been like without actually having to go through with it. A major sticking point, of course, was my underwear. I do remember that. The ribbed-knit vest was relatively harmless, but the knickers were a disaster. And there was no way around them.

So I was quite relieved when I found that I couldn't get out of the cabin. Dutifully, I tried my best. I worked on the lock. I pushed the door. I shook the handle. I beat my fists against the door and kicked it. Then I sat down on my bunk and thought things over; I was engulfed by a happy feeling that I would not need to face my sailor.

My state of bliss lasted perhaps three minutes before outrage took its place. An urgent anxiety relating to the unavailability of bath and toilet nagged at the back of my mind. And what if the SS *Gripsholm* were to hit an iceberg? I would descend to the ocean floor, a prisoner of my cabin, while Ruth sailed away to safety with the war bride and the sergeant in one of the lifeboats.

"Help!" I shouted, throwing myself against the locked door in earnest. "Help me! Help!"

In due time, a steward on duty arrived and, sounding petulant, asked from the other side of the door what the matter was. I told him, close to hysteria, what the matter was.

Apparently it wasn't the same steward bribed by the war bride to lock me in. Or so I surmise. In any case, he went to get someone with the right key and they let me out; and though the general outline became clear enough over the next few days, I have never to this day really found out the details of my captivity.

Slightly disheveled from my jailbreak, somewhat flustered and rather late, I went to the bar to meet my sailor after all.

☆

The first person I saw in the bar was Ruth, flanked by her two suitors. The war bride immediately announced guilt for my incarceration by exclaiming, "What the hell are you doing on the loose?" while the sergeant and Ruth both looked mystified by his outburst.

"Come sit," Ruth said, pointing toward the chair next to her.

But I shook my head. I had seen my sailor at another table. He was sitting with the older man, and they were drinking something dark pink from little glasses. They leaped up joyfully when they saw me, and the older man immediately produced another little glass into which he poured some of the pink stuff from a bottle. Ruth was staring at me, grinning; the war bride was staring at me, scowling. He looked gratifyingly outraged as I lifted my little glass filled with the dark pink stuff that later experience revealed to have been Cherry Heering. I drained it in a few large gulps.

Cherry Heering makes an excellent topping for chocolate ice cream, and it might be rather good warmed, set ablaze, and poured over thin, crisp pancakes. As a digestif, however, it lacks the essential digestibility, and if you are thinking of drinking it through the evening, consider a single-malt scotch—or almost anything else—instead. Not that I got drunk, exactly. And I didn't get sick exactly either. What happened was that the entire evening, from the time I took my first sip of cordial to the moment when I gratefully shut the door of the cabin again behind me, is covered in my memory in a thick layer of dark pink malaise. The whole experience of my first kiss and of my general dissolution from a properly dressed and coiffed adolescent girl to a random collection of limbs and body parts trailing a variety of loose garments is considerably less vivid to me now than the despair I felt even at the time about my shameful ignorance about everything. Until my entire, inappropriate wardrobe, from borrowed dress to unsuitable knickers, lay about me in disorder, dislodged from its original position, I had had no idea how appallingly innocent I was. How lacking in even the rudiments of an education in basic existence. At least, I seem to recall, even in the middle of mounting panic I was making a list for myself of What I Should Know About for Future Reference.

It would be nice to think—it would add a furbelow of wit to the occasion—if I could report that my gym knickers saved my virtue. But they didn't because my virtue was never in danger. I suspect that my sailor, though not nearly as innocent as I was, was sufficiently inexperienced so that his friend, the older man with the bad skin, had worried about him and had been instrumental in organizing this date. And though the sailor accomplished most of the things one is supposed to accomplish on a first date, and possibly a bit more than that, it was without expertise and without enthusiasm.

I don't remember the exact order of events: I downed several Cherry Heerings and then my sailor led me out onto the deck where there was dancing in progress. After watching a few dances we retreated into a dark corner where my sailor offered me my first cigarette, which I accepted and which increased my malaise tenfold. Then he began tentatively to peel me and duly provided my first kiss. The experience suggested that, like me, he felt the entanglement of tongues and the general enterprise of making oneself busy in someone else's mouth lacked a necessary charm. But we went through with it.

At this point it seemed about time to call it a night and go our separate ways to bed. With that in mind I said "Brrrr" several times and clutched my arms around my still more or less covered bosom, signifying chill.

"Poor baby," he said—it was the only English he knew—and he shepherded me downstairs to a small lounge, a deserted lounge with a piano in it. The peeling process continued. I think I was pretty much divested when he retreated slightly from what he was about to ask me how old I was. He did this by pointing at himself and making a count of eighteen on his fingers and then pointing questioningly at me.

"Fifteen," I said, putting up the fingers of both hands once and then the fingers of one hand. I was still fourteen, of course, but it was, after all, only a lie by a few weeks.

"Poor baby," said my sailor and withdrew even further, leaving my ribbed cotton underthings where they lay at half-mast. I suppose neither of us had any idea what we were supposed to do next. I wanted desperately to be back in my safe warm bunk, but it seemed churlish and—worse—childish to flee. I still have no idea what my sailor wanted or what, if anything, he expected from me. What he did was sit down at the piano and start to play it. He wasn't bad. He went through a couple of Strauss waltzes quite creditably, and then he played "Alexander's Ragtime Band" and "Lady Be Good."

I managed to reclothe myself fairly completely by the time a bell struck six. "Goodnight," he said politely, and left.

✡

One or two loose ends remain, trailing from my memory untidily like threads from a petticoat. Did the gray man, as we were leaving the bar, really give me a little rose bouquet, a single rose tied to a piece of greenery? And a small box containing a Woolworth ring? It seems unlikely but then it's equally unlikely that I would make them up. I think I remember stuffing them both, the ring and the rose, into the wastebasket under our unkosher toothbrushes. Then I got into my bunk as quickly as I could, pulled the sheet over my head, closed my eyes tightly, and remained unkissed for at least the next three years.

✡

For the rest of the voyage I spent most of my time with a few of the younger refugees. Bruna was occasionally with us, but I remember none of the others except the sick boy on crutches who liked our company. Like Anne Frank, of whom we had not yet heard, he had spent the war in a Dutch attic. He was afflicted with a rheumatic illness that would not allow him to spend too much time in the sun—in any sense of the phrase: it was unlikely, that is, that he would live for more than a few more years. But despite this—or perhaps even because of this—he was extraordinarily pleased with trivialities: the feel of the deck chair, the taste of his coffee, the sound of the dance band hacking away at "Jealousie." He read almost constantly and spoke rather little, though I remember he teased me a bit about my extreme youth—I was the youngest of the group—and about my extreme seriousness.

He had found a stack of *Readers' Digests* somewhere and read the jokes and the riddles in it aloud to us. And though I don't think I paid very much attention to him at the time, in my memory it's his gnarled image, valiant on crutches, stalwart in good cheer, that comes to me most warmly, the one keepsake of the voyage I cherish in recollection.

✡

Having achieved my kiss, my next and final enterprise before I stepped onto American soil was to see the Statue of Liberty before anyone else did. So on the day we were due to sail into New York Harbor I got up at dawn, stood up on the deck, and looked earnestly westward. Every time a tall outline defined itself in the far distance I felt a rush of adrenaline, a sense that this was it and if I wasn't exactly on American soil yet, I was at least in American waters. Then when the outline was revealed to be only a tanker or a lighthouse after all, my excitement abated and I waited for the next possibility to disappoint me. It was several hours before I finally gave up and went down to get some breakfast before it would be too late for them still to be serving it.

And there at breakfast was Ruth. She'd been among the missing all night long and when I'd woken up that morning, her bunk had still been empty. I had had a fleeting thought that she might have fallen overboard, but my sister wasn't someone you could easily imagine falling overboard. She might jump, possibly, on a dare to see if the best time she could make in her Australian crawl was fast enough to keep up with the ship. And if that had been the case, I was secure in my belief that her Australian crawl could keep up with anything and that she'd emerge from the Atlantic no worse for wear except for being a bit damp.

Still, it was a relief to see her at breakfast, devouring several croissants and a pile of scrambled eggs. She was still in the dress I'd last seen her in the night before, my cousin Clare's yellow taffeta dance dress, which looked a bit deflated. Ruth, however, was triumphant. She'd been with five or six other economy-class passengers, and they'd crashed the first-class final-night party. They'd been thrown out, she said. Three times. Finally, someone in first class had admired their persistence—or been drunk enough not to care any more—and had taken them under his wing as his "guests." After the dance band packed up and left they'd ended up in his stateroom drinking scotch and playing penny poker for the rest of the night.

"I'm beat," she said, yawning with deep satisfaction at a night well spent. But since it seemed likely that we were about to disembark she assumed there would be no time to rest.

In fact, she'd have had two days. We were towed into harbor, advancing slowly through a chaos of other ships and tankers and barges right under the majestic nose of Liberty. By that time, by the time we got to her, jaded by lighthouses and other mistaken sightings, I'd pretty much lost interest. Besides, she paled beside New York's gleaming, astonishing outline. Which itself began to be a bit tedious as we sat there through a day and then a night and then another day, the unchanging backdrop to our growing impatience and dwindling expectations. It began to seem highly likely that we'd never land—that we'd be sent back whence we had come and ultimately drift forever in mid-Atlantic like the Flying Dutchman.

Discussing it, Ruth and I recall that there was a labor dispute of some sort. Longshoremen or customs or harbor control. Who knows? Our mood, the almost universal mood among the *Gripsholm*'s passengers, packed and waiting, was souring more by the minute. The wire-haired, muscular young American and his Sweetie-Dahlin' had been observed inhaling each other until the moment we'd come into harbor, when they'd entwined ferociously and parted with such reluctant force that one mentally heard the noise of suction as they separated. Now they were observed, singly and divided, looking longingly over the railing at the shore. During the two days while we waited, stalled, they did not, at least not within our sight, come together again. I suppose when you're ready to leave, you're ready to leave.

The gnarled boy, uniquely, remained cheerful. He could wait happily for a good long time to see his relatives, he explained; he'd never met them before and he wasn't anxious to meet them now. At least on the *Gripsholm* he knew where he was.

"Yes, we know where we are and we know that we'll never get out," someone lamented.

"Oh, be glad you're here in such a nice safe place. Just look over there," the gnarled boy said, pointing toward the tip of Manhattan. "Those things that look like cars. They can't be cars. They're too huge. They're as big as tanks. And there are so many of them. Thousands and thousands, millions of them. What if the people here are the right size to fit those tanks? What if they're hostile? Do we really want to meet them?"

Though we knew of course he was joking, we contemplated this in silence. For the first time it occurred to me that perhaps, that very likely, I didn't.

And then suddenly, and entirely without warning, debarkation was underway. Everything was in motion and at the brink of panic. The immigration officials had come on board and a line had formed to see them; we were to be stamped and approved in order of appearance for entry into the Promised Land. People were running around trying to find out where they should go and what they needed to show when they got there. Most of the passengers had been made furious by the long delay and uncertainty. The decks and gangways were in chaos. I looked for Ruth, whom I found looking for the sergeant. He had offered to take her two Swiss watches and the gold and platinum jewelry we had carried with us for seven years all the way from Karlsruhe; he had told her that as an American and as a serviceman he could get these valuables through customs more easily than she could. Now, with watches, bracelets, and necklaces in pocket, he had disappeared.

"Shit," Ruth said. Along with a great many other Europeans we tried to get into a line that turned out to be for Americans only; so we found another line, already very long and filled with angry people pushing each other and shouting.

I had lost my pigskin suitcase, also a relic from Karlsruhe. I was sure I would never see it again but suddenly it appeared, solitary and abandoned, in a corner. Much of what I'd packed in it seemed still to be there, but someone had stepped through the suitcase. There was a large, jagged hole clear through it from top to bottom.

"Shit," Ruth said. "Can you believe this?"

So we arrived in New York two days late with a ruined suitcase and without the precious watches and jewelry, which we never saw again. It was not the best augury for what life might be like in America.

CHAMBER MUSIC

❧ I don't know how we managed to find Mother—or did she find us? I suppose both Ruth and I must have changed enough so it would have been difficult for her to recognize us as the same people who'd left her, two children, seven years before. And I certainly wouldn't have known her if my life depended on it; the Mother I had in my mind, the pale, tall, gently phlegmatic phantom with a sweet and unambiguous smile, did not share the smallest element of biology or character with the real thing. The Mother I had in mind, now I come to think of it, was composed in about equal parts of the idealized Anglo-Saxon mother of literature—Mrs. Darling, say, of *Peter Pan*—and my nursemaid, Dada, with whom I'd spent most of my Karlsruhe childhood. As the German nanny, Dada would have done rather well in England. She had the looks and the softness of personality for it, and though Mother later insisted that Dada didn't have the brains of a chicken, I suppose I had found her image psychologically useful as a bridge between my native country and my adopted one. Dada, with her light brown hair pulled back into a chignon and her starched white apron announcing cleanliness and domesticity, was something of a Teutonic archetype; and she had, in fact, followed her Teutonic programming after she left us, had joined the Party and become an enthusiastic Nazi. But that was later when I was already in England, and it naturally had nothing to do with my maternal imaging.

In any case, we did find each other, Mother and Ruth and I. The most likely scenario is that it was Ruth, who now says that she can't remember, who recognized Mother. All I seem to recall is that our reunion occurred among the luggage and that there was about equal confusion sorting out everyone's identity and finding our bags. Our four trunks, two apiece and too heavy to move without help, were lying with a great deal of other people's stuff waiting to be stamped by customs. My broken suitcase and the missing watches and jewelry remained broken and missing, symbols of the disheveled state of our arrival.

While we waited for a porter, I must have stared at Mother for a long time—and I think she didn't easily take her eyes away from me either. I was caught in total disbelief that this was She, was Her, was It—but at the same time I knew that, unarguably, it was. The moment of recognition was like that grim, shocked instant immediately after an accident when you don't believe that the blood on the windshield comes from your head at the same time that you know, with absolute certainty, that it does.

Mother was with a couple neither Ruth nor I had ever met before: a small, brittle, colorless woman, who at first I briefly considered might in fact be her, and a large, flaccid, colorless man. They introduced themselves as our distant cousins, the Dryes, with whom we were all to spend the night before going to New Jersey to Aunt Liesel's new house in Vineland. After a few weeks in Vineland getting used to America, I was to live in Great Neck in a house next to the one where Mother was living. The people I was to live with and with whom I was apparently expected to pass the rest of my life were also from Germany. They had two small children. I was going to help take care of the children.

I am not sure what Ruth and I were expecting. Mother hadn't written much about plans for our arrival, and I suppose that both Ruth and I must have assumed there would be an apartment somewhere where Mother and the two of us would live. We both had had the expectation of coming home, taking it for granted that there would be some sort of home to come to. I know that it had not occurred to either of us, pried loose of England, that we would be cast adrift in America. We hadn't deeply considered what sort of home would be available, though I suppose I was hoping for something exciting and exotic: skyscrapers and Al Capone and palm trees and swimming pools. My sense of American geography and history was uncertain, and I think more than anything I expected to be surprised.

In the event, in fact, surprise was exactly what I got. I was smitten by it at once during that first night that Ruth and I spent, sleepless, on the Dryes' pullout sofa. Elmhurst was nothing, thinking about America, that I would have easily imagined. There was a single window in the room, which looked out on a brick wall; my unforgiving memory of that is vivid, and the brick wall remains among the most palpable artifacts I have in mental storage. The smell coming from the airshaft, however, has diminished somewhat through time, although the atmosphere it brought in with it, the wind of defeat and exile and hopelessness, stays with me.

That weather of despair always hangs at the edge of my memory of my first two years in America; it threatened to cover the world of the refugees among whom Ruth and I now lived. From what I have read and heard in the accounts of those who experienced it, it is very much the same atmosphere that at the time lay over the landscape of what until recently had been the Third Reich, a landscape now in ruins. Germany had imploded; those caught in it, like the survivors exiled from it, were smothered in a cloud of hopelessness almost as dense as that which covered the dead who had perished there, victims and executioners alike.

There is a climate of displacement, a sour, heavy breath that is exhaled by homelessness, discouragement, and a feeling of life without function, and it probably looms over a rather larger portion of the globe than one is entirely willing to admit. Especially, of course, after a war. But even in the normal, embattled conditions of peace the fog of apathy will surprise one occasionally in quite unexpected settings. I recall once when we drove into the featureless wasteland making up the outskirts of Buenaventura in Colombia that it completely obscured the sunshine. And it settles habitually in familiar places as well: the streets of small New Hampshire towns, for instance—like Hillsborough or Hinsdale—where the genetic reservoir of adventure and energy has leaked dry over the last three hundred years and the descendents of the original colonizers endure in their own despairing, rural Elmhursts with a view of discarded trucks substituting for the blank brick wall.

☆

Even on that first evening of our traumatic reintroduction it was obvious that the Elmhurst desperation was almost as foreign to Mother as it was to Ruth and me. She was an alien in the Dryes' apartment, and apparently, whatever sorrows and disappointments had assaulted her in the seven years since we'd last seen each other, she had somehow managed to keep herself in fighting trim.

I'm not sure what it was in her manner that told me this, any more than I can define exactly what could have sustained her over the years, what, in fact, continued to keep her until her death four decades later an ironic, interested, tough old warrior, undaunted by fortune— outrageous or otherwise. She would have put it down to her famous and famously nonexistent sense of humor, of course. I'd offer a more original cause: her uncanny talent for looking monstrosity in the eye and failing to flinch. It wasn't only courage on her part that kept her head unbowed; it was an innate and almost perverse curiosity urging her on to look through the microscope, to sift through the muck, to study whatever horror happened to lie before her. She was cursed with a cool intelligence that did not readily let her go or allow her to relax into the received ideas and preapproved emotions that make life easy and allow one to retreat from it almost imperceptibly. Very good vision was the dominant trait in her character, and it forced her, even in the most catastrophic situations, to see the unpleasant particles that went into making up the monstrous whole and to react to them with interest rather than disgust.

She also had an indomitable sense of who she was. Or perhaps I should say of what she was: she was a doctor. Having been deprived of her function in society by the obscure workings of antagonistic regimes on both sides of the Atlantic was not the same thing as being deprived of her vocation. Scrubbing floors, diapering babies, she was still a physician, impelled by her very essence to reenter her profession at the first chance she had.

But all this is hindsight of course. At the time, meeting this odd duck of a woman who seemed to work at being as far removed from my invented, ideal Mother as anyone in the same species could get, certainly seemed to me by far the most disastrous thing that had ever happened to me. It was incalculably worse than being cast off into the strange, kind, tweedy bosom of Aunt Helen seven years earlier, this second exile into the charge of a stranger stranger than the first exile had been.

In retrospect it appears to me to have been a sort of inadvertent torture, like having your already broken foot stepped on or having a needle stuck through an aching sore. It reestablished the damage done by the first almost-healed wound, doubled it, multiplied it, and rendered the injury unbearable.

But luck had it that my mother's life was long, useful, and surprisingly happy; there was time for the various scars to heal over after all. Now when I look in the mirror, my mother quite peacefully looks back at me. When I leaf through photographs of Ruth and me at various family events through the years I can see not merely a family resemblance but the progression of a specific genetic motif. And unlike most of my friends who find it pretty depressing to discover that they're aging into their parents, I seem to like the model on which I'm destined to mold my waning years.

But let us not wax euphoric too precipitously. First we had to get through the night in Elmhurst and then the summer in Vineland, New Jersey.

✡

Vineland, New Jersey, had, *faut de mieux,* become the center of our exiled tribe. For in the end, all the family on my mother's side had come to America: Mother, grandmother, aunt, uncle, cousins. Ruth and I were the last to arrive. And the chicken farm that Aunt Liesel and Uncle Julius had bought with the money saved from their days as two of Limburg's grandest entrepreneurs, being the only property owned by any family member, became the meeting place for all of us. It was there that I spent most of my first three American summers.

Vineland, established in the mid-1800s, was, and still is, the center for the surrounding agricultural communities. They are communities mainly of truck farms since the climate of southern New Jersey is apparently good for tomatoes and other vegetables. In 1946, however, Vineland had become a town of chickens. I have no idea how they got into it. My guess is that a family of Jews who had fled fairly early on from the Nazi regime for unknown and probably random reasons had bought a poultry farm from someone in Vineland; eggs might have seemed a promising career for someone starting out fresh in a new country. When the poultry farm of those first immigrants prospered, when the chickens thrived and the eggs multiplied, more German refugees moved in: not farmers experienced with livestock, but erst-while professors, innocent about the land, former doctors, lawyers, businessmen. They were eager to try this novel chicken venture, which offered at least a reasonable livelihood for the outlay of rather modest capital.

And by and large they seem to have succeeded. Philadelphia was close and so was New York, with its insatiable appetite, growing larger daily, for almost everything and certainly for eggs. In Vineland, by 1946, if you weren't in chickens you were in chicken feed or chicken sexing or egg distribution or poultry shed building, something, in any case, which was ancillary to the raising of fowl. They ruled the town.

Aunt Liesel and Uncle Julius had settled in a little white house neatly nestled into a street of other little white houses. There was a garden that wrapped around the house's front like an apron, protect-ing it from the messy business of what went on in the back where rows of long sheds held hundreds upon hundreds of white chickens. This was still during a time before the raising of chickens had become to-tally mechanized and the poor creatures had been reduced to being mere egg-laying protoplasm and protein; but even then, egg farming was becoming mechanical. You don't raise chickens by the tens of thousand and expect them to retain much of their natural charisma. The enterprise lacked charm. But at least in those days you knew you were dealing with flesh and blood, not to mention chicken shit. You had to collect eggs manually twice a day, see to the water's being fresh and the feed troughs being full; you had to clean out the coops and spread new straw and sawdust on a regular schedule.

I have known chickens in other countries, in other times, and un-der other conditions. I'd met a few as a child—in the Black Forest and on the farm in Wales that first summer we were in England and we had raised some for eggs for a short time in Leeds. More recently, I've been introduced to the pampered poultry kept almost like pets by several of my friends and admired some quite remarkable chickens wandering around Cielole, a little town not far from San Giminiano. Chickens can be excellent and interesting creatures, talkative, temperamental, and exceedingly beautiful, each one with a quite distinct personality of her own. What seems to be essential for the growth of a decent, natural sort of chicken with a character you can respect—the sort of bird, in short, that you can actually love before you regretfully eat it—is its existence within chicken social norms. A hen to come to anything needs society: space and communication and hierarchy, and, emphatically, the presence of at least one resident rooster to make life interesting.

I suppose my uncle's chicken farm, which had none of this, embodied the first step down from the natural chicken state, the first degradation of Chicken into Product that by now has become complete.

Uncle Julius hated his chickens. I think that for him they embodied every inch of the vast downward slope, from his former life in Limburg as the owner of Limburg's largest department store, to his current life in America as not much more than a farm laborer. He spent his day outside in the chicken coops, feeding hens, collecting eggs, cleaning out. He spent his nights washing off the eggs and putting them in large square cartons of five dozen each. They had to be sorted according to size and color—the larger and whiter the better in those days—and they had to be tested to make sure there were no cracked ones among those packaged. "Crackers," my uncle called them, and put them aside for use in Aunt Liesel's kitchen.

Neither of my cousins, not Kurt, not Clare, went anywhere near the egg business: not, I think because of any reluctance on their part but because it was tacitly understood that their father and mother held them above the menial labor the farm entailed. They were the hope for the future, destined for better things.

Uncle Julius did, however, have one helper; the second black man I had ever spoken to. The first black man I had ever spoken to, a Kenyan in his thirties, had visited us in Leeds and had spent a weekend with us there at the end of the war. My firm belief at the time had been that he was an African prince, or possibly even a king; and in retrospect, considering the cut of his dark blue suit and his slightly amused manner, this still seems not unlikely. He was something quite elegant I am sure, though I am still unclear whether the source of the elegance lay in diplomacy or in the Church. He had an Oxbridge accent so I imagine that he had an Oxbridge education as well.

Not even the darkness of his skin suggested any kinship with Uncle Julius's helper; it was dark and lustrous and bore no resemblance to the old-coffee grayness of the farmhand's. They were as different from each other as I was from Shirley Temple.

I think Uncle Julius's helper had a Biblical name, Samuel or Josiah or Amos, something on that line, although his existence was anything but Biblical. I never saw him dressed in anything but the ragged pants and white undershirt he wore for his chicken chores. As he lumbered among the sheds carrying sacks of feed or wheeling barrows full of shavings he always kept his head down and slightly turned away so I am not sure, even now, what he looked like except that he was tall and loose limbed. He was indistinct and miserly of speech, and the only time I saw him smile was when he visited the dog my uncle kept perpetually chained by the chicken coops—how they would have been appalled in England—a captive guard, deprived of liberty for the sole purpose of keeping raccoons and foxes away. Now and then in the evening after his day's work was finished I would see my uncle's helper carrying odd bones or broken eggs or scraps from his own supper out to the dog, who had no name. And the two of them would sit there amicably for a while and wait for the sunset together.

The first time I spoke to him was when Aunt Liesel sent me to his place one Saturday morning to give him a piece of her apple cake. He had put a little oil stove into one of the smaller chicken coops and turned it into a makeshift home. I was amazed when that life-in-a-box was revealed to me, neat, crowded with oddments of crockery and chairs and a tiny table and also blessed, incongruously, with stacks of *National Geographic*s, which filled up the entire space under the neatly blanketed cot. I had been quite reluctant to go there; I suppose I must have been infected by my aunt's evident apprehension at the thought of going there herself. But when I opened the door to the little shed where my uncle's helper lived there was a sudden strong whiff of pipe tobacco and it reminded me comfortingly of Uncle Bourke.

✡

Vineland, New Jersey, is not a likely place for one's first, passionate discovery of beauty; but Vineland, New Jersey, nevertheless, is exactly where I first did discover it. I'd made a stab towards esthetics before, of course, whipping myself up to great enthusiasms for Shelley and Byron and Keats. But these had rather more to do with their profiles than with their poetry. I knew that "Hail to thee, blithe Spirit" was famous, and in some abstract corner of my mind I think I could understand that "My heart aches, and a drowsy numbness pains/ My sense" might be beautiful. But I took this pretty much on faith and on the witness of other people, and I certainly wasn't roused to any deep yearnings of the heart. The deep yearnings of the heart I reserved for my contemplation of the poets' likenesses and a consideration of their untimely deaths: during most of my adolescence, in an abstract and idealistic sort of way, I was an obsessive necrophiliac.

It was the Rose of Sharon bushes in Aunt Liesel's front yard that introduced me to real beauty and to the effect that such beauty has on the unsuspecting spirit. When she first moved to Vineland she planted a couple of the bushes toward the side of the yard, to screen the henhouses, and now, six years later, their flowers made valiant headway in the heat and humidity of the summer. In the drowsy evenings, they touched the heavy, sugared scent of a neighboring honeysuckle with an edge of tartness. Even now when I walk in a garden where the smell of hibiscus is mixed with sweetness the Vineland summer comes back to me in its totality with its poignant mixture of misery and loveliness.

The misery, of course, is easy enough to explain. It was the result of being cast adrift on an alien shore. There is no mystery about the misery. I wasn't even exactly homesick for England. I had just turned fifteen after all, and at fifteen, eager to get to the next page, try the untrodden path and leave the old behind you, you're not really anxious to go back anywhere where you've been before. There was, in short, a certain advantage, a certain adventure, to leaving England. The problem was that I knew I could never return there and that there didn't seem to be any advantage or adventure to being here in a dull, hot place that was not my home.

The element of loveliness, however, was complex, far more complex than that of misery. It comes into my mind now not as anything specific, but as an atmosphere that incorporates diverse and opposing elements: night and day, indoors and outdoors, silence and sound. The image of the huge red flowers of the Rose of Sharon bushes returns to me on a melody of a Schubert trio, which in my memory drifts from the little white house on a stifling, honeysuckle-laden summer night, and which in turn ushers in a sense of unutterable loneliness and desolation. Loneliness and desolation overwhelmed me in those days. But they themselves were beautiful in some deeply occult way; or at least they were necessary for the perception of what was beautiful. The profundity of my unhappiness gave everything a new resonance and seriousness; it enriched even trivialities and made whatever was at all meaningful, overpowering. I suppose wretchedness can be a sort of lens through which you see the world enlarged, enhanced, and clarified. It perhaps has a similar effect to finding out that one has only a month to live: it intensifies what is important and diminishes what is not. It makes one pay attention. In Vineland, I paid attention and found that I had an appetite for things of which, until then, I'd been completely ignorant.

✲

Music, for example.

I am not naturally musical; but it was understood by almost everyone in the Europe of my childhood that an ability to torture the

piano was required for civilized life. Ruth had learned to play in Karlsruhe and was old enough when we arrived in England that when she
decided she had been cultivated quite enough already and needed no
further refinement, her opinion counted. Di and Val, however, were
taking lessons, and had been for years. And by the time I was nine, it
became my turn too.

My first teacher—I forget her name—was a young woman just
slightly on the far side of thirty, dark haired, dark eyed, and soft-
voiced. She touched the notes delicately, almost as if she were afraid
of making too much noise, and she seldom spoke except by way of in-
structing me. At the end of one lesson, I seem to remember, she sighed
for the past, lost musical talents of her own early teachers and of her
invalid mother with whom she lived. She seemed gently absent even
when she was there, which was every Wednesday afternoon at four.
She came, punctually, each week, for several months. And then one
Wednesday she didn't come.

I heard later that the previous weekend she had drowned herself.
She had put stones in her pockets and walked into the Aire River,
which passed close by her house, just like Virginia Woolf—and in
1941, the same year as Virginia Woolf, who perhaps had been responsible for giving my teacher the blueprint of her suicide.

She was replaced by Miss Ramsbothame. It was Miss Ramsbothame's top, in fact, rather than her bottom, that was ovine. She
was a tall, plain, gangling woman, with a desperation of red-gray
hair around her near-sighted eyes; but she knew music, and as soon
as she heard me stumble through my scales she knew I was a lost
cause. So after a minute or two listening to me demolish the first
bars of *Für Elise* she would take over herself and play for me. She also
taught me a few of the basics of musical construction, chattering
about themes and variations, harmony, polyphony, and syncopation,
leitmotifs and sonata form: anything rather than having to go
through the pain of listening to me thump on the keys. And in the
process of heading me away from the piano she gave me a far more

useful education than I would ever have had if she'd tried to force me toward it.

Even so, I remained abysmally ignorant. When I arrived in Vineland I had heard no serious music whatever; and for years, for decades, Bach and the baroque continued to elude me. So did the pre-baroque and, not surprisingly, anything later than the turn of the twentieth century—nothing contemporary for my money nor even anything delicately impressionistic. You could have your Debussy and your Delius along with your Hindemith and your Bartok. But at least I began to listen. And I found that what I most longed for, what my frayed heartstrings cried out for, was something with a touch of Romantic yearning to it. Possibly even Romantic agony. It was emotion, not formal enchantment, that drew me toward itself and told me that Suffering was Beauty.

Not that I should be ironic about something so compelling and sustaining—a solace, but more than a solace—an emerging part of myself. That summer at Aunt Liesel's house I discovered a depth of feeling that had lain dormant throughout my English childhood. Some idle segment of my mind opened itself; and though the Romantic spirit may have been responsible for turning the key, very soon a more eclectic range of sounds began to drift in. Even in my ignorance I found that the elegant phrases of Haydn and the witty fragments of Mozart that came my way were remarkably satisfying.

And in Vineland, music was everywhere. There were the quartets and trios played at my aunt's chamber music evenings, there were the Schubert *Lieder* and Chopin études that my cousin Clare practiced daily on the small grand piano in the big front room. But whenever someone wasn't playing or practicing, there were also the records to which Aunt Liesel listened while she was cooking and cleaning and ironing and mending. In a household where a rigid control seemed to govern a great part of daily life, music was the one area of exception. Music was free, and even I, the lowliest and youngest person there, was given unconditional access to the phonograph.

✡

When I think back on Vineland, it strikes me now that her music was perhaps the one element that my Aunt Liesel had brought with her to America whole and unblemished. The rest of her life had taken on an altered, diminished form—everything from her furniture to her interaction with those around her, which in Limburg had been swathed in the comfort of a long tradition of money but which in Vineland scraped against a constant, irritating necessity of daily and unaccustomed chores. Duty in Vineland was unending and unglamorous: a battle of screens and sprays against the well-armed hosts of mosquitoes, a war of soap and bleach and spices against filthy overalls and moldy bathrooms. It was a job in itself simply to close all the windows against the midday heat and then to open them again to catch any possible evening breeze; and there were always too many broken eggs waiting in the refrigerator for culinary inspiration. There was no one to help in the house: Clare was taking a degree at Glassborough State Teachers' College; Kurt had begun working with a local real estate company, selling chicken farms. Under the pile of house chores and farm chores and her own unbending sense of obligation, my aunt's life had become all but invisible.

But among the chicken coops, in the little white house with its linoleum floors and Montgomery Ward furniture, the Limburg luxe had miraculously survived. It had seeded itself in my Aunt Liesel's chamber music evenings when, once a month, she would invite a few of the neighbors in to play and to listen. She was an excellent amateur violinist, though she preferred to play second violin, leaving the role of first to an Italian neighbor, a professional who played freelance for orchestras in Trenton and Philadelphia. Sometimes the evening began slowly, haltingly. And it was interrupted at least once or twice for *Mandeltorte* and coffee. But despite these hesitations, music would fill the room: Mozart quintets, Haydn trios, Beethoven quartets—varied now and then with Brahms or Dvořák or César Frank.

The pieces they played they had played so often they must have been familiar to the point of being habitual; yet they did not become mechanical. Aunt Liesel went dutifully each week to the temple and allowed the blue-eyed young rabbi to hold her hand, as he held everyone's, as if reluctant to let it go; but I doubt if she worshiped at the temple. It was music that commanded her awe and the reverence of her friends who played it with her. They were immersed, as it were, in a deep meditation on their own shortcomings as they tried to breathe it into life. They tapped their feet, counting the measures: one-two-three, one-two-three, one-two-three. And their bows arced together and they bent forward furiously over their task.

And as they strained—one-two-three, one-two-three—to keep time and fuse their separate voices into an offering worthy of what they dimly reached for, Limburg began to drift into the room. It filled the air with a sort of yearning; and when the room at last overflowed with it, it floated out of the windows of the little white house and spread out over the humid summer fields. And the soul of a vanished world flowed out over Vineland and mixed with the scent of the honeysuckle.

UNDERSTANDING MOTHER

⌒⌒⌒ It was in Vineland and in the depths of adolescent despair that I discovered I had something of a knack for the paranormal that seemed to be shared by other members of my family. It was luckily a talent I'd no idea I possessed earlier while I was still in England, where I would have been obliged to try to smother it. To be respectable, you can do only one thing with a flair for the paranormal in England: you can see ghosts. To attempt anything else, anything more personal and inward such as prophetic visions or spiritual healing or even telepathy, is looked down upon as being foreign and trying too hard—a sure indication of a lower-class mentality; though Aunt Hilda, who sometimes heard voices, was not considered déclassé but simply mad.

Ghosts, however, are all right. I suppose they are all right in part because if you live in the sort of place where they are likely to appear it is probably very large, quite old, and somewhat prestigious. In any case, in England everyone I knew believed in ghosts and a great many people I knew, including Aunt Helen, had actually communicated with one or two interesting phantoms—ancient figments walking the battlement or appearing ephemerally in the dark corners of one's midnight awareness in an alien and uncomfortable bed.

One might be tempted, perhaps, to interpret English ghosts as Jungian harbingers of some sort of general historical guilt or at least some sort of general historical embarrassment; but they are seldom inclined to bring anyone a personal message. A proper English ghost is part of the environment, the effluvium of a long history, natural to the landscape—observed but not really engaged with. He, she, or it exists, apparently, on a quite different plane from the one inhabited by mortals and is invariably too self-involved, or perhaps too well behaved, to interfere with living persons.

Which is to say that English ghosts have little in common with American ghosts. I suppose we have such a short history to call our own on this side of the Atlantic that we cannot easily imagine unreconciled moments of the past becoming so palpable that they engender actual, ectoplasmic manifestations. And our American ghosts are nasty things—bred, perhaps, from our dour, Puritan beginnings—punitive and terrifying creatures, sent by the devil or other entities hostile to our best interests. American popular culture is filled with lethally haunted houses, diabolically possessed children, and avenging spirits that rise from tribal graveyards to destroy us by way of our television sets. Our specters, aberrant phenomena with vengeful intentions, are the vaporous equivalents of flesh-and-blood outlaws and vigilantes: violent and destructive, they direct themselves towards and against us.

But for the English, ghosts haunt a landscape quite aloof from ours—born in another dimension it is only occasionally that they drift, harmless and even amusing, into our own. No one I knew in England, not even one of those who had actually seen a ghost, asked himself why someone might become aware of such a manifestation or wondered what it signified. No one worried that the appearance of a ghoul in a remote castle hallway might foreshadow the downfall of the castle or the empire or suggest the death of the person seeing it. No one supposed that hearing loud crashes made by an energetic poltergeist in the manor kitchen could be the symptom of other mayhem or that the ability to hear and see these mystifying things was a sign of a rare and mysterious perception that should be explored and could prove to have further and more interesting applications. The paranormal for the English was Out There. If it touched on the real world, inhabited their own lives, or existed, God forbid, in their own skins, they didn't want to know.

The spectral manifestation to which Aunt Helen bore witness, for instance, had been a poltergeist, not seen but only heard, dragging its chains along the cold stone corridors during a nice summer weekend she and one of her sisters had spent at the country house of friends. The poltergeist, she reported, had groaned mightily as it went on its spectral way, and she had at first taken its loud and lengthy agony as poor Aunt Violet with a case of stomach flu, making a wretched trip to the bathroom. Being English and shy of mortifying Aunt Violet even further in her extremity, she had not rushed out with offers of comfort and paregoric; when she saw her sister perfectly well next morning, sitting down to a large country breakfast, she was pleasantly surprised. Aunt Violet, having of course heard the same horrible noises during the night and naturally mistaking them for Aunt Helen in a crisis of nocturnal misery, was equally amazed and equally pleased to see her sister in excellent spirits, helping herself to kippers and eggs. They were both quite charmed by the incident—and so were their hosts who hadn't heard boo from their poltergeist for years and were afraid they might have annoyed it somehow and caused it to leave them in high dudgeon. Far from attributing any sinister meaning to the affair, everyone involved remembered it with offhand pleasure in much the same way one might note the sighting of a rare specimen of flycatcher in the neighborhood.

✶

I doubt if any of my blood relations have ever seen a ghost even back in the Middle Ages, when seeing ghosts was pretty common. If they had seen a ghost, they would have taken it personally and worried about it. They would have felt obliged to develop a philosophy around the sighting, a theory of history and a system of prophecy going back a millennium into the past and forward a millennium into the future.

All members of my family are terminally devoted to reason; we are genetically logical people with an absolute need to establish a rational order upon the environment in which we live. Since the environment in which we live is constantly slipping into disorder and flirting with madness and marvels, we must remain constantly alert, ready to catch any inexplicable phenomena that might come our way so that we can wrestle with them and mortify them until they agree to fit themselves into the natural order. It is a tiring routine, and it keeps us on edge—always waiting for the next monstrosity to appear. We are seldom taken by surprise when the morning deals us a couple of monstrosities before breakfast; in the course of the day we expect a few freaks of nature, which we will then attack with algebraic logic and ingenious theories until they're reduced to a manageable size.

But we do not see ghosts. Had any member of my family seen one, that person would have gone to great lengths to rationalize, socialize, and naturalize it into something compatible with Newtonian physics, unlike the Harveys and their circle, who have always been matter-of-fact about bizarre events and don't feel that the odd occurrence here and there requires them to reorganize their entire cosmological system into a new, orderly, reasonable arrangement. If a ghost appears, it can simply be filed away under "ghost appeared," and no one feels the urge to explain matters any more definitively than just that.

Although ghosts remained aloof and invisible to my parents and cousins, my aunts and uncles and ancestors from time immemorial, other aspects of the mysterious and arcane have not been so fugitive. Despite our annoyingly sensible genes, many of us have a powerful sixth sense and an undeniable sensitivity to the metaphysical currents that slip through our rational defenses. I suppose they should wreak havoc with our nicely ordered calculations, but we have long since stopped classifying our paranormal sensitivities as being in any way peculiar. I think we catalogue them as simple extensions of more conventional intellectual processes, psychological attributes that are completely normal although presently still not understood. We treat them accordingly—in the same way the Harveys treat their ghosts—without much fuss. We're an anxious lot, of course, with a penchant for prophetic dreams and unpleasant intuitions that routinely force us to get the hell out of harm's way every two or three centuries—at a time when most people, less endowed with clairvoyant instincts, are still unaware that the political climate around them is becoming lethally hostile.

✴

So my mother took her sixth sense quite for granted, accepting its directives, I suppose, in much the same way she would respond to her senses of smell and touch. She did what it suggested without thinking twice about it—as she'd done what it told her to do when, at the last minute, she'd taken the train to Marseilles instead of the train to the boat with all her goods and chattels in its hold waiting for her in Holland.

I would guess that turning your back on all your possessions and leaving them behind because you've had a hunch that things will go from bad to worse in the Netherlands demands a considerable faith in hunches. More than once a tacit intuition had saved my mother's life, and I suppose it had saved Ruth's life and mine as well. Intuition also played a part in her professional expertise where it manifested itself in an uncanny ability to diagnose medical conditions invisible to the naked eye. She specialized in pregnancies, which she would announce confidently a month or two before they actually occurred. Celebrity pregnancies she could actually identify—or perhaps I should say pre-identify—via television. After staring intently at the image of some starlet on the *Ed Sullivan Show*, she'd announce, "She's going to have a baby." And sure enough, planned or unplanned, welcome or unwelcome, a baby would invariably make its appearance within the year. I have no idea how my mother did this, and it is quite possible, of course, that she cast such panic in my heart with her infallible birth prognostications that I have come somewhat to exaggerate her genius at them. They were certainly frequent enough and accurate enough to give a sexually active, unmarried daughter of childbearing years cause to be terrified.

Her insight into other medical matters was also a bit unnerving; she seemed able to diagnose sickness in passing, with the merest flicker of a sidelong glance. I am pretty convinced that her assessments were largely correct. She would name whatever illness we happened upon—while we were shopping at Kline's, say, or walking in Union Square—in her best sotto voce mode, which is to say in a stage whisper you could hear for miles. And I have often wondered how many of the weak and the wounded, having heard themselves pronounced destined for agonized death within a month, went home and shot themselves.

My mother had certain favorites when it came to diseases: she preferred those with moral overtones. So she was fond of emphysema (caused by smoking) and coronary disease (caused by overeating.) But she adored syphilis. She was sure that, until the introduction of penicillin, syphilis was a cause in the demise of any male who had died before he was forty. Not *the* cause, necessarily, but *a* cause. She didn't claim that all young men had positively died of it, just that they'd probably had it at the time of their death. It weakened them, she said, and weakness of any sort, moral, psychological, or pulmonary, was something she scorned. In her roster of those venereally compromised she included Keats and Chopin—though they were known to have succumbed to tuberculosis—as well as Schiller, Nietzsche, Schubert, and every single Christian saint and martyr, who must, somehow, have been touched in her imagination with the same green, syphilitic tinge apparent in the Grünewald Crucifixion, a version of which still hangs in the Karlsruhe Kunsthalle. She was quite adamant in these diagnoses; nothing would dissuade her. And recently, mulling over the spread of various newer diseases, I have thought that she was probably not altogether wrong.

☆

My mother was of course totally unaware that her gloomy outlook on health and history was at all odd. And she was also completely unconscious that her gift for telepathy was in any way unusual—she accepted it as incidental. It had no importance in her scheme of things. But one Thanksgiving—my first American Thanksgiving I believe—an old colleague of my mother's invited us to his house on Staten Island; he was a plastic surgeon, and it was a large and luxurious house with a big, book-lined living room where he put on a demonstration of telepathy to amuse us. He gave occasional semiprofessional shows of his mystic powers to leaven his serious, professional life in surgery. He performed the usual tricks—having us all think of little tasks for him to do while he was out of the room: sit in this chair, kiss that child, walk three times around the long oak coffee table. One of us would take his hand, and he would close his eyes until the message of what we had set for him to do reached him through our touch. At first with hesitation, then with more certainty, he would complete his task.

"Helene," he said. "I'm getting strong thoughts from you. You try doing it."

It was astonishing. She understood the thing to be done—take a book from the shelf, fill a glass with water and drink it—as soon as she opened the door, and she did our bidding immediately, as quickly as if we had shouted the order to her out loud. I was amazed; we were all amazed; and she was amazed at our amazement.

☆

It was during my first summer in Vineland that I recognized that I might have inherited a minimal sampling of this familial talent for the extrasensory. My cousin Clare had been given a Ouija board for her birthday. She was probably my only female relative with no psychic gifts whatever, and she had almost given up trying to use the pointer, which in her hands—or perhaps I should say under her finger—tended to wander in incoherent circles or to mosey around letters at random. "What will my husband do for a living?" she or one of her college friends would ask. And Ouija would spell out IMSKAQLZHAX.

I came in one afternoon to join them, put my finger on the pointer, and lo! to the same question its answer made perfect sense. "SELL EGGS," it read. Everyone stared at me, and I was transformed in a second from insignificant adolescent into potent witch. My presence at Ouija sessions was suddenly in great demand.

Through high school and during my first years of college I sharpened my talent for sorcery. In time, I dispensed with board and pointer and simply put an ABC on the floor with an upside-down water tumbler as the guide. Whenever I felt particularly dejected or ignored, I nibbled at the sweet taste of power that my mysterious gift bestowed on me. There was never a scarcity of other girls waiting to participate in fiddling with the occult. I even branched out, briefly, and took requests to put curses on people—usually on the unfaithful boyfriends of other girls in the dormitory.

I have several quite banal and fairly obvious theories as to why some of these maledictions actually came to pass, but no real explanation. In any case, there seems to be a negative balance between sex and witchcraft, and my spell-casting career blossomed very briefly at the late end of my adolescence—a time when my romantic life was sputtering to its dismal start. As soon as I managed to put Eros on any sort of regular schedule I completely lost the knack. Now, on the rare occasions when I can't resist trying to sling a whammy towards a public figure in need of a little anathema, my attempts are abject failures: far from becoming frogs or moral lepers disgraced in full public view—or, for that matter, far even from losing any election—those I curse inevitably flourish. Most of them have achieved high places—including the White House and the Supreme Court.

✶

But Ouija and casting spells were merely frivolous sidelines to a much more central function of the telepathic prowess I'd inherited through my mother: it was because of my extrasensory intuition that I could understand what she was talking about. She had a habit of speaking elliptically, launching thoughts into the blue like little helium balloons detached from their moorings. I suppose that thought flew through her brain so randomly and rapidly that she had no luck tying it down securely into words—especially, of course, into English words—and she'd leave her listeners without the foggiest idea as to what the hell she was getting at. Despite her heavy accent, her syntax and vocabulary were usually quite clear, but who knew what her reference was? Out of the blue, she might ask, for instance, "What happened to them then?" without offering any further context; or she might evoke a grander, more historical perspective with "That's how Napoleon would have done it," while failing to indicate what "that" or "it" might be.

But I invariably knew what she meant. "He's ugly," she announced once in the middle of nothing in particular, and I understood immediately that she was speaking of Max Rosenberg and that she was conveying her explication of why Max's wife was having an affair that, until the annunciation of that "he's ugly," I hadn't known about. That the affair was with their mutual dentist had to be explained to me, verbally, later—some things are not telepathically communicable.

This unshakable affinity with my mother embarrassed me acutely for years. Being alone in knowing what someone means brings one into an involuntary and inexorable alliance. It's a little like inadvertently meeting a neighbor you barely know at the Nairobi airport or being fellow Anglophones in a roomful of chattering Portuguese. The congruence of two even slightly related lives meeting in a strange universe sets up a deep and rather thrilling sense of comradeship, an inadvertent intimacy. And in the case of my mother and me, any intimacy was too close. When I first met her again on the New York dock I probably felt about my kinship with this alien organism pretty much the same way Luke Skywalker must have felt when he discovered Darth Vader was his father. How could I be the daughter of a woman who was the absolute antithesis of the image that the word "mother" brought to my mind?

And yet, even as I yearned to push her away from me and deny that we had any connection to each other, I proved our intimate ties with every word that I understood and that she had failed to say. It was a total calamity!

✻

During my first three years in America I lived with the Steinhardts at 30 Nirvana Avenue, two blocks from Great Neck High School where I studied and from which I graduated in 1949. The Reichenbergers, with whom my mother was living while she was reading for the New York State Boards, were at 28 Nirvana Avenue.

Immortalized in *The Great Gatsby* as West Egg, Great Neck had been a bastion of Long Island social order for more than a century. The rich had long since settled there—unless they were even richer, in which case they had an estate in King's Point, beyond my range of acquaintance since, of course, no one from King's Point came anywhere near a public high school. Those who served and serviced the rich and the even richer lived in Little Neck, the East Egg of Fitzgerald.

It had been ever thus. But by 1946 Great Neck was a town in transition; more and more new people, displaced in one way or another from their prewar securities, were moving in. The United Nations was getting established in Lake Success, just south of the town.

Asians, Africans, and a strange variety of Europeans from countries not represented on our imaginary map of that white and temperate continent were actually looking for apartments in town.

And even before they arrived, even before the war, the streets around Nirvana Avenue had turned into something of a settlement for German-Jewish refugees—for Reichenbergers, Steinhardts, Hubers, Wallachs, Lebachs, people who'd had the foresight and stoicism to up-root themselves from their comfortable world at a time when it was still possible to bring a little money with them.

This little world of exiles, clustered around the north end of Nirvana Avenue and reestablished in somewhat diminished and hum-bled circumstances in their new life, had still not entirely acclimatized themselves to America. They were apt, by and large, to take peculiari-ties of behavior and extremes of temperament as unsurprising, traits to be studied and possibly assimilated since very likely peculiarities and extremes were the standard here on this strange, new planet. Gen-erally insecure and still quite tentative, the newcomers were inclined to take the outrageous as not much more weird than anything else.

This was lucky for me. At fifteen, when the wrong label attached to your tennis shorts is cause for self-flagellation and social ostracism, the wrong mother points toward the end of the world. As I saw it, I had the mother of all wrong mothers. It was bad enough that this dis-approving, dark, intense foreigner had been foisted off on me in place of the graciously maternal personage I had imagined; it was worse that she palpably and unapologetically seemed to find me wanting in every area of my existence: in talent, grace, charm, and certainly, under-standably, affection. I thought I could see it in her eyes whenever she looked at me, and—although I had learned in England to be consis-tently polite towards my elders—I developed an automatic, quite in-voluntary sneer that switched itself on as soon as I found myself in her presence.

Great Neck was a fine place to work out such discomforts. De-spite their hard name and my prickly apprehension, the Steinhardts cushioned my malaise in the pleasant daily routines of their life and allowed me to flail through my maternal miseries—as well as the general anxieties of puberty—in remarkable comfort. I learned how to make *Weinschaum* and *Mandelkuchen* for the Steinhardts' monthly parties, how to stuff the Thanksgiving breast of veal, and how to squeeze juice from oranges for breakfast. I went to Silver Point Beach where the Steinhardts shared a cabana with several of their neighbors, and I played my first (losing) game of strip poker with the boys in the cabana next door. But best of all, on the third floor of 30 Nirvana Avenue, I had my own private small apartment with my own private bath. Somehow, quite suddenly, I had been accorded the status of grown-up. From my little maple desk, when I paused from writing tortured sonnets at my almost new Remington typewriter, I could look down on the beautiful, huge old cherry tree at the center of the Steinhardts' garden and watch the seasons pass.

Over the three years I lived with them I grew very fond of them all. I must have set a disastrous example of filial respect for the children, Roger and Carol Ann, but their parents seemed to be quite pleased with me. In fact I suspect that impatient, moody, generous Joe—a man probably not unlike my father—counseled my mother on more than one occasion to shrug off my growling hostility and try to ignore it. He may have known a bit about parental displeasure since he must once have been a rather appealing sort of bad boy himself. Like many former bad boys, he had grown up to be somewhat too anxious and too strict with his own children, but he was tolerant and warmly amused with everyone else's.

As for Ellen, as soon as I met her I adopted her as my confidante and guide in the New World. Born to considerable wealth—her father had owned a large label manufacturing company where Joe had worked—she approached her reduced life with gusto, intelligence, and a wry, unflickering edge of comedy. She had furnished the house handsomely with the rescued remains of her family's art collection. I remember some nice seventeenth-century Dutch landscapes and a lovely wooden Madonna from the early Renaissance that stood non-chalantly next to the sofa and looked out onto the quiet sidewalk of Nirvana Avenue.

So for three years I nursed my resentment in comfort at the Steinhardts', while my mother, preparing to become a doctor once again, studied for the New York State Boards. For most of those years I was in a state of extreme confusion. In my conscious thoughts I recorded emphatically that the gods had made a terrible mistake in assigning me *this* for a mother, and I would have been delighted if she had evaporated from the face of the earth. But quite against my will and contrary to the current of my aversion, my subliminal self seemed to have been caught in a sort antithetical, sub-rosa arrangement: it certainly didn't have my approval. But apparently, somehow, during the process of assigning daughters to mothers, the gods had programmed me to understand what and how mine was thinking. And if you understand what and how somebody is thinking, empathy is unavoidable.

I was trapped in a paradox—one of those nasty Cassandra inconsistencies that force you into battle with yourself.

I managed to wage a few battles with my mother as well, of course. I recall one involving the pressure cooker. Pressure cookers, I'd just read, had been known to explode, so I had decided to boil the potatoes the slow, old-fashioned way, thereby annoying my mother, who said that this was a waste of gas and, hence, money. She got very angry about it. I told her that perhaps I didn't share her values: I thought wasting gas and money was preferable to losing my life—but then, since she'd left my upbringing to total strangers, she probably considered my life quite insignificant. In another disagreement, which I think also addressed inappropriate cooking techniques, she accused me of being insane and I laughed and said that very likely I was insane; after all, most experts considered mental instability to be inherited.

In a matter of months my goal in life had changed: I was no

longer trying to be an English schoolgirl; I was in the running for the Queen of Sarcasm, skilled in the use of my weapon, a tongue sharpened to wound.

And anger in Great Neck was a far cry from anger in England, where any confession of real annoyance was considered an unfortunate sign of bad breeding. People got irritated there, of course, as often as they do anywhere else—one can't help feeling angry any more than one can help feeling dyspeptic. But like dyspepsia, which some cultures alleviate or even celebrate by public belching and farting, anger—which those same societies vent in intrafamily screaming and extrafamily blood feuds—is usually smothered by the English. Deprived of air, it dwindles to disdain, turns gray, and shrivels but never quite disappears. Once when Valerie had teased me I knocked the glasses off her nose and jumped on them—an act so outrageously beyond family norms that it remained unacknowledged and unaddressed. Valerie wore her second pair of glasses for the rest of the year, and I was told to sit quietly until I felt better; which, of course, my rage unvalidated by either comfort or punishment, I never really did. In England, my anger was not avoidable but it was always unsatisfactory.

And then too, it was dangerous. I understood that I had been taken on by all four Harveys as an integral part of their family, but it was, nevertheless, *their* family. I had arrived late and been taken on in an adjunct position. The very fact that I was bad tempered underlined my difference from them. I was unlike them in shape, thought, and sensibility, needing to camouflage my volatile and foreign soul to earn it a place in a wing of their peaceful house. The knowledge that I was an accessory, a temporary addition, had been central there to my definition of myself

My relationship with my mother presented me with no such misgivings. I could do battle with her quite casually. It was inexplicably comforting to be able to exercise my blatant hostility, which felt not only justified but totally safe. She was my mother, after all: our bonds were biological, psychic, and inexorable. I could loathe her at leisure, and what could she do to me that she hadn't already done?

☆

It took more than two decades for the two of us to come fully to terms with each other; but while I was still in Great Neck I had already begun to discard my adolescent perception that my mother's main business in life was nagging and disapproval. I realized—it was something of a shock—that I really liked her rather better than I liked any of the other mothers around. And she never criticized me about important things—my choice of friends, my study habits or lack of them, where I spent the money I earned babysitting, how I used my time. What was infuriatingly regular was her nagging about what I wore, how I dusted, the level of flame I used on the stove—mere triviality, all of it. It was her way, I suppose, of trying to signal to herself that she was still the parent that neither she nor I, after our seven years of separation, actually recognized her to be.

And then in the summer of 1949, the two of us went shopping. We had both reached a turning point in our lives. She had passed her Boards and begun an internship at the Booth Memorial Hospital on East 15th Street. She had become a doctor again, and she continued to be a doctor until, in 1976 at the age of 82, she finally retired from running the emergency room of the New York Infirmary. As for me, I'd just been given a grant from the Great Neck Women's Club and also a year's scholarship for tuition and maintenance from Mount Holyoke College.

So my mother and I were spending the afternoon at Ohrbach's to buy me some college clothes.

The New Look had arrived: the postwar, romantic look of prodigal fabrics, bouffant sleeves, and extravagant skirts that flared down to midcalf from their wide-belted, tightly cinched waists. I'd been relying on a few ancient skirts and dresses, augmented by the odd

222 • THE TIGER IN THE ATTIC

castoff given to me by Ellen or one of her friends. Everything I owned was a good three years old and in well-to-do, fashionable Great Neck, declared me Out. And here we were in Ohrbach's Juniors and College Shop, whose racks were loaded beyond capacity with dresses, skirts, coats, suits, blouses. Many of them were wildly elaborate; most of them had been copied, I suppose, from designer outfits shown just weeks before on Paris runways.

My mother was enthusiastically pulling out one thing after another, inspecting it, and then either replacing it or setting it aside for me to try on. We began slowly, two or three outfits at a time, and then gradually worked ourselves into a frenzy of acquisition. I still remember some of what we bought. There was a black taffeta number—a "cocktail dress" with balloon sleeves and black velvet collar and cuffs; a sort of flamenco dance dress with an uneven hem, also in black taffeta but with a ruffled, rustling, magenta underskirt; a navy blue two-piece suit with a vestigial peplum and a Peter Pan collar on its tight little button-up jacket; a brown and yellow wool suit with yellow velveteen buttons and trim; a long maroon and blue plaid jacket; several pairs of slacks for it to go over; many pieces of lingerie; and two pairs of pajamas.

It was as close as I've ever come to living one of those dream fantasies that have probably been dear to the female psyche since prehistory and certainly since long before the fairy godmother did Cinderella's instant makeover. From Bette Davis's blossoming in *Now, Voyager* to Richard Gere's upgrading of Julia Roberts in *Pretty Woman*, it is one of Hollywood's central stories. I saw something just last week, I think, though I can't remember what, in which the heroine, looking as much like a frump as a film star can look, entered Macy's or Bloomingdale's or Barney's and emerged through the same revolving door seconds later transformed into an embodiment of chic and glamour. Minions—beauticians, doormen, sales personnel—followed her with her purchases, a mountain of bags and boxes overflowing with those tools that will, of course, change her life. Or perhaps I only thought I saw it, or I may have dreamed it—the myth of the Woman Transformed is such an archetype that it seems to live within us, a constant undercurrent to feminine thinking.

But I should admit here that while the black taffeta outfits and the maroon and blue plaid jacket were very nice in their way—they became popular items for borrowing and exchange in my freshman dorm, thus adding considerably to my prestige there—the transformation of which they were a part had very little to do with appearances. What they had to do with was my feelings about my mother. The woman was the most enthusiastic shopper I'd ever seen, and, more important, she shared my taste. The things she pulled from the racks were things I liked. The things I liked best were the things she liked best. No shadow of disagreement hovered between us about our final purchases.

She must have had very little money but she paid for everything. My savings from babysitting had been put aside with the money from the Women's Club grant and the Mount Holyoke scholarship. And when we were finished, completely exhausted from the day, she treated us to an early dinner at Child's.

It was an experience extraordinary for its triteness: shopping as a female rite of passage and bonding. And like many other trite rituals, its effectiveness was astonishing: I had a revelation of a sort. For the first time I could acknowledge—though this still took years more for me to assimilate completely—that I was my mother's daughter. My children would be my mother's grandchildren. My philosophy, my politics, my *Weltanschauung* would descend from the same line of insight and outlook as those of my mother and my grandparents, and their mothers and grandparents ad infinitum.

My bad temper and my taste in fabric were the progeny of a long history of moody people with a taste for black taffeta. And if you are angry and yearn for dark, rustling textiles there is no point trying to stifle your irritation and claim to like pastel tweed. You convince no one, since you fail to convince yourself. And so it was in Ohrbach's Juniors and College Shop that I gave up for good any last lingering hope I may have held of becoming a mild-tempered English schoolgirl with a penchant for heather wool; and I took up instead a lifelong stab at trying to become myself.

It was pretty much a case of Hans Christian Andersen in reverse, I suppose. Having grown up inadequate, clumsy, and totally inauthentic among swans, so to speak, I had just discovered to my slight regret but also to my great relief that I was in fact a somewhat unconventional but entirely recognizable duck.

✫

In the spring of 1978, when my mother was already very ill, my sister used to visit her almost daily in the apartment on East 19th Street where she had been living for twenty years. It was an apartment, I suspect, very like one she might have chosen to live in had she been allowed to stay in Karlsruhe: two light, high-ceilinged rooms with polished parquet floors, a Danish modern sofa, chairs, and coffee table, some good Oriental rugs, a Kollwitz lithograph. She had seldom turned willingly towards the past, and she had rarely talked about it—but during those last months a natural impulse to weigh her life in the balance and test its worth now and then overcame her.

One morning when Ruth was there my mother became ruminative. "I've had a difficult life," she announced. She was speaking in German.

I stage the scene in my mind: Ruth is putting away the groceries she has just brought by and is somewhat distracted by the task at hand. "Hmm," she agrees.

"And it didn't do me a bit of harm," says my mother.

I have thought that this equivocation would do quite well as our family motto. We could perhaps even design the family crest around it, with a creature—probably an earthworm rampant—in the process of being cut in half. The top half would have a little balloon coming from its oral orifice with "I've had a difficult life" written inside; while the balloon emerging from the bottom half would be inscribed "and it didn't do me a bit of harm." My optimistic vision is that, in the tradition of worms, both halves could be expected to be fruitful and prosper, producing in their turn generations of ready-to-be bisected, equivocating, invertebrate multitudes, which will ultimately inherit the earth.

WEATHER

⟅⟆ I've lived in rural New Hampshire for the last thirty-five years: the weather here is unreliable, often extreme, and always a large consideration in daily life. Our winter plans for a party or an excursion to a nearby town to see a movie have to be distressingly tentative. And between the beginning of December and the end of April, next to the penciled notations in my diary marking the arriving flights of family and friends at the Manchester airport or the departing flights of myself leaving it, I am usually careful to add a superstitious question mark. The only daytime soap opera I watch is the Weather Channel: before I take a trip, I check it at least five times a day.

My city friends, who rarely think about meteorological matters and then mainly in terms of umbrellas and parking places, find my concerns amusingly eccentric and obsessive. And I suppose that I do dwell a bit intensely on the approaching blizzard and the oncoming flood. I worry about the climate more earnestly than most of my contemporaries—who seem to assume that technology will protect them from major meteorological disaster. I measure weather as a basic in-gredient for survival, as essential to my life as food or shelter, health or status are, though far more capricious. It is the single aspect of my environment that is so far beyond any dream of my control that it would never even occur to me to question it.

☆

It was probably in Leeds—long before I ever saw northern New En-gland—that I began to appreciate the weather's sinister supremacy.

Memory takes me back to Twenty-Three the Towers. It is No-vember 1944. The allied armies are marching through Europe, and the allied air forces are hurling bombs into Germany. Victory is in the air. So, unfortunately, is a large amount of soot. The fog is so thick that if you go outside you can't see more than three inches in front of your nose, which, if you take a few good breaths, you have to blow to get rid of the oily black deposit that's formed at the back of your nostrils; it tastes like vinegar mixed with coal dust. Everyone is staying indoors, but even there a slightly greasy black haze shadows the floors and tables and smears the windows through which, anyway, nothing is visible. No one is home except Aunt Helen and me. Uncle Bourke went to work at the prison yesterday and has been unable to get back; there is no traffic, and the trams have stopped running.

But Aunt Helen is planning a party. She has been planning it for months—since August or September when our armies marching through France and Italy became sure enough of victory to make a tentative celebration possible, a species of preparatory festivity to get us into the mood for real jubilation when the war is really over. This party is by way of being our experimental, first, introductory about-to-be-post-war party. Some fifteen or perhaps twenty guests are ex-pected for lunch. Since it is fated that I will never meet them I have no idea who they are to be. I think the deputy governor of the prison is one of them—as well as of course his wife; perhaps a couple of the directors of the school board on which Uncle Bourke serves and quite likely one or two of his fellow church wardens—also with spouses. And I am quite sure that Aunt Helen has invited several of the company of actors who do repertory at the Theater Royal where we see every play they put on.

On the sideboard in the dining room Aunt Helen and I have already laid out a cold buffet. At one end is a ham; a mound of mustard pickles in a silver bowl is at the ready to decorate the first slice. Next to that a salmon mousse is shimmering in pink splendor and a bowl of potato salad sits in front. I am the assistant cook and also the scullery maid. I have washed and dried all the Indian Tree pattern lunch plates and set them up in two piles beside the potato salad; I have polished the silver and laid out the smaller forks and knives (the ones we use for lunch) in two neat rows. The smaller, lunch-sized damask napkins are piled beside them and at the sideboard's far end is dessert: a huge blancmange as well as my three pies, apple, jam, and lemon curd. I have been in charge of pie making for two years now—ever since I made the discovery in my domestic science class that my bad circulation and usually freezing hands make me a natural pastry cook.

We have been saving coupons for this feast for a month.

The fog continues unabated through the morning. A faint gray cloud settles on the salmon mousse, and the blancmange is becoming mottled. Aunt Helen covers them with wax paper and finds lids to put over the other food. The ham is hidden under the silver dome we use to keep the Sunday joint warm.

Silence. No one appears. At noon, the world outside the windows is as dark as if it were midnight and Aunt Helen has switched on all the lights in the empty dining room. At five minutes after twelve the phone rings. Aunt Helen answers it. And then it rings again.

"I think I shall go and lie down, dear," she says at twelve thirty; the phone by now has rung many times. "I have a bit of a headache."

After she has left, I sit in the dining room for a while to watch the groceries wilt; then I put away the plates and cutlery. This is a time before refrigeration has come to Twenty-Three the Towers, so I have no idea what I should do with the food. Aunt Helen reappears at five or so. The blancmange, the salmon mousse, and the potato salad go into temporary storage in the larder. Aunt Helen says that they can still be distributed to our neighbors if the fog lifts enough by tomorrow to get them there. After tomorrow they will have to be thrown into the garbage bin. Meanwhile we wrap the pies and the ham for more permanent keeping. They will last almost for ever, even while they are growing daily and eternally a little less appealing.

"Oh for the wings, for the wings of a dove," Aunt Helen declaims, sighing.

"That you might fly, fly away, fly away," I finish for her. This is her favorite song, which she often quotes or hums to herself while we are washing up.

"Not today, my darling," Aunt Helen says, looking towards the befogged window. "No dove in its right mind would fly anywhere today."

But, even though the evening should be getting darker, the black murk seems to be becoming opalescent. At around seven, Uncle Bourke returns; the trams are running again, and a faint breeze appears to be stirring the cloud made visible by the dining room lights. Smoke is swirling gently at the window, and it is becoming thinner by the minute. It seems likely that by tomorrow we may be able to see the sun: in time to bless our neighbors with salmon mousse but too late for the party.

That is my first introduction to the phenomenon that I ponder in silent, incredulous wonder—the fearful, arbitrary, though unostentatious power of simple weather.

☆

It was another November storm that set the scene the last time Val and I saw each other: early November in 1999, about eighteen months before Val died. It was unsurprising that the weather was foul; in England you can pretty much count on bad weather in November. These days it's not likely to be fog. It's rain and more rain and a high wind to drive it all the way down to your skin.

Val was already pitifully thin and easily tired—weakened by three (or was it four?) operations to remove the obdurate, recurring tumor that finally killed her—but she drove in to meet me at the station in Bath. And despite the downpour—or maybe because of it, because of that heightened sense of life one has under duress—we were both in a celebratory mood. "This is such fun!" Val said several times as we splashed our way through Bath. The car windows were leaking slightly, and we both thought this exceedingly comic, registering our joy with squeaks at each drip that fell on us.

"I think we need some coffee," Val announced. "We hardly ever drink coffee at home. I've never learned to make it properly. But I know just the place where we can get some." And we stopped on the outskirts of Bath to park behind an old hotel, a rather grand, historical, old hotel that she had wanted to look into, Val said, for years. She'd never quite dared to try it on her own.

We were still in the car park when a black-tied, morning-coated gentleman rushed out to shelter us with an enormous umbrella—we were already drenched since both our own umbrellas had blown inside out as soon as we'd opened the car doors. Entirely unfazed by Val's guilty confession that we weren't staying, that all we wanted was a cup of coffee, he opened the hotel's great double doors with the solemnity of Saint Peter uncoupling the gates of Heaven and escorted us to a fire-warmed nest he informed us was the library. Then, clucking sympathy for our dampened state, he draped our soaked raincoats over a radiator.

He had apparently already ordered coffee up on our behalf. It arrived magically as if it had been lying in wait for us, to be served from a silver tray by a sort of footman—uniformed and begloved and far above anything like a waiter—with the requisite cream and brown sugar and a pair of crumpets dripping butter. Bathed in the sudden balm of all this civilization, beyond the reach of the storm, soothed by the relief of being warm and being dry and by the sheer extravagance of cream and butter, the edges of our propriety entirely melted away. The world seemed to have retreated to an earlier time, and, cradled in a sense of safety from all outside perils, we ourselves had also regressed alarmingly. We giggled furtively at each approach of the footperson and snickered as we dared to ask for seconds.

The library sofas and armchairs, I noticed, were upholstered in the same pattern of chintz as those in the drawing room with the old tiger-skin rug.

The keeper of the silver tray looked upon us indulgently, looked upon us, in fact, with pleasure. Even the lesser staff lurking in corners smiled at us, gratified to have so easily supplied these two slightly dotty and rather elderly ladies, leaking rain puddles onto the Kerman rug, with so much joy.

Restored and comforted, we drove on to Batheaston. Despite the obscuring rain, the dining room of Valerie's ancient stone cottage had a splendid view of the Avon and the hills beyond, a swirling, blurred panorama of mist and clouds. George's garden, tumbling down steeply into the valley, was drained of color, a muted cascade of dying delphiniums and roses for whose lovely unruliness he offered unneeded apology.

That was the last time I saw Val, as I say—the last time I was in England. Diana had died some years before, while she was on holiday with her daughter. She caught one of those strange new plagues that have taken to flying in from the exotic corners of the world. There was no cure for the virus—if that's what it was—and it did its work quickly: Di came down with something that looked like the flu on Christmas Day and she was dead before New Year's.

Since Val died there seems no urgent reason to return to England again, although for one reason or another it's likely that some day soon I will.

✳

But I doubt that I'll ever go back to Karlsruhe. This is probably foolish on my part—I should steel myself, brush up on my German, spend a few days looking the town over at leisure so as to get my birth-place settled more securely in my mind. But, by and large, I think I'll leave Karlsruhe to itself.

I did go back once. It was a side trip, really, an afterthought that happened almost inadvertently without my quite intending it because my husband, Peter, was offered a six-week residency at the Rockefeller Center on Lake Como and because I joined him there.

I was writing fiction at the time—short stories, mainly—but I'd been wanting for a while to try to work on essays instead. I was think-ing of autobiographical essays, which are not nearly as simple as you think they're going to be. First you have to remember what the facts were. And when you can't—or at least when you can't be sure that what you remember ever actually happened—you have to forgive yourself for inventing things that will support the alleged facts and that convince you enough so they'll be likely to convince other people as well. If fiction is, to a large degree, the art of lying cogently, auto-biography is probably the art of lying cogently to yourself—and for that, to do it properly, you need a fair amount of space and time and quiet to cushion the exercise.

Lake Como seemed like the perfect place to begin. The domes-tic partners and spouses of residents at the Center were treated almost as generously as the residents themselves, and I had been given my own studio to write in, a delightful little summerhouse made of stone with windows around its entire, rotund circumference. It was in the middle of the front garden of the Villa Serbelloni—which contains the main dining hall, residences, and offices for the Rockefeller Center com-plex—and it was a spectacular place for writing. It was surrounded by lawn and laurel hedges, and since it had a full view of the front entry I could study the Villa's comings and goings whenever I got bored.

I had wanted to start my essay project by writing something about England—a memento of Leeds, perhaps—but as soon as I be-gan an outline and sketched in a few notes to prepare the first essay, I found that it was heading itself inexorably towards Karlsruhe.

Well—we were in northern Italy, after all, which, in both miles and concept, is not so very far from southern Germany. You could hear the whistle of the express train between Frankfurt and Rome passing by punctually each evening on the opposite shore of the lake, retracing the journey of the train between Rome and Frankfurt, which came through just after lunch. Both trains stopped at the Como railway station. A few hours before or after Como they also stopped in Karlsruhe.

✳

The Rockefeller Center's compound includes a variety of buildings: several villas, a monastery, a ruined castle, a lake-side conference center, boathouse, stables, gatehouses, the odd cottage or two, greenhouses, sheds, and barns. Many of the buildings have been converted into studios. If you climb to the top of the hill where the castle is, you confront the impressive range of white-topped mountains that are the Italian Alps; if you walk down the steep path through acres of formal gardens, meadows, woods, and olive groves, you come to the old town of Bellagio, a steep maze of stone façades and cobbled streets dating back to Julius Caesar, where you can now avail yourself of all the essentials for modern life. There are several hotels for vacationing Italians who like to spend summers here and a landing from which a ferry will take you to any town on the lake—the only way, in fact, to get to most of the small towns and the best way to get to Como, the single large one.

The area all around the lake is blessed with a mild climate and the rather odd miniclimate that prevails on the arm dividing the lake in two, the peninsula where Bellagio is, is milder still. Even in February there were flowers in bloom in the gardens of the Villa Serbelloni. Once it snowed—but it snowed huge, fairy-tale flakes as light as air, which floated down on us like rose petals.

Sometimes it seemed to me that there was a sort of temporal

miniclimate at the Villa. We were required to dress for dinner as though we were back in some earlier, more ceremonial age; during conferences, when the Center's population doubled, there was even a formal seating chart and one would search out one's dinner partner so as to walk together into the dining room. Such antebellum customs belonged to a quite different time than the technological expertise of most of the people observing them—the innovative thinking that had brought many of them to Bellagio in the first place. Looking around the assembly nibbling on their *pesche agli amoretti* the full length of the damask-covered banquet tables, one understood that the polyglot conversations, the saris and caftans and kilts scattered among Versace gowns and well-worn dinner jackets, were the signatures of an ambiguous chronology. They spoke of a pleating together of past with present, of an inexplicable shrinking down of the temporal dimension, as though it had become subservient to the space that contained it.

You sense that phenomenon quite often, of course, in many very old places, as if time had folded in upon itself and moments of history, divided by centuries, had become suddenly simultaneous.

Peter and I had a grand room, furnished with sixteenth-century chests and paintings and an even grander, futuristic sort of bathroom, all smoked glass and chrome. We were on the second floor of the Center's main house, the Villa where Stendahl had spent some happy summers. Our balcony window looked over terraced gardens and onto the footpath where Pliny the Younger had walked. Further down we could see Lake Como, and directly across from us, on the other side of the Lake, was the village where Mussolini and his mistress had been captured at the end of the war.

Under these circumstances—and with the train on its way to Frankfurt and again on its way back coming through twice every day—my childhood seemed to be remarkably nearby in time as well as in space. It was quite natural and effortless, in such an atmosphere, for my mind to turn towards Germany: it would have been an effort, in fact, to turn it anywhere else. And so, without quite meaning to, I found that I was writing about Karlsruhe. And without quite meaning to, I found that I was going there.

✷

It was certainly the logical thing to do. After Peter's residency was finished we had planned to travel around a bit and Karlsruhe was in a straight line from Lake Como, a mere two or three hours away. We decided, sensibly, that we would go there directly from the Center on the same train that had been whistling at me so invitingly for the last six weeks.

But somehow, once the decision had been reached, I kept finding reasons why we might go in some other direction, after all: Venice before it got crowded, Milan to meet friends—or perhaps a week in Munich because the art there needs to be visited at regular intervals? Peter noticed that the closer the time came to go there, the more inventively I was avoiding Karlsruhe; I passionately denied avoiding anything.

In the end Peter dragged me there, though even as he was dragging me I continued to insist that I wanted to go. We went, at my insistence, by way of Venice—not exactly a short cut. And when we were actually on the train heading towards Karlsruhe, in another blithering exercise in unconscious balking, I refused to spend the night there, declaring that there wouldn't be any decent hotels and it would be better to stay in Stuttgart.

But, finally, we were there.

It was April, and there were pansies and tulips in planters everywhere. Peter and I walked from the station through streets, which, to my astonishment, I remembered—not in terms of discrete memories, not in my thinking, exactly. They were just familiar; I knew them in the deep, ineffable way one knows places in dreams. And in fact, there, in living metal on Karlsruhe's street corners, were the sculptural fantasies of bronze flora and fauna lurking in bronze fairy-tale trees that do still pay me the occasional nocturnal visit. Far down Kaiserstrasse I recognized the block where my grandparents' apartment had been, though it was, in fact, utterly changed, having been destroyed by bombs and replaced by a row of modern office buildings. The *Kronenapotheke*, my father's pharmacy, was also gone, but the corner of Zähringer-strasse, which had been the view from my bedroom window, was exactly as my fickle memory tells me it had always been.

For some reason—tombs, even those of close relatives, are not high on my list of enthusiasms—I had declared that the main purpose in this Karlsruhe visit was to find and photograph my father's grave, which meant that we first had to find the Rathaus so as to get a map that would take us to the Jewish cemetery where my father's grave was.

We walked along the cobbled pavement of the Kaiserstrasse; its tram tracks and its trams were still extant, but cars were now banned. In their place, a couple of mimes and a quite excellent, silver-painted mechanical man were performing for the edification of strolling shoppers. The Rathaus, in one of the neat, neoclassical squares that form the town's center, was just past another one of my dream icons: the miniature pyramid, symbol of Masonic virtue, that presides over the tomb of the Margraf who had himself buried in the heart of this town he had founded and built.

We were directed to the Oberbürgermeister's office as the best place to make our inquiries, and there a very agreeable young man took charge. He spoke perfect English, and he gave us not only a map of Karlsruhe but two books recently published by the town: *Juden in Karlsruhe.* The first volume was a general history of Karlsruhe's Jews; the second was a catalogue of the fate of Karlsruhe's Jews from around 1930 until the end of the War. There was a picture of my mother in it and another of Ruth among a group of Hachshara girls. There was a picture of the *Kronenapotheke* too, taken at the time my father had bought it.

"Let me give you a bag for those," the young man said. "It's a very nice bag. Completely ecologically correct." And he handed me the town's official tote, a reusable cotton carryall with a picture of the Rathaus on it.

✳

Karlsruhe is an elegant town: the courthouse where the Supreme Court meets is just across from the new opera house—a fine piece of architecture, as handsome in its way as the old Schloss. There were banners in front of the opera announcing an impressive schedule for the upcoming weeks: performances of the *Ring* cycle, *Don Giovanni*, and *Bluebeard's Castle.*

Peter and I were now fully equipped for completing my stated mission of photographing my father's grave. But I said we should wait a bit before we went out to the cemetery; there was so much to see. We could at least walk a little in the Schlossgarten on whose semicircular paths Dada had taken me, first in my stroller and later holding my hand, every day that the sun shone.

So we walked around the Schlossgarten—Peter declared himself impressed but demurred at my near insistence that we should keep going beyond the neat flower beds and well-trimmed lawns, deep into the wilder woodland. And then of course there was the Kunsthalle, the museum—we had to see that, I said. My husband, who is usually avid for a new museum, suggested mildly that we mustn't forget that the cemetery closed at five.

Meanwhile, however, we did go to the museum. In the modern wing, there were Noldes and Beckmanns and an astonishing number of paintings by Otto Dix, who seems to have been the town's sardonic favorite—or possibly a relative of the director of acquisitions. Several of the Dix pieces seemed strangely familiar, as though I had seen them many times before. The work in the museum's other wing included some excellent examples from the Middle Ages and early Renaissance, as well as the Grünewald *Descent from the Cross*, with its green-fleshed and tragic Christ that has haunted my memory since childhood.

So, I thought, I must have been in the museum often as a child; I must have spent some time there. And apparently children were expected to come often to this museum and to spend some time there. A foot or two from the walls a wooden platform ran the length and breadth of every room so that a child standing on it would be on the level of the paintings. And the boxes of descriptive material had been hung on two heights—in each room one box was set at the normal height for adults but the second was low enough so that even a small child could reach it.

What a surprising, superb little town, I thought to myself. And I told Peter that the zoo here had always been extraordinary. "We should really go there," I said.

Peter is not usually assertive about making other people do things they don't seem to be doing. But at that point he grasped me by the elbow and led me firmly out of the museum towards the place where we'd been told the bus for the cemetery stopped to pick up passengers.

"I don't have change for the bus," I protested. But it was too late. The bus had come and stopped and I was on it, having been pushed on by Peter.

✣

Karlsruhe's Jewish cemetery is concealed inside its larger, Catholic cemetery, which wraps itself around it. It is hidden behind a high, dense hedge so that one has to look carefully to find the little gate that is the only way in. Searching for the entrance we passed a fair number of people in the Christian cemetery: women with flowers, whole families coming to visit their deceased uncles, grandparents, friends. But when we finally found our way into the Jewish section we were suddenly entirely alone.

Someone must have been taking care of the graves, most probably members of the small, Orthodox congregation that the nice young man at the Rathaus had told us had reestablished itself in Karlsruhe after the war. The gravel paths were raked, the grass cut, the groundcover weeded. My father's grave, which I located almost immediately as if I'd been drawn to it, as if I knew where it was, was a tidy rectangle of periwinkle. The gray headstone with BRUNO COHN engraved below the two priestly hands raised in blessing looked almost new, as if it had been put there in 1990 instead of 1937. I took two rolls of pictures to bring back to my sister, not quite sure what it was, exactly, I had wanted to prove.

And I wondered why I hadn't stopped at the kiosk at the cemetery entrance to buy some flowers. The people we had passed, the Christians, had all been carrying bunches of flowers. They had come here to decorate the graves of their dear departed. Why had I neglected to follow this simple ritual?

We left my father's gravesite to wander through the rest of the cemetery, which was divided by gravel paths into blocks of twenty or thirty graves. Reading the names of those who were buried there and looking at the dates of their death gave one no sense of any specific order. There was no massing into large family groups, no mausoleums, no obvious arrangement by congregation or by strict chronology—although the more recent interments were naturally kept to the available space, which was, naturally towards the cemetery's edge.

But then I saw that there were no really recent interments. The dead, who had been buried here for well over a hundred years, seemed suddenly to have ceased their patronage.

This strange phenomenon was, however, accounted for. The evidence lay in the clusters of markers crowded together under the high hedges around the cemetery's circumference: modest stone markers easy to miss at first, each less in size than a shoebox, each white or gray with etched black lettering. They were grouped by fives and tens and twenties, apparently not in order to indicate any actual grave—they were much too close together for that—but simply to acknowledge a death. There were hundreds of them.

The names on the markers were diverse and so were the dates of birth, but the date of death—often modified with a question mark— was invariably 1944 or 1945. Occasionally the place of death, Auschwitz, was also inscribed.

Of course there were no recent interments: no one had died because almost no one had lived.

✡

I suppose, on some level of semiconsciousness, I must have known pretty much what I'd find in the Jewish cemetery in Karlsruhe—in any Jewish cemetery in Europe for that matter. And probably my reluctance to find it, to come face to face with the unthinkable, accounts for those odd bouts of ambivalence that seized me on my way there.

It occurs to me, now and then, that instead of taking three or four dozen photographs of a single, ordinary grave that I will never look at I might have been better employed taking a couple of rolls of film of those clusters upon clusters of markers. But who is there now that I could show them to? And besides, the globe is covered with such tragic memorabilia: with mass graves and stones over empty tombs, the sad, paradoxical record of our murderous histories to remind us of who we are.

A couple of years after my brief trip to Karlsruhe I got a form letter from the Oberbürgermeister addressed to the town's former Jewish citizens. He expressed his deep regret and shame at needing to inform us that several graves in the Jewish cemetery had been desecrated. Shortly after that a second letter came with the news that the teenage hooligans who had done the damage had been arrested and were to be tried and that the graves had been put to rights. Yet another letter announced that the town planned to put up a memorial to those of its citizens who had died in Auschwitz: the Herr Oberbürgermeister professed that he would be personally pleased to welcome the return of those of us who would honor its unveiling with our presence.

It struck me that he cared a great deal about the responsibilities of his office. I judged him to be far more passionate about his job than your standard provincial mayor might be expected to be. Like many Germans I know he seemed to be painfully conscientious, as though by flinging the weight of his present goodness against the terrible burden of the state's evil past he could, with every virtuous act he accomplished, redeem some portion of the staggering mountain of guilt built up during the century. I admire him.

I only wish I had his resources. It seems that I have no way now of remembering Karlsruhe reasonably. It is impossible for me to think about the town without evoking mentally those rectangles of stone each of which signifies a death. And then nothing at all comes to my mind. It bleeds to an absolute void where any feeling—horror or fear or anger or compassion—is revealed as fictitious and sentimental. In response to my recollection of the Jewish cemetery in Karlsruhe a blank seems to be all I can conjure up.

So I think, despite the great good will I feel for the town, I will stay away from it. My sister, who of course remembers it much more clearly than I do, has never gone back; and whenever we see each other we seem not to talk about Karlsruhe at all. Instead, our meetings almost always begin with a joint declaration about how astoundingly lucky we've been in the years since our childhood there. It's become a sort of ritual between us, partly thanksgiving for still being able to wobble about at a fair pace on our septuagenarian legs, largely appreciation for the extraordinary privilege of having been granted such reasonable and ordinary lives.

But always, shaking our heads over the marvel of being pulled away from a world drowning in chaos, we talk about our seven years in England. I suppose I see them in my imagination as being like one of those brilliant days of January that take you by surprise in New England: a rare interval of inexplicable, astonishing sunshine at the very moment when you are least expecting it. Just when the year seems surely sunk in darkness, a morning breaks, radiant with contradiction of the winter, bright with anticipation of the spring.